RENEWALS 458-4574

DATE DUE

NOV 2 9			

GAYLORD   PRINTED IN U.S.A.

THE
CRITICAL
EDGE

Also by Hendrie Weisinger, Ph.D.

NOBODY'S PERFECT (with Norman Lobsenz)
DR. WEISINGER'S ANGER WORK-OUT BOOK

THE CRITICAL EDGE

How to Criticize
Up and Down
Your Organization
and Make It Pay Off

BY HENDRIE WEISINGER, PH.D.

LITTLE, BROWN AND COMPANY

BOSTON   TORONTO   LONDON

COPYRIGHT © 1989 BY HENDRIE WEISINGER, PH.D.

FIRST EDITION

Library of Congress Cataloging-in-Publication Data

Weisinger, Hendrie.
  The critical edge.

  Bibliography: p. 271
  1. Psychology, Industrial.   2. Criticism, Personal.
I. Title.
HF5548.8.W43   1989   158.7   88-23014
ISBN 0-316-92877-1

10 9 8 7 6 5 4 3 2 1

MV-PA

*Published simultaneously in Canada
by Little, Brown & Company (Canada) Limited*

PRINTED IN THE UNITED STATES OF AMERICA

Contents

Dedicated to my friends,
who give me the Critical Edge.

Acknowledgments

I certainly could not have written this book without the support of numerous people. Thank you, Richard Pine, for the title and belief in the subject matter. Thank you, Victor Tabbush and Ernie Scalberg, for allowing me the opportunity to present my thoughts at the UCLA Graduate School of Management. Thank you, John Willenborg, Steve Garris, and the University of South Carolina Daniel Management Center, for helping me take criticism to the corporate communities throughout the United States. Thank you, Temple University, Wayne State University, University of Colorado, for bringing me to your communities. Thank you, Wess Roberts, for creating opportunities for me to implement my work in a top company. Thank you, Sharon Wago, for believing in my work on a yearly basis in a most gracious manner.

Thanks to Ken Blanchard and BTD, for always being supportive, and to Ken, for speaking so highly of me. Thank you, Joe Cosby, for doing the same and helping me become a better communicator of my thoughts.

There are many more. Thanks, Fredrica Friedman, for your productive criticisms, which made this the best book possible and stretched my abilities. Thanks, Mary Sutter, for quickly responding to all my needs. Thanks, Debbie Roth, for your editorial support. Thanks to Little, Brown for giving a big push.

There are still more. Thank you, Kathryn Welds, for your abundant enthusiasm and all the sources of information you provided to me. Thanks, Alex Gross, for your constant optimism and friendly criticism. Thank you, Robert Braun and Joan Friedman, for constant support and thoughtfulness when I was under the gun. Thanks, Paula

La Brot, for your continuing support with a smile. Thanks, Robert Levy, for the art lessons. Your contribution made the first chapter. Thank you, Lenny Levine, for being the best *consigliere* and showing me that you can never lose your family. Thank you, Mel Kinder, for your street wisdom, for sharing your wonderful insights about the process of criticism, and for giving me 6528250. Thank you, Kenny (P.S. No More B.S.) Cinnamon, for once again demanding that the book must be written and for your inspirational comments that could show anyone Who's The Boss. Thank you, Ron Podell, for never being too tired or busy to help me. Thanks, Ron, for going through the Epic. Thanks, Ronnie and Don, for being great cheerleaders. Thanks, Mom and Dad, for so many super times.

Thank you, Lorie and Bri, for being Lorie and Bri. You are the reasons I work at home.

And thanks to all the others who have helped me. This book is yours, too.

PART I

BACK TO BASICS

CRITICISM affects almost all aspects of your job: the quality of the work you do, how you feel about it, your relationships with your boss, co-workers, subordinates. Used productively, criticism is a powerful tool that helps you improve your work, enhance your working relationships, increase your job satisfaction, and achieve better overall results. Improperly used, it impedes performance, demoralizes you, discourages you from wanting to try again, and creates friction in the workplace. In short, the ability to give and take criticism significantly determines how well you do on the job.

Part I will present an overview of the criticism process by introducing some basic criticism concepts, principles, and issues — all of which must be understood if you are to be a productive criticizer — and basic techniques that will improve your results at work. This section will then culminate by presenting a general model for giving and taking criticism productively. With the basics in hand, you will be able to begin to tailor your general criticism skills to specific encounters, such as criticizing your boss, peers, and subordinates (these specific encounters will be the subject of Part II).

Mastering the basics is the beginning of getting the Critical Edge.

Chapter 1

The Power of Criticism

BEING CRITICIZED can be a devastating experience. It can make us cry and feel ashamed, even humiliated, to the extent that we want to run away so we can sulk and lick our wounds in private. For many of us, a simple criticism like "Brush your teeth, your breath smells," or "Here, I'll do it, you're making a mess," or "How could you make such a mistake?" has the same effect as that of a knife being pushed into our heart and slowly turned.

It is a lonely feeling to be criticized. When you're wrong, you stand alone. Certainly, it's hard to feel loved by your spouse when he or she is carping at you for not picking up after yourself, or watching too much television, or always cooking the same thing. And who of us feels appreciated when our boss is aghast at our work after we have made our best effort?

Criticism hurts. It almost makes you feel as if you are once again a little child getting scolded for not washing your hands before dinner, or coming home with dirty clothes, or forgetting your lunch box and books. All of a sudden, you feel, "Mommy doesn't love me. Daddy doesn't love me." Who wouldn't want to cry?

But we don't always cry or bury our head in the sand. Why not get even? "Gee, don't wear that dress . . . It makes you look fat." "Hey, let me tell you about my boss — the guy's a real jerk." We think, "Ahh, this is better. Let's see how they like it. They're just as bad as I am." We can throw knives, too. We can be powerful, too.

On the other hand, giving criticism is often no picnic either. We think, "How can I tell her she's lousy in bed? It would kill her. And I love her." "I know he worked hard on this. How can I tell him he's off the mark? I don't want to discourage him." Are we so humane that we are most concerned with not hurting the feelings of those we criticize? Maybe. But for the most part, giving criticism is difficult because it elicits the same feelings in us that our recipient is apt to experience: embarrassment, guilt, anxiety, and anger. Sometimes these feelings arise because giving criticism puts us in a paradoxically tough position — we like the person but must tell them something displeasing. Other times such feelings arise because we know that the recipient of our criticism will respond negatively and thus make us deal with a distressing situation. And sometimes we experience these feelings because giving criticism, despite its necessity, is proof that we aren't always the nice guy, a fact that rubs our self-esteem the wrong way. Whatever the case may be, these feelings are good reason for us to remember that "If you can't say something nice, don't say anything at all."

Either way, giving or taking criticism can create emotional havoc that makes it impossible to feel good about ourselves and/or others. Criticism, for too many of us, is a totally negative experience. Yet making people feel bad was far from criticism's original purpose.

CRITICISM — THEN AND NOW

It's impossible to understand how criticism has evolved into its present form without getting a cursory education in art and philosophy, since it was in these areas that criticism had its roots.

The word "criticism" is semantically derived from the Greek adjective *kritikos,* a word coined by Aristotle that means "able to discern or judge accordingly." However, it was actually his teacher, Plato, who organized the first school of criticism.

At this time, criticism was seen as an intellectual activity; the objects that deserved the intellect's attention and criticism were literary works, especially poems, which at that time were the acceptable literary vehicle for expressing one's thoughts, values, and philosophy of life. Plato taught his students to criticize on the basis of the Greek term "mimesis." In a criticism of this sort, the poem is considered an imitation, a representation, or a copy, and is definable in terms of whatever it copies — nature, a picture, another poem. Plato assumed the mimetic orientation to be the fundamental method of criticism, and he criticized some poets because in his system of thought their works were often copies of copies of reality and thus twice removed from it. For example, the poet who introduces a shoe into his poem copies the shoemaker's copy of the Platonic idea of a shoe.

The mimetic theory is important because it introduced the criterion of accuracy into the concept of criticism. Previously, the act of criticizing was often no more than an exercise in sophistry. Itinerant critics roamed the countryside, arguing the merits of everything from art and philosophy to politics and literature, for no more than a speaking fee. The same Sophist might argue either side of an issue with equal lack of conscience for two different audiences. The right answer could as easily be ill served by a bad argument as could the wrong answer by a good one. The mimetic theory took issue with this practice as it raised certain questions in the context of poems: What sort of accuracy does the poet seek? Should the poet introduce objects not in nature into his poem, as in myth and romance? Is there not some sense in which the nature we experience is created by the nature poets have insisted we see? The importance of these questions is that they made critics consider on what basis they were evaluating a poem. To be a good critic, then, one must criticize on the basis of well-defined criteria relative to the object of criticism.

Well-defined criteria, however, did not mean simple criteria. In fact, many of Plato's students, notably Aristotle, did not assume accuracy as a canon of judgment for valid criticism. One of Aristotle's famous remarks, "Not to know that a hind has no horns is a less serious matter than to paint it inartistically," raises the question of what Aristotle really meant by imitation and suggests that no simple criterion of accuracy was in his mind. What is important is that these points — that criticism should be based on well-defined criteria, and that there are no simple criteria — became fundamental and constant tenets of criticism throughout the ages.

Aristotle's and Plato's theories were quickly dispensed with upon the rise of the Church and the waning of classical society. The Vatican saw little value in any theory of criticism at all. Criticism was sacrilegious in a society in which the divine word was believed to be passed from God to the Pope and by word of mouth on down. This societal view of criticism prevented new thinking from emerging; the Dark Ages began their tenure.

Following this period, criticism entered its Neoclassical era and came under the influence of the empirical tradition, to which such men as Francis Bacon and John Locke belonged. For critics of this period, art represented not merely ideal completions of nature but the truth implicit in generalizations from sensory data. In this context, criticism became highly objective, since the object was evaluated against external criteria; the critic's task was to evaluate how close the art came to representing these external (or larger) truths. Personal opinions did not affect objective nature. As was the case with critics in classical times, the Neoclassicist did not make room for his own subjective evaluation.

However, in what will soon emerge as a pattern, when subjective critical thinking and personal expression are suppressed, revolution is ignited. Here it took the form of the Romantic movement, which spurred criticism up its evolutionary ladder. The Romantic movement was a philosophical revolt in the eighteenth and early nineteenth century against the artistic, political, and philosophical principles that had become associated with Neoclassicism. In contrast to prescribing adherence to objective realities, Romanticism advocated freedom of form and spirit, with emphasis on feeling, originality, the personality of the artist himself, and sympathetic interest in primitive nature and the common man. This "romantic" orientation arose in part from a larger movement based on a radical epistemological change that took place in the later eighteenth century. It came to be thought that the mind was not merely a passive receptor and combiner of sensory data, as the empiricists seemed to believe, but was at least in part a creator of nature. As this idea was developed by a series of philosophers from George Berkeley through Immanuel Kant to Friedrich Schelling, the theory of the constitutive imagination gained strength, and the idea of art as primarily a copy of an exterior reality waned. By the end of the nineteenth century it was not impossible to understand Oscar Wilde's witty insistence that nature copies art more than art copies nature. The theory of imitation gave way to the idea of creation. Critics emphasized the power of art and language to create or at least give significant shape to nature.

While the idea of art as creative or constitutive of reality arose, criticism began to emphasize the presence of the artist in the poem. Before the mid-eighteenth century — before the epistemological revolution and the emphasis on individual freedom in politics, economics, and religion that accompanied it — not much attention had been paid to the artist himself nor to the idea of the poem as an expression of the artist's inner being. But with the shift in emphasis toward the subjective, the poem came to be considered less in terms of what it copied in the world than what it expressed of its author. The relationship between author and work became the major critical issue.

Theories of creative spontaneity and preferences for feeling over rationality accompanied this development. The individual and the particular became more important than the general. Biographical criticism began to flourish. Interest in how a writer composed and in other aspects of creativity became common. The psychology of the author emerged as a subject for study. In essence, what the Romantic period contributed to the arts was the realization that the artist cannot be separated from his work; rather, his thoughts and feelings are integrated into what he produces. Similarly, the concept of criticism was transformed from an objective measurement into a position colored by the critic's personal values, beliefs, and feelings; thus criticism, by definition, can never be objective.

Another philosophical orientation that affected the concept of criticism is that in which a poem is seen in relation to its readers. There have been many theories of what the results of the poem should be: moral betterment, scientific or other learning, hedonistic pleasure, or psychic therapy. This "affective" orientation is significant because it emphasizes "intent": What is the purpose of a poem? This critical question was then turned back upon criticism itself: What is the purpose of criticism? This philosophy is often espoused by Existentialists, such as Jean-Paul Sartre. He believed that there is no destiny and that events can be explained as a matter of randomness. Thus, the only means to explain one's behavior is the intent that one purports to have.

These three philosophical approaches to criticism — mimetic, expressive, and affective — have all shaped the concept of criticism by emphasizing three of its most important components: a criterion for the criticism; a realization that criticism is subjective; and clarification of purpose.

But philosophy has not been alone in shaping the concept of criticism; criticism must also be looked at in the context of its environment. For example, in the eighteenth century, exceptionally wealthy and powerful monarchs dictated the taste of the day, and no one dared be a critic at all out of fear of decapitation. Louis the XIV (and those like him) had little patience for dissent over his politics or his taste in furniture. But history repeated itself, this time more dramatically. Just as the Romanticists revolted against the Neo-classicists for stifling their creative spirit, so did the common man revolt against a society that restricted or inhibited his critical thinking, his right to expression, his freedom of spirit. The American and French revolutions ended this period of stifled criticism, and attention was again focused on the nobility of the common man. A sign of the times was Gustave Courbet's painting of the Stone Breakers, which heralded new attention to everyday life, in contrast to pictures glorifying the life of Napoleon, painted just a short generation before.

It was then that criticism took on expanded meaning. Previously limited to the art world, criticism became a tool whose intent was to evaluate all aspects of society. The English divorce courts, school systems, the Church, all became targets of criticism. The *Zeitgeist* of allowing critical thoughts had arrived and pertained not only to the whims of philosophers and artists. For example, Sigmund Freud changed the rules of criticism with regard to man's psychology and the causes and effects thereof. Previously, man's behavior was thought to be best explained in strict physiological terms; Freud's criticism of this explanation brought attention to the importance of the psyche. And at the same time, his work influenced the field of literary criticism, with critics in this field beginning to analyze poems using psychoanalytic criteria. Within a few hundred miles of Freud but unbeknownst to him, Albert Einstein was working on the theory of relativity, which did to physics what Freud had done to psychology. At the same time, Wassily Kandinsky was painting the first abstract painting. The Expressionists were painting their psyches rather than their subjects. While these events shaped history, they also affected the concept of criticism. Far from following the mimesis theory of judging against specific criteria, criticism now became a means of challenging old ways and introducing new ideas. It was a means of offering one's thoughts based not on fixed and specific criteria but based rather on any criteria that reflected the times.

In retrospect, we can see that this has always been true, that criticism (its type and quality) merely reflects the times, as did the expressive orientation reflect the Romantic movement. But it is also true that criticism — as evidenced by the likes of Freud, Charles Darwin, and Galileo — can change the society that fosters it.

During the last few decades, the concept of criticism has continued to be redefined by society. In particular, there have been three recent sociological developments that have shaped criticism's current status.

In contrast to the stoic quality of Plato's criticism, today's criticism is much more emotionally loaded. Buzzwords and phrases like the "Age of Narcissism," the "Me Decade," and "Looking Out for Number One" have become part of our vernacular and indicate humankind's concern with itself. Many of these phrases grew out of the human-potential movement of the sixties, which proposed that investing in yourself was the number-one priority. Asserting yourself became a daily routine, and the need to be perfect flourished. This emphasis on self-concern affected the process of giving and taking criticism, because both the giver and the taker became much more emotionally involved in the criticism process than had been common in previous eras, when criticism was characterized by a more intellectual attitude. Consequently, today's criticism, whether it's of our work, the way we look, or the way we act, is interpreted as a measure of our personal worth rather than an objective appraisal of what we produce. Today, criticism is an ego indictment.

Second, today's society is characterized as never before by the need for interpersonal communication. The very fact that the population has drastically increased over the last hundred years causes us to interact with those around us much more frequently than people did a century ago. Indeed, while the computer age is in midstream, interpersonal communication still reigns as the number-one means of transmitting information. Thus, the need for effective interpersonal communication has carved out a strong place for itself in today's world. Marriage counselors, psychologists, and popular studies like the *Hite Report* testify that communication is the building block for successful relationships. Business schools and their graduates report that the most important determinant for success is good interpersonal communication skills.

In this context, it is not surprising that today's concept of criticism has taken on its greatest meaning in interpersonal relationships. Most people, for example, will define criticism as a remark or comment that is made directly to them or as something that they say to another person rather than the act of objectively judging some inanimate object, such as a painting or a book. Criticizing the latter is usually, and with conspicuous neutrality, termed a "review," as in *book reviews, movie reviews,* and *restaurant reviews.* Yet seldom do we say to our spouse, "Stop reviewing me" or complain about a boss "who always reviews me"; instead, it is common practice to tell our spouse to "stop criticizing me" or to resent a boss who is overly critical. Indeed, "literary criticism" is now thought of as a branch of criticism, when in fact it — and not today's focus, interpersonal criticism — is the original tree.

Third, in today's society, critical thinking and freedom of expression are strongly encouraged, and, more than ever, we tend to scrutinize every fact that is presented to us. (This does not mean that we know what criteria to use!) Although this is probably good for our intellectual growth, our mental set consequently tends to be to find what's wrong rather than what's right. Few news shows, for example, start out by reporting the good events of the day. Instructors teach critical thinking by having students find the faulty logic of a philosopher. As a result, by contemporary definition, criticism has taken on a skewed meaning of being negative rather than retaining Aristotle's original definition of "judging accordingly." To this point, most dictionaries define "to criticize" as "to stress the faults of: cavil at." Criticism is said to be "the act of criticizing, usually unfavorably." The synonyms most often suggested for "criticize" include *blame, censure, condemn, denounce, reprehend.*

Stephanie Hughes, a sociologist, for her dissertation at Boston University studied how people give and take criticism. Among her findings was that "flaw-finding seems to be the most dominant, the traditional, and the expected response to attempted change or innovation." She reported that negative criticism (emphasizing the negative) is the standard technique by which most reviewers judge books and films, by which government agencies assess various options to reach their goals, and by which business and industry evaluate products, procedures, and personnel.

When this negative definition of criticism is brought into interpersonal relationships and is combined with today's zealousness in protecting one's ego, it becomes obvious why most people experience criticism as a highly charged, negative emotional encounter; a personal attack; a hurtful exchange. No wonder people hate criticism.

CRITICISM HAS POWER

Although the concept of criticism has evolved over time, one attribute of criticism has remained constant — its power to motivate, influence, and change behavior, and even shape the course of history. Again Freud, Darwin, and Einstein exemplify this point, as do, on a lesser level, the contemporary movie critics, book critics, and restaurant critics whose opinions have the power to create a success or failure. That criticism can evoke such strong responses testifies to its enormous power. And in today's world, its power is greater than ever. Nowhere is this more obvious than in the context of work.

A Michigan woman sued her employer on the grounds that her boss's relentless and disparaging criticism resulted in severe emotional and physical stress. A jury awarded her twenty-five thousand dollars. She represents the thousands who come home distraught because of their boss's critical comments. "A constant stream of negative criticism not only impedes job effectiveness, but also is a frequent cause of depression and anxiety," says UCLA psychiatrist Dr. Ronald Podell.

Jan Kemp, an instructor at the University of Georgia, publicly criticized what she termed the university's "preferential academic treatment of athletes." Ms. Kemp claimed that the University of Georgia stretched normal academic procedures in order to keep athletes eligible for revenue-producing sports. The university responded by dismissing her. She represents the thousands who are afraid to voice their criticisms for fear of getting fired.

Consider Michael Gould. During a seven-and-a-half-year tenure as chairman, he helped turn J. S. Robinson into the fashion leader among Southern California department store chains, only to resign in March 1986 after the parent company criticized him for allowing costs to get out of hand and profits to slip. His career represents all the times we do our best and then receive little appreciation for our efforts.

In the wake of the space shuttle *Challenger* tragedy, numerous sources reported that NASA's morale was destroyed by the barrage of government and public criticism. The fallout included employee insecurity, psychological distress, and group dissension. This represents the times that criticism has made us feel down about where we work, insecure about our jobs, and part of a losing team — but, of course, "It's not my fault."

Poor interpersonal relationships, low self-esteem, psychological distress, job dissatisfaction, impaired job performance, low morale, high turnover, and group dissension are only some of the counterproductive results that criticism's power brings forth. And these results are to be expected when one remembers the contemporary definition of criticism.

But criticism's power should not be viewed as limited to having negative effects. Criticism also has the power to help us avoid failure or to turn a failure into a success. Reebok president Paul Fireman criticizes every one of his company's shoes to ensure that each product is a hit instead of a miss. Winston Churchill said that criticism helped him avoid making many wrong decisions. He viewed criticism as a way to solve problems. "I do not resent criticism," Churchill said, "even when, for the sake of emphasis, it parts for the time with reality." For Clarence Darrow, criticism was a legal skill that helped him win many cases. In preparing for a trial, he criticized his own briefs numerous times; this helped him anticipate his opponent's objections before his day in court.

Criticism can help make relationships more harmonious, solidifying them with honesty and trust. It can inspire innovativeness and creativity. Norman Vincent Peale agrees. He believes his work would stagnate without criticism. "I used to get criticized a lot more and I don't get criticized as much now. It makes me feel like I'm slipping."

Criticism has positive power. It can change organizations, remodel them for the better. Television is a prime example. Often accused by educators of causing the minds of children to stagnate and of giving them poor role models, the industry is making a concentrated effort to improve the quality of its product. In an address to the American Psychological Association, Rhoda Barauch, director of the Institute of Mental Health Initiatives, in Washington, D.C., stated that "networks are responding to our criticism. More and more shows are attempting to provide positive role models to children by demonstrating how difficult emotions, like anger, can be handled productively instead of slamming doors, going to a bar, becoming verbally abusive, or [resorting to] violent behaviors."

Despite these potentially positive effects of criticism, the man on the street still responds to criticism as though it were a four-letter word. What about you?

Think back to the last few times you were criticized or had to give criticism on the job. What were your thoughts beforehand? What did you think as you said or heard the words? How did you feel? How did you act? What were your reactions? What were the results? Was it easy or difficult? Why? If your answers are like those of the sixty-five hundred people surveyed as part of the research for this book, they are apt to include:

- "I find it very embarrassing to give criticism."
- "I don't like to criticize someone, because I don't want to hurt his feelings."
- "Criticism is difficult for me to take because it means I'm not doing my job."

These responses and literally thousands like them indicate that giving and taking criticism is one of the most difficult and uncomfortable tasks we face at work. Yet the capacity to use criticism productively has been identified empirically as a key attribute of effective CEOs, managers, supervisors, and entrepreneurs, as well as of line employees. It can make the difference in how you feel about your job, your superiors, peers, and subordinates, and in how they feel about you. In fact, how you deal with criticism can make or break your career.

Michael Lombardo and Morgan McCall, Jr., of the Center for Creative Leadership, in Greensboro, North Carolina, studied why some executives continue to move forward while others are stalled. They concluded that two major reasons executives are derailed from the track of success are that they are insensitive to others and that they are unable to allow room for the views of others. These are two major characteristics of giving destructive criticism.

Richard Pascale and Anthony Athos, Stanford and Harvard Business School professors, point out in their book, *The Art of Japanese*

Management, that a key characteristic of effective managers, and what often makes certain managers rise above others, is their ability to criticize — their ability to effectively communicate negative information to — their subordinates.

Harold Geneen, famed president and CEO of ITT, writes in his autobiography that being open to criticism helped him achieve his success: "I tried to welcome criticism. . . . Being open to criticism usually pays unexpected dividends."

If giving and taking criticism is such a key determinant of personal career success and so important to reaching peak productivity in a company, why does it so often produce such stress in both the giver and the taker? Why does it trigger such interpersonal tension?

This is the paradox of criticism. On the one hand, we know that critical evaluation and feedback are inherent and necessary in any group; we know they will help us, the recipient, or our firm. On the other hand, we all know from experience that criticism usually creates discomfort both in ourselves and in others. We need it, yet we avoid it. Indeed, it is the rare individual who goes to work hoping to be criticized.

The goal of this book is to help you resolve this paradox by teaching you how to transform the necessary exchange of criticism from a destructive, damaging experience into a motivating experience. A "both lose" interaction that elicits negative emotion, tension, and decreased productivity can become a "both win" communication that encourages trust, heightens self-esteem, and boosts productivity.

THE CRITICAL CYCLE

Why we do the things we do is one of psychology's oldest questions. The contemporary psychological answer is that our responses to our environment are explained by a complex interaction of our thoughts, feelings, and behavior. These three factors are dynamic, and they continually influence each other.

When we respond over and over in the same way to the same situation, the responses we make become strongly associated with the situation, and we develop what psychologists call structured response patterns. Ultimately, when we encounter the specific situation, the structured response pattern emerges automatically, as if it were instinct.

When it comes to criticism, most people have developed structured response patterns that treat criticism as an ax or a sledgehammer instead of a tool for growth. For example, when criticizing someone, our typical attitude is that we are telling a person that he or she did something wrong: we are accusing. Our common emotional posture is anger, which makes the encounter emotionally distressing both to ourselves and the other person. And the usual behavioral mode is aggressive, attack-oriented, and negative. The recipient of the criticism usually responds with retaliatory comments or becomes silent and withdrawn.

Since the three factors that dictate our actions — thoughts, feelings, and behavior — interact with each other, the likelihood is increased that as soon as one part of the pattern is initiated, the others will automatically follow. Thus, if you "think" negative, you will "feel" negative. If you feel negative, you will "act" negative. And if you act negative, you will continue to think negative. In short, every time you give or respond to criticism counterproductively, you perpetuate the cycle, a "critical" (in the contemporary negative sense only) cycle.

Let's take a closer look at some key concepts that explain how our thoughts, feelings, and behavior are shaped into structured response patterns to criticism. We must master these concepts and related techniques if we are to harness the positive power of criticism.

Cognitive Appraisal

Many types of thought affect how we construe criticism, but the most important ones come from a type of thinking process called cognitive appraisal. This is the mental process that helps us define and interpret what is happening around us. Its roots lie in the individual, unique factors — our early childhood experiences, how we've been educated, our natural talents — that shape our personalities. Because cognitive appraisal has these roots, each of us has a unique way of appraising the situations we encounter in daily life.

The way we "appraise" criticism is crucial in determining how we respond to it. As the Greek philosopher Epictetus said two thousand years ago, "Men are not troubled by things themselves, but by their thoughts about them." Psychologists today agree that it is not events per se but the meaning we assign to those events that gives them the power to affect us for good or ill. Albert Ellis, originator of rational emotive psychotherapy, elaborates on this point by proposing the ABC principle. Here's how it works: *A* is an antecedent event. In this case, your boss criticizes you, saying that your work is sloppy. *C* is the consequence; let's say anger, hurt, defensiveness. According to Ellis and other cognitive theorists, the mistake that people make is to identify the event (*A*) as the cause of the consequence (*C*). In fact, the real culprit is *B,* the belief you hold about the event. If being criticized is appraised as a negative event, then the ensuing response is apt to be negative. Thus, it is how you appraise criticism, not the criticism per se, that causes the counterproductive response. Since most people appraise criticism as a negative event, it is only natural that they tell themselves that they are in trouble when they are being criticized or are about to perform an unpleasant task when giving criticism. Furthermore, the negative private speech that runs through our minds — "I am being put down, I am a failure, I am going to get fired" — strengthens our general belief that criticism is indeed a negative event. The point is this: As long as you believe criticism is negative, you will continue to give and take criticism counterproductively.

It is important to note that cognitive appraisal is not a static but a dynamic process; how you view an event can change. For example, your initial reaction to criticism may be defensive, but after a day or two, you may come to agree with what has been said. Obviously, the criticism has stayed the same, but how you appraised it has changed. Crucial, then, to dealing with criticism is knowing how to appraise it and how to get others to appraise it.

It is also important to remember that people can appraise the same event differently. In fact, since our perceptions are always uniquely individual, it is unlikely that the appraisals of two different people could ever completely coincide. A big new project, for example, will have different implications for an already overworked word processor, an ambitious manager, and a hungry subcontractor. Similarly, the same criticism can take on different meanings for different individuals and thus cause different reactions from each of them. One person may appraise the criticism as an intentional put-down and thus respond with angry words, while another appraises the criticism as a knock to his self-esteem and becomes depressed. Yet another may be grateful for having been told how to improve. How often after delivering a critical remark are we surprised at the reaction it produces, especially when we intended our words to be helpful? "You took it the wrong way," we protest (never thinking we said it the wrong way). The fact is, there is no right way or wrong way. There are only different ways.

To criticize productively, you must use the fact that different people appraise things differently as a means for understanding and resolving conflict rather than promoting it. Productive criticism entails clarifying not only how you appraise the event but, of equal importance, how the recipient appraises it.

Since one can always interpret an event in numerous ways, the question of what makes us prone to interpreting criticism as a negative event in the first place arises. The answer lies in psychological learning principles.

HOW WE LEARN ABOUT CRITICISM

Psychological learning principles help us understand how our responses to particular events are developed, strengthened, and maintained, i.e., why we begin and continue to appraise criticism in a negative light. There are three learning principles that, as applied in our society, help us develop and maintain our criticism habits.

Classical Conditioning

One of the most important ways in which we develop response patterns is through classical conditioning, as proposed by Ivan Pavlov, a Russian physiologist. In essence, the learning principle behind classical conditioning holds that if a stimulus initially having little power to evoke a particular response is continually paired with a stimulus that has strong power to evoke that same response, the weak stimulus will inevitably pick up the "stimulus power" of the strong stimulus and will, in itself, be able to evoke the response in question. As an example, think of how you jump up each time your telephone rings.

Pavlov demonstrated this principle in his classic experiment with dogs. He first observed that upon having meat presented to them, the dogs would salivate. Because the meat evoked the salivating automatically, Pavlov called the meat an unconditioned stimulus. The dogs' salivating, which seemed to be an automatic reaction to the meat, was called an unconditioned response. Pavlov's next step was to introduce a neutral stimulus, one that had no meaning to the dogs. He chose the sound of a bell. He then followed the procedure of ringing the bell moments before he presented the meat to the dogs. After he did this several times, the dogs began to salivate upon hearing the bell. The meat did not even have to be presented for the dogs to salivate. The bell had now picked up the stimulus power of the meat, or, as Pavlov put it, the bell had become a conditioned stimulus. And because the dogs would still salivate automatically upon hearing the bell, even in the absence of the meat, their response was dubbed a conditioned response — they had been conditioned to respond in a predictable way.

In a similar fashion, almost all of us have become classically conditioned to respond negatively to criticism. No one is born with the ability to give and take criticism. Nor is one born predisposed toward thinking that criticism is either positive or negative. It is a neutral stimulus, but one that, since early childhood, for most of us, has been paired with negatives.

Consider, for example, a litany of a single day of parental criticisms, entitled "Saturday with a Teenage Daughter." It was discovered in a Rhode Island church periodical by child psychologist Dr. Charles Schaefer and is quoted in his book, *How to Influence Children*.

> Are you going to sleep all day? . . . Who said you could use my hair spray? . . . Clean the dishes off the table. . . . Turn down the radio. . . . Have you made your bed? . . . That skirt is too short. . . . Your closet is a mess. . . . Stand up straight. . . . Somebody has to go to the store. . . . Quit chewing your gum like that. . . . Your hair is too bushy. . . . I don't care if everybody else does have one. . . . Turn down the radio. . . . Have you done your homework? . . . Don't

slouch. . . . You didn't make your bed. . . . Quit banging on the piano. . . . Why don't you iron it yourself? . . . Your fingernails are too long. . . . Look it up in the dictionary. . . . Sit up straight. . . . Get off the phone. . . . Why did you ever buy that radio? . . . You've been in the bathroom long enough. . . . Turn off that radio and go to sleep.

Criticisms such as these serve the purpose of building an association between criticism per se, the act of being criticized, and the resulting negative feelings and actions. Eventually, because of the repetition, one needs to be criticized only once, no matter how tactfully, to experience distressing feelings and act defensively. It's as if we automatically respond negatively. Furthermore, there is a good deal of research that indicates that these early exposures to criticism, like other early childhood experiences, are permanently coded into the neurological workings of the brain, making us that much more likely to repeat our learned patterns of responding.

If our early learning experiences weren't enough to classically condition us to react negatively to criticism, our contemporary experiences help. Newspaper headlines and stories frequently pair criticism with negative implications and behavior:

- From the *Wall Street Journal:* "Critics fault Mr. Trautlein for failure"
- From the *Detroit News:* "Rocket assemblers criticized in NASA probe . . . [for] failure to follow approved procedure"
- From the *Los Angeles Times:* "GENERAL MOTORS STUNG BY CRITICISM"

We see reports and headlines like these almost every day, and each time we read them, our mind is classically conditioned to the belief that criticism is negative. In the end, just the thought of criticism automatically elicits negative thoughts, feelings, and actions. Mel Brooks sums it up: "I get anxious two weeks before my movie opens up just thinking about the critics."

Modeling

Psychological research has also taught us that observing other people can teach us what to do and how to do it. The girl who learns how to calm her baby brother by watching her mother is using modeling. The father who teaches his son to throw a football by saying "Watch me first" is using modeling. Unfortunately, in the case of criticism, we frequently model behavior that has counterproductive results for ourselves and others. Think back to how your parents, brothers, and sisters in your childhood criticized each other. Chances are that if your parents expressed criticism through yelling, name calling, or sarcasm, you probably do the same. If your parents responded to criticism with retaliatory comments or by leaving the room, your reactions are likely to be similar. You have learned these patterns by observing others. And what you have learned confirms and reinforces your conditioned belief that criticism is negative. While it is true that modeling does not solely explain where the sense of criticism as a negative event originated, it significantly facilitates this negative perception, because by modeling we observe how our society typically gives criticism and responds to it. We then deduce from our observations that criticism is a negative event.

Likewise, when a senior manager criticizes his subordinate in a destructive manner (or responds to criticism defensively), not only is he making the immediate situation worse, but equally important, he is giving his subordinate a counterproductive modeling of how to give (or take) criticism. The subordinate goes on to criticize her own subordinates in a similarly negative manner. The trick, as we shall see, is to make modeling work for you.

Operant Learning

A third psychological learning principle that helps explain the shaping of our ingrained criticism behavior is operant learning. Our behavior "operates" on our environment (or on another person) to produce specific results — we take an action and see what occurs. If our behavior produces desirable results, we tend to repeat it, because it is thus reinforced or encouraged. If the results of our actions are undesirable, we don't repeat the behavior.

Examples of operant learning are all around us. The child learns to throw a Frisbee by throwing it in different ways until he discovers the way to pitch it with accuracy; he then knows how and can do it again. Mixing a recipe to taste is operant learning, too. Sometimes we get the results we want on the first try. Other times, we try a hundred variations before we get what we want. In any case, the action that we "keep" is the one that succeeds.

Many of us have learned our patterns for giving and taking criticism through operant learning. For example, a man may discover that if he doesn't want to hear his wife's criticisms, all he has to do is insult her and she will back off. The fact that his wife always reacts in the same favorable way serves to increase the probability that he will insult her in the future whenever she voices her criticism. Although his insults are hardly productive for their marriage in the long term, he does get a desirable immediate result: his wife stops criticizing him. His wife meanwhile "learns" that if she walks out of the room, she won't have to hear his insults. Her behavior, too, produces a desirable result. Because they both get what they want, at least temporarily, their actions will tend to be repeated.

In the same way, a worker may learn that if he responds to his co-worker's criticism with anger and retaliatory criticism, the issue is dropped. An engineer at an aerospace company recounted: "For years, I responded to my colleagues' criticisms with anger. I found it to be a pretty effective way to keep them silent and their noses out of my work. It wasn't until years later that I realized I was hurting myself. I probably lost plenty of opportunities to improve my work by responding so counterproductively." During those years, his co-workers learned that giving him no criticism was the best response, since it ensured that they would not have to deal with his wrath.

This example illustrates an important paradox about operant learning in the context of criticism. Because unproductive responses to criticism are somewhat reinforced — they stop the criticizer and help the recipient avoid confronting the criticism — it is difficult to conceive of trying new ways of responding, even though these new ways would yield better results. Consequently, the negative pattern continues, and both the giver's and the taker's belief that criticism is indeed a sledgehammer are reinforced. (As we shall see, one way to break this pattern is for the recipient to respond productively, even when the criticism is negative, or for the criticizer to continue to give criticism productively, even when the recipient acts defensively.)

Many times, we reinforce behaviors in the people we work with that we later criticize. The boss who tells his subordinate not to worry that his report was a few hours or even a day late is in effect communicating that it's okay to be late. Six months later at a performance appraisal, the first problem brought up is the subordinate's tendency to be late on his projects. The fact is, the boss has encouraged him to hand in his work late. As with modeling, we need to learn how to use operant learning to facilitate the criticism process rather than impede it.

To summarize, our everyday responses to life's events stem from a complex interaction of our thoughts, feelings, and behavior. Our thoughts influence how we feel and act, and these responses then validate that our thinking is "correct." If we appraise criticism as negative, as most of us have learned to do, then it will follow that we will experience negative feelings when we are criticized. If we are thinking and feeling negatively, it is natural that our behavior will also be negative. And again, each of these responses — thoughts, feelings, and behavior — validates the appropriateness of the others. For example, if you feel distressed, it seems only logical to assume that what you are experiencing is in fact a distressing event. And if you feel angry, then it seems only appropriate that you act in an angry manner. Each of these factors thus perpetuates the others, creating a cycle that inevitably keeps itself spinning. Furthermore, the time it takes for the patterns to occur can be as brief as a millisecond.

In short, every time we respond to criticism with negative feelings and behavior, we perpetuate and strengthen our belief that criticism is negative, and we keep the cycle in motion. It is irrelevant whether the initial reaction is negative thoughts, feelings, or behavior. The result is the same — a Pavlovian negative reaction to criticism.

Thus, in order to create the positive power of criticism and consequently get positive results, criticism must be communicated — and received — in a way that does not trigger negative reactions. Stated another way, we must break the critical cycle by reconditioning the thoughts, feelings, and behavior that we associate with criticism. To this end, we must first redefine criticism as a results-oriented interaction whose goals include improvement and motivation.

A NEW FRAME OF MIND —
TAKING CRITICISM TO TASK

Learning how to give and take criticism productively begins by re-defining it. Its contemporary definition and use — flaw finding, letting a person know he did something wrong — must be changed to a definition that integrates both the early orientations of criticism — judging accordingly (part of the objective orientation) — and its contemporary qualities as an ego-invested process, an interpersonal communication process, and a means of communicating negative information. In this context, the definition of the verb "to criticize" becomes "communicating evaluative information to others in a way that enables them to use it to their advantage."

This redefinition is more than just playing with words. For one thing, it shifts the emphasis from communicating negative information to communicating evaluative information, thus reminding us of the expressive approach to criticism — that criticism is our opinion, not absolute fact. It points out that the proper use of criticism is to encourage improvement, not to remind us of failure. This definition also emphasizes that criticism is an active process in which both giver and recipient take part so both can benefit, personally and interpersonally. Most important, it stresses that criticism is between people, people who have feelings. While Plato, Aristotle, and their students criticized inanimate objects — statues, pictures, and poems — we criticize each other.

With this definition, criticism becomes a tool that facilitates growth. Our cognitive appraisal of criticism is changed, thus enabling both the giver and the recipient to respond differently. The criticized behavior is identified not as an irrevocable act but as a behavior that can be changed. The criticizer is now challenged to perform a TASK — to Teach Appropriate Skills and Knowledge. The underlying message becomes "I am telling you this because I think it can help you and/or can help our relationship." By the same token, the recipient, instead of thinking "He is always pointing out my flaws," is more likely to think "He is trying to help me." Both giver and receiver are now participating in a growth process.

When this definition of criticism is assimilated into our thinking, we can begin to bypass our own and others' negative Pavlovian reactions. We can begin to apply psychological and communication principles that will sharpen our skill in using criticism as a catalyst in helping others (and ourselves) improve. In the workplace, this yields better results.

Working with Criticism

NBC *Today* host Bryant Gumbel once said, "I hate criticism, but I need it." How well put. The ability to give and take criticism is, without a doubt, one of the most important determinants of career success.

We hate it, but we need it. For most of us, a strong effort of will is required to accept criticism of our job-related skills or capacities. Most of the time, we complain about unfair or insensitive superiors and bemoan our inability to criticize them back. Or we grumble about co-workers who are always telling us what we did wrong but never seem to listen to our evaluations of their work.

Yet, when we examine the productive qualities of criticism, we can see how its help is invaluable to individual and organizational success. What follow are some positive functions of criticism.

Productive criticism provides feedback that enhances job results

It's hard to do a job well if you don't know whether you are on target. It's well validated by psychological research that a person's job performance deteriorates when feedback is withheld. Criticism is a special type of feedback. It lets us know what aspect of our work or behavior we need to modify, correct, or strengthen so that our results can improve. Without this evaluation and feedback, we tend to repeat what we've been doing. We fail to show improvement because we don't know that we need to change. In this context, criticism gives us direction that steers us in a straighter path toward our goals.

Productive criticism leads to ongoing personal and professional development

While it is true that criticism helps us develop skills that will improve our day-to-day work and our results, it also has an important role in spurring professional development. A sales manager's criticism, for example, not only lets a sales representative know whether

her closing strategy is effective but also provides her with the seasoning that enables her to mature professionally, to perfect her craft. Here, criticism is a tool that helps people develop over time. The importance of criticism in this context is evidenced by the fact that many companies demand that their workers actively seek out criticism. One case is that of Matsushita, the giant Japanese electronic company in whose corporate philosophy self-criticism is treated as one of the disciplines of personal development, a tough, difficult process to experience but one that needs to be endured. Sir Laurence Olivier speaks here: "Above all, do not despair when the hand of criticism plunges into your body and claws at your soul: you must endure it, accept it and smile."

Productive criticism reduces stress and creates psychological security

A Los Angeles County employee said it was difficult for her to do her job because her boss never told her what she was doing well or what she needed to improve. She said: "It was like working in a vacuum. I would do things every day, but I never knew how I was doing — whether I was meeting my boss's standards, or whether I was on thin ice. Over time, I found that my job became quite stressful because I didn't know whether I was making any progress. I began to feel as though I was just a body that nobody paid any attention to, that my actions were inconsequential. I felt very alone."

A recent study by the American Management Association found that one of the four major causes of job stress is a lack of feedback, especially criticism. Productive criticism helps reduce stress because it lets a person know where he or she stands, how he or she is doing. When a person is unsure whether his performance is up to his boss's or organization's standards, feelings of anxiety are sure to arise. Consequently, he begins to question whether he has a future with the organization. Feeling insecure, he may do nothing in response, with the result that his innovative or risk-taking behavior is inhibited, or, more frequently, he may begin to look for a new job. Productive criticism not only reassures him of his firm's belief in him but also gives him the confidence to stretch his potential. Creativity and innovation are frequent results.

Productive criticism helps improve interpersonal relationships

When best-selling authors, collaborators, and psychologists Mel Kinder and Connel Cowan write their books, they criticize each other. Says Kinder, "We're eager to hear each other's criticisms; we each want to know how the other thinks. We find that allowing this type of exchange not only helps us write better books, but also makes it fun, and exciting." Adds Cowan, "It's pretty easy for Mel and me to criticize each other. It's been so helpful; even if it hurts, each of us knows it's usually helpful. In fact, I would say that we look forward to each other's criticisms."

Good interpersonal relationships engender greater productivity, higher morale, and job satisfaction. Productive criticism facilitates the development of such relationships, ones that are characterized by honesty, intimacy, and trust. It allows both the giver and the receiver to discuss stressful information in a nonthreatening manner. Each person becomes less defensive. There is more self-disclosure, which leads to a greater sense of trust, thereby increasing each person's openness toward the next encounter. The relationship solidifies and in itself becomes a source of nurturance and support. Both parties come to look forward to sharing their thoughts, because they know the information will help them grow. Each time criticism is productively communicated, the relationship becomes stronger, whether it's with a boss, a subordinate, a co-worker, or a client. This is one of the reasons many sources, including the *Wall Street Journal,* report that one growing corporate trend is to spend more and more time and money training not only managers but also line employees in how to criticize each other.

Productive criticism helps develop the ideal organizational climate

When Henry ("The Fonz") Winkler was given an Emmy award for his role in the long-running television show *Happy Days,* he said in his acceptance speech that the cast had become a special group of individuals who had transcended the "forced" roles of working together. Individually, the actors were excellent. But together, they were even better. Why? Said Winkler, because they supported each other. They helped each other stretch their talents. It wasn't "as if" they were a family, they *were* a family. It was this "feel" that Winkler believed was at the core of the show's outstanding success.

Whether it's a sports team, a Fortune 500 company, or the cast and crew of a television series, organizations achieve their outstanding results when they jell, or, as group dynamic specialists say, "when the whole is greater than the sum of its parts." When this happens, as Henry Winkler described it, the group is functioning in an ideal organizational climate.

Although nobody knows exactly what an ideal organizational climate is, it would be hard to refute that it is supportive, cohesive, emotionally energizing, and self-evaluative. Productive criticism is a vital catalyst for such organizational development because it helps build and maintain all of these qualities.

For example, productive criticism builds support since it helps people develop their skills. This enables them to experience a sense of growth, resulting in increased self-esteem and job satisfaction. Cohesiveness is fostered by honest, intimate, and trustworthy relationships in which critical information freely passes among individuals without fear of negative consequences; each knows the information is intended for the good of the relationship, the good of the group. Learning how to do things better through this productive criticism and getting excellent results lead to a sense of excitement, an emotional charge, that makes work fun and makes it easier to sustain best efforts, as echoed by Kinder and Cowan. Knowing what is expected and the specifics of how to do it, again through criticism, creates a psychologically secure environment that gives individuals the confidence to take innovative risks. And productive criticism's orientation toward improvement forces the members of the organization to continually renew themselves by asking "How can we be better?" When these ideal qualities are present, there is a mesh that makes peak performance the norm.

In sum, productive criticism allows you to improve your job skills, increases your interpersonal effectiveness, enhances job satisfaction, moves you up the organization, and helps you achieve your long-term goals. Given these distinct and far-reaching positive attributes, and in light of the fact that criticism is an everyday occurrence with every job, the plan is clear: to learn how to give (and take) criticism in a way that not only produces the desired results but also enables people to feel good so that they want to change, want to improve, want to excel.

Equally important is to learn how to criticize (or take criticism) without feeling embarrassed, angry, fearful, or inept. Just think how many times you may have said "I don't know how to tell you this, but . . ." or something else expressing similar unease with the process of giving criticism.

When we can do both these things, criticism can fulfill its TASK, as poet Ralph Waldo Emerson described it: "Criticism should not be querulous, and wasting, all knife and root puller, but guiding, instructive, inspiring, a South wind, not an East wind."

Chapter 2

The Critical Factors

DURING the last ten years, I have extensively studied what it is that makes criticism productive. From these studies, seven factors emerge that set the stage for productive criticism. The critical factors are:

1. Productive criticism is strategic
2. Productive criticism protects self-esteem
3. Productive criticism is timing-oriented
4. Productive criticism is improvement-oriented
5. Productive criticism is interactive
6. Productive criticism is flexible
7. Productive criticism communicates the Helping Spirit

By being aware of these characteristics and actively building them into your specific criticisms, you will be able to increase the chances that the recipient of your criticism will respond productively. You will be able to become a productive criticizer.

All of the factors are equally important, but at times the significance of one may exceed that of others.

PRODUCTIVE CRITICISM IS STRATEGIC

People who are productive criticizers actively take responsibility for how they communicate. They see themselves as a directed force, with the goal of getting their recipient to take their criticism productively. They recognize that the communication process itself is influential and that the more active they become in it, the more they can influence how their recipient responds.

This active philosophy is crucial because it entails advance planning. Instead of making spontaneous negative remarks — caustic, sarcastic, blaming, or accusatory "you are wrong" statements that produce resentment instead of results — the active critic thinks through the criticism beforehand, which enables him or her to devise the best way for making a mark. The critic thinks strategically. Productive criticizers implement this factor by asking themselves several questions:

- Exactly what do I want to communicate? What do I want to change?
- What are my motives for expressing this criticism? (If a subordinate's performance made you look bad, you may be angrily passing down your boss's criticism in a nonproductive manner. Beware those times when your motive is to get even.)
- How can I communicate this information so that the person will be receptive to it?
- What specific solutions and goals can I offer and what can I do to help the person achieve these goals?
- What is a reasonable time frame in which this change can occur?

Strategic planning forces you to become aware of what you want to accomplish; it helps you develop an improvement-oriented behavioral style of criticizing. Many people may feel that they do not have the time to plan in advance how they can best criticize someone. It is indeed true that things happen on the job that demand an immediate response. And because of the spontaneity of the situation, we are caught off guard. Our destructive patterns of criticizing quickly emerge, making the situation worse. The Critical Edge is lost.

Fortunately, we also know of specific times at work in which we frequently have to point out a wrongdoing. Most sales managers have a pretty good idea of the criticisms that they will eventually have to give their new sales recruits. The same is true for a supervisor of student teachers, nurses, or flight attendants. Alfred Hitchcock said he always knew he was going to have to criticize his lead actors and actresses for "not looking startled enough."

These situations, the criticisms that we know we are going to have to give, usually make us anxious. We know we will have to point out a wrongdoing, which is apt to elicit all the negative feelings and thoughts that we associate with criticism. Paradoxically, these same situations provide us with a rich opportunity to develop the skill of giving productive criticism because they allow us to practice in advance. The sales manager who knows he is going to have to criticize his subordinate's first-time sales presentation for being too long and impersonal can begin to think, "How can I say this so that he will be most receptive?" The nurse who knows that she will have to tell her student practitioner that she is neglecting her patient's need to talk will be able to plan in advance the best way to do it. When the moment of truth comes, you are ready. Instead of blurting out destructive comments, you can make your point skillfully because of your preparation and thus positively influence behavior.

In addition to asking themselves the questions given earlier, many people have found it to be very helpful to write out their criticism in advance of saying it; putting it on paper helps them clarify exactly what they want to say and how they want to say it. Others have found that rehearsing criticism out loud before they deliver it can be effective, because they can get the feel of how they will come across, how they will sound.

When we practice handling frequent and expected criticism situations, not only are we learning how to deal with them more effectively, but we are also honing our criticism skills for those situations that are unforeseen. This happens because we are getting in the habit of asking ourselves "How can I communicate this information so the person will be receptive to it?" The constant practicing of this type of thinking allows you to integrate it into your daily communication patterns and enables you to answer the question more and more quickly, even in the most delicate and pressured situations. Whether you need to talk to the company mailroom staff about its failure to get your report out to its destination on time or have to criticize a co-worker at a staff meeting, your immediate thought will be strategic: "How can I best say this?" This reaction inhibits the destructive words that you might have used. Thus, a strategic approach to criticism can help you develop an effective spontaneous style.

This concept, which psychologists call response generalization, is well illustrated by the workouts of professional athletes. Jack Nicklaus practices hitting out of a sand trap every day so that if need be, an excellent effort is second nature in a tournament. Boston Celtics superstar Larry Bird launches hundreds of jump shots before each game so that he can make the same shot when necessary during play. His constant practicing helps him make split-second decisions — whether to pass, shoot, dribble, or jump in a fluid motion that looks choreographed. The principle to extract is this: The more you practice in structured situations, the better you become in spontaneous situations.

In sum, the strategic factor is important because it helps you to think through what you want to communicate and the best way to do it, and to develop the skill of doing it under the gun.

PRODUCTIVE CRITICISM PROTECTS SELF-ESTEEM

There are many ways to define self-esteem, but a good working definition is "the confidence and satisfaction that a person possesses about himself or herself." Productive criticizers act on the assumption that a person's self-esteem is his or her most important possession. They are keenly aware that if they threaten it, defensive behavior is quick to occur. This is well validated by dozens of psychological studies indicating that when a person receives information causing self-esteem to be reduced, psychological distress is experienced.

"Sticks and stones may break my bones, but words will never hurt me" runs the proverb. But if ever a proverb was wide of the mark, this one is. As the majority of people would ruefully admit, words can do more lasting damage than most physical blows. Peter Sellers's statement that "two lines of negative criticism could kill me" is an understatement for some.

When criticism attacks self-esteem, it emotionally scars even the sturdiest ego. Ultimately, negative criticism can seriously undermine the way people feel about themselves. The recipient's self-image, the inner sense of value as an individual, is weakened. When we take this into consideration, it becomes obvious that one of the reasons people respond defensively to criticism is to protect themselves from feelings of hurt, from having to think less of themselves. An advertising director, for example, who tells his assistant "You made the layout too crowded, you didn't use the right colors, your concept makes no sense" is apt to trigger defensiveness, as is the manager who criticizes his sales rep with "You blew it. You didn't pay attention to your prospect. You didn't listen. Perhaps you're not right for this job." Criticisms like these attack the self-esteem — they emphasize that the recipient didn't do well and imply that he might not have the ability to do better. These messages stab the ego.

On the other hand, when criticism is given in a way that protects the self-esteem, it becomes more productive, because the likelihood that the recipient will process the information with an open mind is increased. If the criticism does not threaten or attack, the negative Pavlovian defensive reaction is short-circuited. This frees the recipient to respond differently, more productively. When this happens, the criticism has the opportunity to fulfill its TASK. For these reasons, the criticisms in the previous paragraph would more likely be effective if communicated in these terms: "How about spacing the pictures out and using some brighter colors?" and "You might find it more effective if you periodically ask your prospect if she has any questions. This will keep her involved."

Besides allowing you to get through to your recipient, criticism that protects the self-esteem has other benefits. One is that it paves the way for future criticisms. Since the recipient's ego has been left intact, or even enhanced, her perception of you is likely to improve to the point where she sees you as a credible source, someone whose opinions deserve to be considered carefully. Consequently, your later criticisms are welcomed, even sought. Another benefit of criticism that takes the ego into account is that it improves the quality of the relationship. Your conscious effort not to attack or wound communicates that you appreciate and value the person. The recipient's sense of this helps you both build and maintain a supportive relationship that is characterized by trust. (Similarly, an empirically identified trait of effective marriages is the spouses' ability to criticize each other productively.) IBM's Tom Watson, Sr., said it cogently: "Always protect the person's self-esteem. Enhance it if you can."

Note that if you think strategically, it will be easier to protect the recipient's self-esteem; planning how to do it will help you inhibit the traditional put-down comments.

PRODUCTIVE CRITICISM
IS TIMING-ORIENTED

There is a time and a place for every endeavor. Criticism is no exception. Critical remarks that otherwise might be offered and accepted in a positive way can be rendered ineffective — not because of their content, but because of when and where they are made, because of the recipient's state of mind at the time, and our own mood, too.

Productive criticizers, when they criticize, are very much alert to the time, the place, the presence or absence of other people, and the psychological state of the criticized person. They recognize that each of these factors can serve as an obstruction to their goals. They also know that each factor can be used to help them reach their goals. For example, a boss's well-put criticism of a subordinate at a group meeting may be rebuffed because the subordinate feels that she has to defend herself in front of her peers. Or she may nod her head in agreement but internally be focusing on what her co-workers are thinking about as she is being criticized.

Conversely, a boss may intentionally criticize a subordinate in front of her peers because he anticipates that her reaction will be less argumentative than if he did it privately. He believes that her past behavior reflects a strong need to impress her peers as being open to criticism and that the group atmosphere will pressure her into thinking about the criticism. The point is that there are no rules as to when and where to criticize. What must be developed is the skill of using environmental, situational, and psychological factors to increase receptivity.

Timing is also important, for many times, although the criticism may be valid and accepted, it is given too late for the recipient to do anything about it. David Puttnam, former Columbia Pictures president, illustrates this point with a reference to the film *Heaven's Gate,* the biggest financial disaster in film history. "Look at *Heaven's Gate.* Notice nobody criticized Michael Cimino when he should have been criticized — when he was actually making that movie. When something could have been done. Instead, they [studio executives] waited until it was finished. By that time, it was too late." Inappropriate timing here almost put Columbia Pictures out of business.

It is equally important, and perhaps more difficult, for productive criticizers to create an environment that increases their recipient's openness to criticism. This can be as simple as meeting in the recipient's office, holding all telephone calls, picking a pleasant nonwork environment, or actually creating a situation that illustrates the criticism. A Warner-Lambert manager once demonstrated a perfect blending of these strategies. He wanted to criticize two subordinates for being too competitive with each other. Their lack of cooperation was resulting in frequent power struggles that led to costly project delays. He planned his criticism and took them both to lunch at a local Chinese restaurant. Before the waiter took their order, the manager subtly remarked, "Well, I like everything. You two decide what to get." This prompted a short discussion, and the dishes were mutually selected. After all was happily consumed, the manager remarked: "I really enjoyed that. You guys did a good job in ordering. Everything went well together. And when we get back to the office, I will expect the two of you to cooperate in the same manner." This example is not as out of the ordinary as most would think, and it does illustrate the art of giving criticism. (The manager also had the subordinates pick up the check to cement their feeling that they had truly cooperated with each other!)

Besides being aware of the mood of the recipient, productive criticizers are aware of their own mood. They recognize that their criticisms will probably not be productive if delivered in a mood of anger or if they feel uncomfortable. In fact, attributional psychology — the study of how you deduce information from your environment, to what you attribute your own or others' thoughts and feelings — points out that when the critic gives his criticism in an angry mood, the criticism, even if well grounded, is perceived by the recipient as not being valid because it comes from the critic's anger, not from a valid frame of reference — "He's only saying these things because he's angry. When he calms down, he won't mean it." Therefore, productive criticizers delay their criticism until they feel that they have both the physical environment and the psychological environment working for them and for their recipient.

Overall, being timing-oriented helps make criticism productive because it prompts you to decide actively on where best to do it, when best to do it, and if you are ready to do it. This has the additional effect of increasing the critic's general sensitivity to the recipient, which becomes a building block for empathy and rapport, qualities that always enhance the criticism process.

PRODUCTIVE CRITICISM IS IMPROVEMENT-ORIENTED

Psychologists Abraham Maslow and Carl Rogers have written extensively on people's inherent desire to develop themselves, to improve. Criticism that is improvement-oriented becomes productive because it facilitates this desire, enabling both the critic and the recipient to use the specific criticism as an opportunity to develop their potential.

Most criticism, however, stifles this desire by placing strong emphasis on the negatives. The criticized behavior is usually defined as irrevocable. The recipient is told what he "did," thus placing the action in the past; any chance of change for the better is precluded. Since there seems to be little chance for improvement, the recipient, in order to protect his self-esteem, defends his actions rather than looking for ways to improve. The Critical Edge is lost. Furthermore, even if one feels that people lack an inherent wish to improve, the fact remains that a constant barrage of negative criticism will undermine any recipient's confidence, making it difficult for him to believe that he can improve.

Making criticism improvement-oriented has the opposite effect. For the critic, it creates the mental set of using criticism as a teaching and educational tool. The TASK becomes to figure out "How can he do it better? How can I help him improve?" The critic begins to formulate specific ways in which he can help the recipient. He becomes solution-oriented. Here we see the meaning of T. S. Eliot's words: "Great critics are those that bring something to their subject."

One way productive criticizers make criticism improvement-oriented is to move the criticism forward, into the future. They emphasize what the recipient is "doing," not what she "did." Change becomes possible as the critic begins to stress how the recipient can do it better "next time." This lets the recipient feel secure in knowing that she will get another chance. She also can feel confident because her critic believes she has the ability to improve. With this in mind, the recipient can begin to focus her energy on improving her future performance rather than on defending past results. Criticism becomes a "put-up" instead of a put-down.

Although, to reiterate, many believe that the need to improve oneself is inherent, it is not uncommon that we find our boss, co-workers, subordinates, acting as though they felt no such need. Productive critics quickly point this out to those they spot who exhibit this "temporary" mind-set. Stanley Marcus recalls how his father did this to him: "He ran his hands over the inside of a shoe and asked, 'How can we improve it?' I pointed out that the store buyer said 'We don't have to improve it, because we've already sold 10,000 pairs.' But my father ran his finger down the inside of the shoe and said he wanted the lining scathed down. I said people never will notice the difference, but my father said maybe not, but those who do will appreciate it, and you'll sell more. The customer didn't say do it, my father did, and it cost us an extra 25 cents a pair. That was a great lesson to me: How do you make it better?" Over the years, Stanley Marcus became committed to always making sure his merchandise got better.

PRODUCTIVE CRITICISM IS INTERACTIVE

Conventional criticism is almost always a one-way process. The critic speaks and, having spoken, assumes he or she need not say or do anything more. When criticism is approached from this one-way perspective, counterproductive effects are almost sure to arise. The burden of resolving the criticism is placed solely on the recipient, who may not have the resources to improve the situation independently. Psychological distress is inevitably experienced. The pressure and frustration inherent in being told to solve a problem alone, a problem on which your job may depend, almost always lead to destructive anger. When this fails to get productive results, a sense of hopelessness and/or depression begins. The recipient becomes impotent and does nothing to improve the criticized behavior.

For his part, not seeing any change, the critic becomes frustrated and angry, too, frequently interpreting the recipient's honest but ineffective efforts as showing a lack of motivation. Instead of change for the better, the result is mutual resentment.

When this mode of criticism is practiced daily in the working environment, it undermines many of the qualities of an ideal organizational climate. Teamwork, group cohesion, and mutual problem-solving efforts become almost nonexistent as the style of the organization forces people to resolve things on their own. Since peak performance requires the aforementioned qualities, these organizations become far from excellent, to say the least.

Significant, however, is not just that a one-way perception of criticism has negative effects but, more to the point, that the one-way perspective is a misconceptualization of the criticism process. This is demonstrated by the following experiment.

Sociologist Stephanie Hughes gathered data for her dissertation, "Criticism and Interaction," by testing the way people use and respond to criticism. She had two groups of female volunteers. One group was instructed to invent a new game played with dominoes. The second group was told to respond to half of the women's suggestions for game rules with positive criticism (focusing on both the positives and negatives of a suggestion but emphasizing the former) and to half with negative criticism (focusing only on the negatives of a suggestion). The volunteers were then paired off, with each member of the first group talking to a member of the second group. Hughes analyzed the attitudes and feelings aroused in both sets of volunteers using the two different types of feedback.

Her findings indicated that when the critics knew they were to use a negative approach, that expectation colored their attitude. Many subjects said they felt hostile or competitive toward the person suggesting the game. For instance, one critic said she found herself "trying to pick up on something about the other person that bothered me, so I could give negative criticism." Another said, "Giving negative criticism puts me in a negative state of mind, so I can't think highly of anything that is suggested." Hughes concluded that expecting to give negative criticism actually creates a negative mindset.

The responses of the volunteers who received the negative criticism indicated that they, as well, were strongly affected. They were influenced to a considerable degree by even the slightest downgrading of their suggestions. Many who at first thought their ideas were reasonably good decided after even mildly negative criticism that the ideas were not only "less good" but were more or less "bad."

Clearly, the person criticizing and the person being criticized both contribute to the effects of criticism. It is an interaction — the attitudes, feelings, and behaviors that each person brings to an encounter affect how each responds to the other. Thus, productive criticizers make the assumption that how you give criticism affects how the recipient takes it: If you give criticism productively, chances increase that the recipient will take it productively; if you give criticism destructively, chances increase that the recipient will respond destructively. (Productive criticizers acknowledge, however, that even if criticism is given destructively, the recipient can still respond productively.)

Acknowledging that criticism is an interaction helps make criticism productive for at least two reasons. First, it gets the critic to recognize that he is, in part, directly responsible for how his recipient responds. The critic's awareness of how he criticizes is consequently increased, making it easier for him to think strategically and to remember to protect the self-esteem. Second, by accepting responsibility for how the recipient responds, the critic becomes more involved. He begins to ask himself, "How can I interact positively with the recipient? How can I get him involved in the criticism process in a productive way?" His criticism changes from a monologue to a dialogue — an exchange of information — which helps set the stage for making criticism a genuinely helping process.

On the other hand, the recipient recognizes that she, too, shapes the course that the criticism is to take. By interacting productively, not defensively, she is able to keep herself — and the critic — on track. Asking for suggestions, clarifying points, and not interrupting the critic are ways in which the recipient can do her share in making the criticism interaction productive.

The concept of interaction carries an important corollary: Behavior is a process, not an event. Most of us think of our daily activities as a series of discrete events that have little if any bearing on each other. Something happens, it is over and done with, and we start afresh with the next event. The fact is, human behavior is not a series of detached events but rather what ecological psychologists Herbert

Wright and Roger Barker call a flowing stream. They mean that each event shapes the course of the following event, that there is a continuity, and that this continuity explains why a "particular part of the stream is holding its course." Criticism is a process, not an event.

Let's suppose that you are criticizing a co-worker. Her immediate reaction is defensiveness. Typically, her defensive behavior elicits your own defensiveness, which causes your co-worker to respond with more of the same. The pattern continues, and escalation is inevitable, all within a few seconds. Both parties will then blame the other for "starting it." The truth is, who is to blame is arbitrarily decided by what you designate as the "starting time." While you have a valid point in arguing that your co-worker's defensiveness triggered your response, your co-worker is equally justified in seeing your criticism as the trigger. Each one's behavior is a starting point for the other's response. Thus, how you give criticism affects how it's taken, and how it is taken will affect how you continue to give it.

When you focus on who started it, you keep the interaction stuck in the past and prevent both yourself and the recipient from moving forward, from becoming improvement-oriented. There is more. Because behavior is a process, this part of the stream is going to affect what happens downstream. Since your co-worker responded defensively to your latest criticism, how do you think you are going to feel the next time you have to criticize her? Anxious, reluctant, scared, guarded, are among the most typical responses. In fact, you might not even criticize at all. Thus you begin to withhold information that could be crucial to improving performance.

Acknowledging that criticism is a process instead of an event helps make it productive because it tunes the critic in to the fact that the interaction is developmental and that he has the power to develop the interaction in a positive way. Similarly, he begins to think of criticism as a tool to help develop the recipient's performance over time rather than an event limited to pointing out what is wrong.

PRODUCTIVE CRITICISM IS FLEXIBLE

"You should" or "You shouldn't" frequently prefaces the criticisms that we give. Those and similar phrases obstruct the criticism process because they reflect rigid attitudes. "Should" and "shouldn't" imply that the criticizer's opinion or method is the only right one. This in itself is enough to put a damper on anyone's willingness to try to change. Furthermore, the assumption that the critic's way is the only correct way perpetuates the traditional concept of criticism as an either/or situation — one in which something or someone is right or wrong and there is no acceptable middle ground, no possible alternative behavior. The criticized person is likely to react defensively — "Why shouldn't I do it my way?" — or to counter with reasons he or she "couldn't" have done it the way the critic wanted. Either type of response results in stubborn disagreement between the two parties.

Rigid thinking takes on extra significance when one considers the study, cited earlier, by the Center for Creative Leadership of executives who were derailed from the track of success. A major reason for this was discovered to be that these executives had trouble making room for others' points of views and ideas. They tended to be rigid thinkers. So do destructive criticizers.

In contrast, productive criticizers acknowledge that what they are saying is neither right nor wrong; rather, they are communicating their own subjective (expressive-oriented) viewpoint. They consciously avoid the right/wrong issue. In so doing, the message they convey is "I am not saying you are wrong. I am saying there are alternatives." The focus becomes what the recipient "could" be doing, not what he "should" be doing. The productive criticizer approaches the recipient in a teaching, advisorial role rather than with a strict authoritative stance, which promotes resistance. By the same token, she recognizes that the recipient's response is not merely defensiveness but another subjective view that, like her own, merits consideration. When criticism is flexible, it provides a framework for a true exchange of ideas, a search for the truth. Because there is no right or wrong, the criticism can be molded to its most useful form. Both parties, not just the critic, contribute information that can lead to better results. This is a sharp departure from criticism that is rigid, that is not malleable, that is presented as a fact. Flexibility makes room for the recipient's opinion. A relationship between colleagues is formed, dialogue is encouraged, and productive interaction is facilitated.

Flexibility has additional applications and consequential merits.

One is that productive, flexible criticizers have a style of communicating that allows them to change how they are criticizing someone as soon as they see that the recipient is becoming defensive. They are flexible in the sense that they do not continue to do what is not working. Changing tacks increases the chance of getting through to the recipient because it nips defensive behavior in the bud. The critic trains himself to be flexible in this way by anticipating how the recipient will respond before he criticizes him and by developing a plan for each one of his possible reactions.

For example, let's say that you are going to criticize a subordinate because you believe that he is not being supportive of his co-workers and that, as a result, he is undermining their work. What will you do if the subordinate disagrees with your criticism? And what will you do if he blames his co-workers for causing his own behavior? What if he says it's your fault that his co-workers don't like him? In other words, anticipate the worst reactions that you can imagine and figure out a plan for overcoming each one so that the criticism can stay on track. If you're ready, and sensitive to the notion of inter-action — watching how the recipient is responding and how you contribute to that response — you will be able to shift gears and substitute a new course of action as you see fit. If plan A isn't working, move to plan B, then to C, and so on until what you are doing is having an effect. You will be particularly flexible in that you will become able to change what you are doing while you are doing it. Many top salespeople use this same strategy. They anticipate their prospective client's objections so that if they encounter one, they can change their selling approach midstream and pursue another course that might enable them to close the deal. In short, when your criticism isn't working, be flexible and try it another way.

Productive critics also make criticism flexible by learning how to communicate the same criticism to the same person in several ways. The father who is always criticizing his teenager for watching too much television by saying or implying "Can't you do something else? Don't you have any other interests?" is wasting his time saying it over and over, since his son's behavior remains unchanged. He needs to develop a way of saying the same thing in a different manner, one to which the son will be more receptive. Perhaps "Today's a beautiful day. How about playing baseball instead of watching it?" or "I bet you'd like the book much better than the movie" or "Gee, this looks like the same old stuff that was on last week. How about finding something more fun to do?" When the content of criticism is flexible, when the same message can be communicated in a variety of ways, the odds grow that the recipient will be receptive, because out of multiple approaches, one usually gets results.

Most people, however, do not take this point into consideration. As a result, they end up saying things like "How many times have I told you this?" or "You never listen." What these people fail to recognize is that they are creating their own problem by communicating the criticism in the same way every time. They need to be flexible and express it differently.

A final point about flexibility and criticism: Remember that there are different strokes for different folks. How you should criticize John is apt to be very different from how you should criticize Jack, which will be different from how you criticize Jill for the very same behavior. People are different, and flexible criticism takes those individual differences into account so that the specific criticism can be tailored to the individual in question.

PRODUCTIVE CRITICISM
COMMUNICATES THE HELPING SPIRIT

Criticism is much more likely to pay off positively when the recipient perceives the critic to be genuinely concerned with his or her welfare. Productive criticizers act on this by demonstrating the "helping spirit."

Showing the helping spirit means giving three important messages to the recipient:

1. I care about you and will prove it by investing my time and energy in helping you.
2. I am confident that you can improve, that you can do the task at hand.
3. I am committed to helping. You are not alone. I will support your efforts.

Demonstrating the helping spirit goes beyond merely saying that you care, that you will help, or that you will be supportive. It means communicating this attitude through action. To act on these points, you must look for signs of improvement, ways to acknowledge it, and ways to help if improvement is not occurring. Acting in this manner serves to remind both the critic and the target that criticism is not a one-shot event but rather the beginning of a process of change that takes place over time. In essence, the critic's actions acknowledge that it is sometimes difficult to improve, that it takes time, and that it can be done.

To be sure, this does not mean that productive critics do not sometimes go at it tooth and nail, but when they do, they still underscore their criticisms with a supportive tone that in the end projects a concern for the welfare of the target and the target's work. In fact, productive criticizers usually increase their helping-spirit efforts as the criticism becomes more intense, more important. This is well illustrated by the actions of former secretary of state William Rogers, who led the investigation of the NASA *Challenger* disaster. Knowing that as the criticisms mounted, NASA's chances for survival became slimmer, and that the entire space program might be terminated, Rogers, according to a *Business Week* article, intentionally "tempered" his commission's criticism. The result was that his report included both valid criticisms and a recommendation for improvement, and today the space program continues to expand.

Significantly, the helping spirit is not something that productive criticizers reserve for giving criticism. They behave in a supportive and helpful manner on a daily basis. In other words, the helping spirit is part of a positive, encouraging management style. Because productive critics consistently act in a supportive manner, their colleagues come to expect that any criticism is in their best interest. The general helping spirit is thus useful to the specific situation.

Author and psychologist Harry Levinson provides in his book *Corporate Leadership in Action* a good example of a productive criticizer who had a reputation for demonstrating the helping spirit — Reginald H. Jones, former CEO of General Electric. He earned this kudos for doing things like sending notes to ill family members of associates, flowers for a death in the family, and personal notes of appreciation for jobs well done to people low in the hierarchy. His everyday supportive and helpful actions generalized to his critical encounters, earning him the distinction of being a gentle, supportive, and effective criticizer. One particular incident bears this out. An associate of several years brought Jones an inadequate report. Jones responded, "This is the very first time I've ever had to do this, but . . . I just don't think it's going to work." His criticism was well taken. His associate acknowledged that due to workload pressure, he had patched the report together and rushed it to Jones. Because Jones was supportive and exchanged ideas in a helpful manner, the associate became less anxious and was able to work up within twenty-four hours a revision that won accolades. And like the true productive critic, Jones passed the credit on: "I said something intuitively to a guy, and it had a tremendous impact on him as reported by a third party. I can't take credit for it." But what he can take credit for is that in his suggestions for revisions of the subordinate's work, there was neither a personal attack nor an emphasis on the negative; rather, he focused on how it might be done better and on points of praise for the positive elements. Certainly, this is the helping spirit at work.

THE WHEEL OF CRITICISM

To repeat, all of the critical factors are equally important. Visualize them as spokes on a wheel, each one connected to the other through the hub, the helping spirit. As the hub, the helping spirit becomes ingrained in all of the other factors, thereby fulfilling its role of setting the tone of the criticism. As the wheel turns, each characteristic takes on temporary priority and exerts its influence on the criticism process. Sometimes flexibility is most important, while in other situations protecting self-esteem might be most critical. The factors are all important in different ways, and they all combine to make criticism productive.

It is now time to look at how productive criticizers blend and implement these characteristics in concrete ways — how they turn the wheel, so to speak.

Chapter 3

Giving Productive Criticism:
A Tough TASK!

W HEN ASKED why Frank Sinatra fired him, public relations kingpin Henry Rogers tells the story of how he blew it. One day he and his partner, Warren Cowan, were summoned to Sinatra's house. "Frank was looking very grim. He said, 'We've had a long association, you've done a good job, and everybody tells me you fellows are the best in the business. Then why the @&*!% do I have such a lousy image?' " Rogers replied, in one word, "You," and was promptly fired. "It was an ill-timed, rude, smart-aleck remark that was inexcusable and I wouldn't have said it to a stranger," Rogers says. "But I not only said it to a client but to someone I genuinely liked and respected."

This is just another example of how ineffective criticism leads to all kinds of bad results. Having the Critical Edge at times like this is an invaluable tool. It will help you use the power of criticism to transform a potentially negative encounter into a positive opportunity for growth, for success. As Rogers puts it, "What I should have said is 'Frank, you don't have a lousy image. Ninety-nine percent of the people in this world think you are the greatest entertainer who ever lived and there is 1 percent with whom you have a lousy image. So let's see what we can do about that 1 percent.' . . . If I hadn't blown it, Frank Sinatra would still be a client today." Henry Rogers teaches us a vital lesson here: It pays to know how to give productive criticism.

This chapter will help you develop the Critical Edge by showing you how to make criticism fulfill its TASK — to teach appropriate skills and knowledge.

TAKING CRITICISM TO TASK

To learn to give criticism productively you must start out by reexam-
ining what you think giving criticism is all about. If you continue
to think of giving criticism as an opportunity for telling a person
that he did something wrong or for pointing out a flaw in a person's
work, then it is a sure thing that you will continue either to experience
psychological difficulty in giving criticism and/or suffer the results
of ineffective criticism. If, however, you begin to think of criticism
as a means for helping other people develop and/or a means for
improving your relationship with them, then you will be able to
generate new ways of communicating those "must be said" negatives
in a productive manner. You can use criticism to motivate, educate,
and influence others for positive change. Learning to take criticism
to TASK is the key.

THE CRITICISM TASK MODEL

The Criticism TASK Model provides a framework that allows us to
develop a new set of criticism skills. It is the basis for all criticism
techniques and will enable you to begin to productively criticize your
boss, colleagues, subordinates, and others in your work environment.

The model is based on the assumption that productive critics begin
by deciding what their task is, what they want to attain as a result
of the criticism. As stressed in the section on making criticism strategic, once you know what you want to accomplish, you can begin
to figure out the best strategy for getting there. Your comments
become productively purposeful rather than flippant, accusatory, or
otherwise destructive.

Although your task will differ with each criticism, there is one
task that supersedes all others. Regardless of whom you criticize, and
no matter what the criticism is, your basic task is always the same:
to teach appropriate skills and knowledge. That is, as a critic you ask
yourself: What do I want to teach the target? Is it appropriate to the
situation? What skills does he need? What knowledge can I impart?

This orientation, based on the premise that criticism is a tool for
growth, helps you mentally reexamine and restructure your thoughts

about criticism. Keeping this TASK in mind always will keep you on track for making your criticisms productive.

Once you understand the model, you can begin to individualize it — discover through application and experimentation how it works best for your own personality type and each specific situation. The Criticism TASK Model consists of three stages:

1. What to do BEFORE giving criticism
2. What to do WHEN giving criticism
3. What to do AFTER giving criticism

Each stage implements different critical factors of productive criticism, for, as we have said, different factors come into play at different times. Furthermore, the fact that the model is in three stages reflects the concept that productive criticism is a process, one that unfolds, with each part influencing what is to come.

As you master each stage, you will find it easier and easier to maintain the Critical Edge; you will be able to integrate the factors of productive criticism into your daily communication style. In other words, mastering the model will help you develop a spontaneous style for criticizing productively.

Stage 1: What to Do Before Giving Criticism

The goal of this stage is to help you focus in advance on 1) what you want the recipient to do, 2) whether the recipient can do it, and 3) how you can help the recipient do it. Aiming your thoughts in these directions immediately helps you think strategically, become improvement-oriented, and become involved in the process.

To meet the goal of stage 1, you must take the following four steps:

Target the Behavior to Criticize

It's very important to be clear in your own mind as to exactly what it is you are criticizing. This helps you in several ways.

First, knowing the specific behavior you want to improve will prevent you from using words like "always" and "never," which are sweeping generalizations and are characteristic of the destructive criticizer's vocabulary. These words not only cast your recipient's behavior in a negative light but also instantly elicit defensiveness. At the first use of these words, the recipient will no doubt interrupt you with several examples that will invalidate your criticism. Before you know it, you are into an argument. The fact is, "always" and "never" invalidate any criticism because there are "always" exceptions. The rule is, Never say "always" or "never." "Sometimes" is a much better choice.

Being specific also prevents you from giving faulty feedback — information that is too vague. Common examples of faulty feedback are statements such as "Your work needs to improve," "Give it more pizzazz," and "Fix the tone." These statements are so nebulous that the recipient has little chance of responding productively. Telling a subordinate that her work needs to improve is better than telling her that her work is sloppy (which is negative criticism) but is still not calculated to achieve results. What aspect of the person's work needs to be improved? Is it her reports? Her relationships with her co-workers? Or how she runs a meeting? Without knowing the specifics, the recipient is unable to devise an improvement plan. What makes it worse is that the critic frequently misinterprets the recipient's unsuccessful attempts at improvement as showing disagreement or a lack of motivation.

Thinking in specifics is likewise important because, inevitably, the recipient will ask you for a specific example that illustrates your general criticism. Let's say you've criticized a subordinate for not working well with his co-workers. He then asks you for an example of what "not working well with my co-workers" means or of a specific time when he didn't work well with them. If you draw a blank, the chances are great that he will simply scoff at your remarks, suggesting that you don't know what you are talking about. (This may be true if in fact you can't demonstrate your point.)

On the other hand, if you are able to produce an example or two, refrain from presenting them like a prosecuting attorney: "You want an example? Three of your co-workers told me you have been late for all your team meetings. You let others do all the work." Communicating examples like this makes them seem like evidence that the subordinate is guilty as charged. This is the beginning of a destructive process.

Just remember that you have a TASK: to teach appropriate skills and knowledge. In other words, use your examples to help the target understand what you are talking about: "Well, not getting to meetings on time and not taking care of your own responsibilities as part of the team seem to me to be examples of this."

Targeting the behavior to criticize allows you to communicate the criticism with precision and accuracy. It lets the recipient know that you have thought carefully about what you are saying. Your criticism becomes more credible, and the recipient is more likely to accept your remarks as reasonable, fair, and worthy of serious thought. Instead of inviting an ill-defined debate or a blanket denial, criticism that targets a specific behavior is more likely to facilitate a constructive two-way dialogue.

Identify Your Criteria

As Plato and Aristotle advocated, a good critic bases his opinions on a specific criterion. In many cases, as Aristotle noted, more than one criterion will be used. Identifying your criteria is important because it helps you clarify your standards, your values, what you think is good, what you think is bad. It helps make criticism much more focused and accurate because you have a specific reference point in mind that you are trying to get the recipient to achieve or reach.

Identifying criteria in advance is also important because it reminds us that our criticism makes sense only in the context of our criteria. Criticizing a saleswoman for doing a poor job makes no sense if she doubles her quota. However, if your criterion for being a good salesman is having happy customers and this particular saleswoman has customers who feel as though she took advantage of them, then your criticism is valid. A principal who criticizes the most well liked teacher for being poor at his job may seem out of line, but not if his criterion is how well the teacher's students do on reading tests rather than the teacher's popularity.

Another reason for identifying criteria is to help remind ourselves that what the recipient is doing might be acceptable — if a different criterion was being used. It is also important to remember that criticism, no matter how objective the criteria, is still subjective, because your choice of criteria represents what you think is important (i.e., your expressive orientation).

Assess the Potential and Time Frame for Change

After you have targeted the behavior to criticize, you must assess whether the recipient is capable of improving his behavior. Most of the time, we assume that the person is capable of improving, but this is not always possible. Telling a computer scientist that she needs to develop more complex software programs is fruitless if she doesn't have the intellectual ability or academic knowledge necessary. Similarly, a baseball team owner is wasting his time if he berates his players for not winning when they don't have the inherent talent. In these situations, criticism becomes an attack that simultaneously undermines the recipient's self-esteem and frustrates the critic because no improvement results.

When you catch yourself criticizing behaviors that can't be changed, engage in some self-exploration by asking yourself "What's my motive?" Almost always, such criticism comes out of anger, hurt, or your own annoyance that the situation can't be different. Acknowledging these feelings may be initially distressing, but it is much more productive than presenting your purposeless criticism under the guise of "I'm telling you this for your own good."

The majority of cases, however, seem to involve behaviors that can be improved. In these situations, the key question to ask yourself is, "How long will it take?" You might be confident, for example, that a new account executive can improve his presentation or closing skills within six months. But the problem may be that you need to see improvement in six weeks. An editor may know that her author can incorporate her suggested changes in three months, but she may need the revised manuscript in two months to meet her publication schedule. Having a deadline that does not allow enough time for improvement is a common problem.

Because most of us do not objectively assess the time frame for change, we develop unrealistic expectations, which lead to criticism that is ultimately destructive. Because change is not occurring as quickly as we need it to, we become increasingly negative toward the recipient. Critical remarks become overtly hostile. The recipient feels pressured, and before he knows it, he is experiencing tremendous stress, which erodes his performance. In the end, everybody loses.

By assessing how long change will take, you develop realistic expectations. These allow you to explore your options prudently. If you estimate that it is going to take a junior architect six months to master certain commercial design skills, you can take that into account and decide how else you can get a certain job done in the interim. For example, you could get someone else to do it, do it yourself, or minimize the junior architect's other responsibilities so that he could concentrate on the task at hand. Or it might be that you have to dismiss him and hire someone else. When a head buyer for an import company recognizes that she is being unrealistic in expecting a new buyer in Tokyo to be able to negotiate deals in the specified time, she can rearrange her merchandising schedule, focus on other negotiations, and plan accordingly.

Bobby Reisman, thirty-six-year-old president and owner of Northeast Apparel, a national retail outfit that does well over a hundred million dollars in sales annually and is still in its infancy, recognizes the need to assess realistically how quickly improvement can happen. Instead of being destructively critical of his West Coast operation and expecting his managers to create an effective operation in a few months' time, he acknowledged that it would take two years. As a result, his employees' feelings of stress were converted to loyalty, and he and his front-line staff were able to make helpful adjustments. Today, the West Coast operation runs more smoothly and is more profitable than ever before.

Choose the Right Time and the Right Place

As was suggested in the previous chapter in the context of becoming timing-oriented, before you criticize somebody, you should make sure you are doing it at the right time and in the right place. You can in this way boost the recipient's willingness to listen, for you are being sensitive to her needs, to how she will experience the criticism.

A common mistake of most managers and supervisors is thinking that the right place for criticism is in their office. Unfortunately, since the traditional way of delivering criticism is negative, and the boss's office is almost always the setting, the boss's office is often associated with negative thoughts and feelings. As a result, the supervisor will operate there at a handicap because the recipient is thinking defensively before the superior even starts. Ask yourself what you think and how you feel when you are summoned to your own boss's office.

Alternative settings include the recipient's work station or a neutral area, such as a cafeteria.

Another common mistake is to criticize immediately after the recipient has demonstrated inappropriate behavior. Doing so stems from the assumption that immediate feedback is the most effective. It isn't always, especially if we are angry or disappointed. These feelings may make us hypercritical. Besides, many times the target knows what he or she has done wrong. Criticism at these times takes the form of "I told you so" and undermines the target's self-confidence. Discussing the event at a later time, when both parties are more calm and likely to be objective, will be more effective.

A good way to monitor whether you are choosing the right time and place is to ask yourself, "If I were the recipient, would I be open to criticism at this moment?" How would you feel if you were criticized in front of others, behind closed doors, or in a setting where the phone was ringing every two minutes? Would you be ready to listen if you were having a hectic day or were in the middle of closing an important deal? These are key elements to consider, since they affect the target's receptivity. Granted, there are plenty of times when criticism is demanded on the spot, but the truth is, criticism is never productive if the setting is wrong. Therefore, it is just as important to know when and where to give criticism as to know how to phrase it.

To summarize, before you give criticism:

- Target the behavior to criticize
- Identify your criteria
- Assess the potential and time frame for change
- Choose the right time and the right place

Together, these steps get you thinking strategically, help you be sensitive to your target's needs, and pave the way for actually giving the criticism.

Stage 2: What to Do When Giving Criticism

The goals of this stage are to present the criticism effectively, to get the recipient involved in the process, and to be supportive. Accomplishing these tasks requires that you implement the critical factors of flexibility, orientation toward improvement, and the helping spirit. To meet the goals of stage 2, the following steps are necessary.

Acknowledge That Your Criticism Is Subjective

Webster's Dictionary defines "criticism" as "an evaluation of merits as well as demerits." But whose evaluation is it? Criticisms are neither true nor false in and of themselves, yet most of the time we communicate our criticism as if it were fact. "Your work needs to be improved," "You need to get along better with your peers," "You're not doing as well as you should be," are all presented as statements of fact, when in truth their content is a matter of judgment. Others might judge the same behavior differently.

Most people forget this, overlooking the point that their own perceptions are usually quite different from those of the person they are criticizing. As a result, when they present their criticisms, they allow little room for opposing views. If there is opposition, it is quickly interpreted as defensiveness. Yet when criticism is presented as a fact, as a "you" message — a statement that *you* are doing or not doing something — defensiveness is to be expected because the criticism is heard as a sweeping generalization, a black-and-white statement that from the recipient's point of view is rarely true. A few exceptions to your "facts" destroy the credibility of your criticism and set the stage for destructive arguing in which both parties become rigid and entrenched in their positions. Furthermore, "you" messages evoke the finger of blame. They imply, "You are at fault for causing this problem," "You should have known better," "You are bad." Most of the time, blame is unnecessary, because people seldom do poor work on purpose; their behavior is usually motivated by a desire to meet their own needs and is not intentionally aimed at making your work harder.

Acknowledging that your criticism is subjective, that it is your own individual perception, removes the notion that the recipient is definitely doing what you claim or needs to do what you say. Instead, it arouses the recipient's curiosity as to why you think as you do — you are inviting the recipient to compare his or her assessment with your perception. You are communicating that there is room for his or her views. Not feeling as though you are saying he is wrong or blaming him for a particular action, he becomes more at ease and begins to make a concentrated effort to capture your point. Instead of inciting an argument filled with accusations, you are able to initiate a constructive dialogue. Furthermore, when you mentally note that what you say may be true only for yourself, you are much more likely to search for the right words, eliminating broad generalizations and statements of blame.

Acknowledging that your criticism is subjective is implemented by using "I" statements and subjective phrases. Some examples are "In my opinion," "I believe," "From my perspective," and "This is the way I see it."

When you make your criticisms subjective, you make them flexible and provide the transition from a one-way monologue to a healthy dialogue, a productive interaction.

Get the Recipient Involved

When giving criticism, it is crucial to get the recipient involved. Otherwise, you will find yourself not only giving a laborious monologue but also facing the Herculean task of trying to help another person improve her behavior without her assistance. Getting the recipient involved in the criticism process is important for many reasons, but mostly because having the recipient interact with the critic in a positive manner greatly enhances the chances for productive resolution. Each party begins to contribute to the task. A synergy begins to build.

One way to get the recipient involved in the criticism process is simply to ask her for feedback about what you are saying. Two effective phrases for asking for feedback are "I'd like to know how you see things" and "Please share your thoughts with me." Note that even when asking for feedback, the subjective mode is used, since it helps you avoid the demanding and challenging tones that seem to accompany phrases like "Tell me what you think." Besides creating interaction, asking for feedback helps you determine whether the recipient understands your point of view. If the recipient does not understand your criticism, it will be impossible for her to respond productively. If the critic finds a misunderstanding, he can immediately clarify the recipient's point of view.

Most critics fail to assess whether the recipient understands. They make an unstated assumption that the recipient comprehends the message. Often, they are mistaken in thinking this. Yet they become angry when the expected results do not appear.

Besides clarifying the matter of understanding, the recipient's feedback also will provide you with his views on the situation and a sense of whether he agrees with your criticism. If there is a disagreement, it is important to find out why. Many times, his reasons for disagreeing will supply you with insights that will change your criticism. Although you can force the person to agree if you are the boss, there is little probability that he will attack the task with enthusiasm and commitment in this case. Knowing that he disagrees permits you to pursue a different avenue or to reassess the validity of your criticism.

A third way that asking for feedback helps your cause is in minimizing the recipient's defensiveness. Most of the time when we are criticized, we are thinking of our rebuttals even before the critic is finished. This reflects our need to protect our self-esteem. We can hardly wait to respond and frequently interrupt to defend ourselves. However, when you let someone know you want his feedback, his receptivity increases because he knows that he will get the opportunity to express his viewpoint. He doesn't have to worry about getting the chance to defend himself. As a result, he is free to concentrate on what is being said to him; that is, he listens better.

A good way to build this point — as well as the subjective mode — into your criticisms is to use the Prediction Technique. You implement this gambit by saying something like "This is how I see things, and I know that you may see things differently, or you may agree."

If, in fact, the recipient appraises the situation differently, you have already given permission, said it is okay, to disagree. The recipient thinks along these lines: "He's right. I do disagree. I'm glad he can accept that. But let me listen to what he says." In essence, the target sees that you can make room for opposing views. She begins to feel comfortable.

The point is, the recipient is either going to agree or disagree with you regardless of what you say. Since we know that most people are mentally disagreeing with the critic as he speaks, it becomes a smart strategy to acknowledge overtly that the recipient is "allowed" to disagree, because she is going to do it anyway, and because most people become more receptive when they know they can freely express their own opposing views.

By predicting the disagreement, you communicate to the recipient that she is safe to disagree with you, as you are with her. The paradox here is that disagreement typically is a prelude to conflict and inter-personal polarity. However, this is the case only when disagreement is not allowed, when each person attempts to coerce the other to accept his or her view as the "correct" one. A power struggle begins.

If, on the other hand, you allow disagreement, then there is no need for coercion. Each person is allowed to hold on to his or her own thoughts. Whether the recipient agrees or disagrees with the criticism becomes secondary here; of primary importance is that no matter how the recipient responds to your "prediction," the criticism process is facilitated.

Getting the target involved, then, is important because it trans-forms criticism from the traditional one-way mode to an interaction in which both parties exchange their views. When this occurs, the critic and recipient can find out where each is coming from, which lays the groundwork for good relationships, greater commitment to resolving the criticism, and a common ground for generating a mean-ingful solution.

Give the Solution

A common reason that most criticisms fail to get the job done is that the critic does not tell her recipient what she wants to happen; she does not give a solution. The recipient then tries, with good intent, his own solutions, which far too often are not what the critic had in mind. Seeing no change, the critic becomes frustrated and angry and destructively critical of the recipient. From the recipient's point of view, this is unfair. After all, he is making a concentrated effort to resolve the criticism. "Why try, if this is what I get for my efforts?" becomes his attitude. He begins to feel that the burden of change is solely on his shoulders. Getting no help, and seeing little positive effect from his efforts, he begins to feel impotent. His self-esteem is diminished. And the criticism remains unresolved. The result is that everybody loses. This sorry state of affairs can be avoided if the critic offers a solution as part of her criticism.

The solution that the critic gives the recipient communicates how she thinks the criticism can be resolved. It is her answer to the problem. The obvious reason for providing this is to give the recipient a clear direction for improvement. Telling a subordinate "You need to be more of a team player" is less effective than saying "You can improve your peer relationships by not canceling meetings with them at the last minute, getting your share of the work to them on time, and verbally being supportive of their efforts." You are suggesting specifics — you are teaching appropriate skills and knowledge.

Besides giving a clear message of what you want, what you expect, offering solutions is important because it demonstrates the helping spirit. The recipient sees that you have taken the time and energy to think about how he can become a better worker. He sees that your intent (the expression of the affective orientation of criticism) is to help rather than put him down. You become an ally instead of an enemy. You are showing the recipient that he is not alone, that you will share the responsibility for resolving the criticism. When this message is communicated, it converts criticism into a mutual problem-solving process, one that is cooperative. Change becomes easier when you have a partner.

Many people, especially managers and supervisors, balk at offering the solution, on the grounds that the recipient should be able to generate the solution himself. "It's his job, I shouldn't have to do it for him" is the attitude. These people need to remember the principle of response generalization — teach people how to respond in situation A, and when situation B comes along, they will come up with a similar response modified to the new situation. Applied here, instead of thinking that you are doing the recipient's job for him, recognize that you are teaching him an example of what constitutes an effective response. For example, if you tell a saleswoman that she needs to improve the way she waits on customers, she will want to know "How?" Telling her "It's your job to know how" will be of little help. However, instructing her to accompany customers to the dressing room not only gives her a specific action to take but also helps her understand what the concept of attentive service is all about. The chance increases that when she later sees a customer who has purchased several items leaving the store, she will spontaneously approach her and ask her if she needs assistance with her packages, then thank her for her business and invite her to return. To reiterate, offering a specific solution helps you teach appropriate skills and knowledge in a general sense.

What about the times when you don't know the solution? Acknowledge this and add, "If we put our heads together, we can figure it out." Again, criticism becomes cooperative.

State the Incentive for the Recipient

There are literally thousands of psychological studies indicating that the best way to change behavior is to reward (and thus reinforce) the desired behavior. Criticism, too often, is communicated with a stick rather than a carrot. No wonder it is frequently heard as a demand, a threat, or an order. The typical reaction is for the recipient to become defensive, and the criticism thus becomes ineffective.

Most people think that they do offer incentives when they criticize, but what they fail to recognize is that the incentive offered is important only to themselves. They misperceive the value of the incentive to their recipient. Trying to get a subordinate to change because it will increase your own chances for being successful is apt to have little effect. Pointing out to a co-worker that you both stand a chance of being given more responsibility if she meets her deadline will have little motivational effect if she doesn't want more responsibility, to say nothing of the effect if she actually wants less responsibility.

For criticism to be an effective catalyst for change, there must be a payoff for the recipient. He must clearly see how he will benefit. He needs to know "What's in it for me?" Offered an incentive he values, he thinks, "Hey, this is for me! I'm doing this for myself." To help you master this point, think about:

- What is important to my recipient?
- What incentives are available?
- What if there are no incentives to give?

Include the Positives

Criticism is an evaluation of both merits and demerits, but few of us can remember the last time we heard positives when we were criticized. The fact is, most of us omit the merits when we give criticism. Effective critics, however, accentuate the positive.

You may feel that including some positives when you criticize is simply a way to soften the blow. To some extent, this is true, but there are several more important benefits to doing this. One is that it requires you to know what the person is doing right. This prevents you from generalizing and destructively labeling the person as "all bad." For example, if you plan to criticize a subordinate for chronically missing his deadlines and yet keep in mind that his report content is consistently excellent, you are less likely to think he is doing a poor job generally. Being aware of a person's merits, whether you express them or not, allows you to approach him in a positive manner. And, when you explicitly state the positives, it conveys that you're aware of and appreciate his efforts. The recipient's self-esteem is intact, if not enhanced.

Your positives must be sincere. Giving a soft-soap job is likely to make matters worse — so if you can't come up with any positives, don't invent them. Also, it's essential that positives you are mentioning be positives from the recipient's frame of reference, not neutral statements. You may think that telling your secretary her letters are typed neatly is a positive, but this may be something that she takes for granted. For her, a positive may be "Hey, I liked the way you worded that last line, gave it a personal touch!"

Be aware also of when in the criticism session you give the positives. The most common sequence is to begin by telling the person all the good things they are doing and then catalogue what is wrong. Why is this ineffective? Let's focus on the sentence structure that typically accompanies this type of presentation. It looks like this:

State the positives — BUT — state what is wrong.

If you recall the last time someone criticized you using this format, you will recognize its problems. When someone starts by giving you the positives of what you are doing, the typical reaction is to think "What did I do wrong? Here comes the ax." You start to anticipate the negatives to come and begin to plan your rebuttal prematurely. And, let's not forget that the expectation that negatives will soon come forth elicits negative emotions. Defensive behavior is brewing. The criticizer's chance for the edge is lost.

One reason for this cognitive response pattern is that people are not used to getting positives in a work situation. When they do, these positives are usually followed by negatives. That is just what happens here. You hear the word "but," and your expectation that the negative is coming is confirmed. The next time is sure to be the same.

Now the other problem with this method of criticism. The word "but" is a negation. Semantically, it tells you to forget about what you have just heard — the positives. You then hear the negative part of the message and leave the interaction with feelings of failure. Even if the positives were well deserved and meant sincerely, the recipient forgets that the critic even mentioned them. He leaves thinking that his boss put him down, with his self-esteem diminished and a stronger view that criticism is to be avoided. And in the process, the critic has made herself someone to be avoided.

Another school of thought favors presenting the merits and demerits in reverse. Such critics start out by telling you what's wrong and then end up by telling you how good you are. This criticism structure looks like this:

State the negatives — give the positives.

Of the two formats, this one is preferable. The problem, however, is that when you start with the negatives, you run the risk of eliciting a defensive reaction, which may make it impossible for you to get to the positives. If you get caught up in a destructive interaction, you might not even feel like giving the positives. Furthermore, even if you do give the positives, the recipient might be mentally stuck on your opening negative remarks.

One solution is to start neither with the positives nor the negatives. Begin instead by focusing on how the person can improve, then conclude by telling the person what he or she is already doing well. This method has the following structure:

State how the recipient can improve — AND —
state the positive things the recipient is already doing.

This format capitalizes on three principles. The first is that most people respond positively when you tell them how to make something better. Recall that self-esteem theorists believe that it is a natural tendency to want to develop oneself. Telling a person how he can do something better (as opposed to telling him what he is doing wrong) taps into that tendency and makes the recipient eager to hear your pointers. This is obviously a good way of making your criticism improvement-oriented and is also a quick and excellent way to increase receptivity. The focus of attention immediately becomes the "next" effort; instead of dwelling on the last one, the recipient looks ahead.

The second principle is that people feel psychologically better when a conversation ends on the upbeat. The second criticism format does this, too, but with this third format, you do not have to contend with the possibility of the recipient's dwelling on the negatives — because you have not stated any negatives.

The third principle involves the word "and." Whereas the word "but" semantically negates its previous message, the word "and" does just the opposite: It integrates the preceding statements. The recipient leaves the dialogue feeling good about himself, thinking "I am doing a lot of good things and I can be that much better if I improve on some others." The principle is that change is encouraged when a person feels good about himself and realizes that he can do better. Although the use of the word "and" rather than "but" is subtle, its long-term effects are powerful. In the end, it helps the recipient realize that he is not perfect, he does some things well and can improve on others, and this is pretty good. The acceptance of this notion is a sign of healthy self-esteem and a token of productive criticism.

Get the Commitment for Action

Giving criticism productively means getting the recipient to take action. Therefore, it is imperative that you get the recipient to commit herself to responding productively. Getting a commitment is impossible if you violate the earlier requirement of getting feedback, because in order to get the recipient to commit, you must know how she assesses your criticism. Otherwise, you will be asking the recipient to do something that she may disagree with or, for that matter, doesn't understand. This will make it difficult for her to commit to act productively, even if she is committed to improving.

Sometimes the recipient will tell you that she is committed to taking action with her own enthusiastically toned comments: "This is a great idea. I can't wait to try it. This really is going to help me." Other times, you will have to ask the recipient if she will respond in the agreed-upon manner. This is a crucial moment and frequently determines whether your criticism will have a lasting effect. Like a sales pro, you must close the deal.

If in fact the recipient says she will respond in the agreed-upon manner, follow up with a statement that binds her to act in the specified way by a specific time, if appropriate. An example might be "Well, since you see this in the same way as I do, when can I expect the points discussed to be implemented in your future reports?" or "when can I expect to see improvement?"

It is important to note here that the superior is asking the subordinate for the time frame rather than dictating it. If you recall, stage 1 requires the giver of the criticism to assess a realistic time frame. But what if that time frame is unrealistic? The result is apt to be poor performance and a stressful situation. By asking the recipient for her time frame, you are able to match the two time frames to determine what is actually realistic. If the recipient's time frame is really shorter than the one you have in mind, all is well, although a huge discrepancy on the short side could also be unrealistic on the part of the recipient; perhaps she wants to be seen in a good light or maybe is afraid of stating how much time she actually needs. If these latter possibilities are suspected, you can expand the time frame to approximate your own: "Well, I don't need it that fast, so you can have a few extra days' leeway."

If the opposite occurs, if the recipient gives a time frame that is much longer than what you have in mind, you should ask her to explain why it will take so long. This question will cause one of two things to happen. First, in the process of explaining, the recipient will come to see that, in fact, her time frame can be shortened to approximate your time frame. Or, the recipient's explanation will help you recognize that your time frame was actually unrealistic and will allow you to lengthen it to accommodate the demands of the situation. This procedure — finding out the time frame of the recipient before you state your own — also helps safeguard against the tendency people have to take as much time as their deadline permits. Although an employee may be able to make corrections in a few days, he or she will be sure to take two weeks if given the time. The aforementioned procedure can be used to assess a realistic time frame, one in which the recipient feels that a commitment to action can be demonstrated.

If the recipient shows any signs of resistance, verbal or non-verbal, then you must find out why; you must know what she is secretly objecting to so that you can deal with those issues. The mistake that most people make is responding only to overt resistance — a verbal disagreement. They ignore the recipient's "soft" signs of reluctance and then act surprised when the target fails to respond as promised. To make the criticism process effective, you must be able to pick up the signs of indirect resistance and be able to overcome them.

Pay particular attention to hesitancy in the recipient's voice, her facial expressions, and her general level of enthusiasm. Rely on your intuition, and if you sense a lack of commitment, say so. Remember, the recipient's showing hesitancy to commit means that she does not fully believe your criticism and/or doesn't buy the solution. Until she does, you will not get the efforts you desire.

A good way to develop your awareness of a recipient's indirect resistance is to recall previous experiences in which you sensed resistance and later found out you were right. Think about those experiences and focus on what it was that caused you to think that the target wasn't really committed. Use these data as a basis for developing your ability to sense lack of commitment.

To summarize, when you give criticism:

- Acknowledge that your criticism is subjective
- Get the target involved
- Give the solution
- State the incentive for the target
- Include the positives
- Get the commitment for action

Incorporating these points into your criticism enables you to communicate effectively the skills and knowledge that you believe will help you and the recipient be more productive, thus increasing the chances that the recipient will respond productively. The task is almost complete.

Stage 3: What to Do After Giving Criticism

The goal of this stage is to ensure that the criticism will be resolved as planned and that the recipient feels he is supported in his efforts to change. Meeting this goal shows the helping spirit and makes you a full-fledged productive critic. To meet the goal of this stage, you need to do three things:

- Follow up
- Follow up
- Follow up

Follow Up on Your Criticism

It is naive to think that after you have presented your criticism, your task is complete. You must ensure that the recipient keeps on track by doing continual follow-up. In the strictest sense, following up means that you observe whether the recipient is responding as agreed upon and that you directly communicate your observations to the recipient. More to the point, though, follow-up means recognizing that criticism is a developmental process, that the process is ongoing. Your long-range task is to use this specific criticism as part of the lengthier process of actively trying to help the target improve on a daily basis. With this type of follow-up, you stay involved in helping the recipient improve. Clearly, this behavior shows the helping spirit.

On a more practical level, if you perceive that the recipient is not responding as agreed upon, you should share your perceptions with him. If you observe that improvement is occurring, share your perceptions. Either way, your response lets the recipient know that you are still involved and intend to see the criticism resolved as agreed.

Most critics commit two fouls at this point. The first is assuming, if they observe no improvement, that the recipient is not committed and is ignoring the criticism. They then begin destructively criticizing the recipient or, just as bad, record their observations and save them for the annual performance appraisal. They forget that developing new habits or improving behavior is very difficult and usually does not happen overnight. An accountant might be able to clean up his bookkeeping procedure in a week, but it might take a teacher six months to improve his rapport with his students.

The second common error is noting improvement but failing to acknowledge it, often focusing on the fact that the recipient is still not performing up to the established standards. Again, change does not happen overnight. If you fail to acknowledge positive progress, no matter how slight it is, the odds are good that the recipient will revert to her old ways, because she sees that her efforts are bringing her no rewards, not even a positive stroke. Since change is hard, especially with no incentive at hand, it's easy for those old habits to reemerge. Besides, if you wait until the recipient is perfect at her task, you will be waiting forever. If B. F. Skinner had insisted that the pigeon hit the lever before it got its first food pellet, the pigeon probably would have starved to death. Note that if you have established a realistic time frame, you will have a guide upon which to base your follow-up observations when looking for improvement.

Here is how you can implement your follow-up:

• As soon as you see progress, speak directly to the person. Your acknowledgment will act as positive reinforcement and will keep the recipient's momentum going, enabling him to do even better. When you thus reward a behavior you want to encourage, you are using operant learning to your advantage by teaching the recipient to repeat successful behavior.

• If you see that the recipient is having difficulty in taking productive action, reacknowledge the criticism and ask how you can help. Most of the time, we tell the recipient to try harder, which may or may not be effective but in either case puts the responsibility of change on the recipient. Asking how you, the critic, can help directly involves you in the process and becomes a built-in follow-up system — as long as you are helping, you are following up. For example, the principal who sits down on a weekly basis to help the teacher revise her criticized lesson plans is following up in a much more productive manner than the principal who merely asks every week how things are coming.

Following up on your criticism is essential because it continues the criticism process. You keep yourself involved and can assist the recipient in improving. Furthermore, by following up on your criticism, you demonstrate to the recipient that your initial expressions of helping spirit were more than just a pep talk. He feels that you are committed to helping him and, inevitably, begins to look forward to your criticisms because he starts to view them as part of a mutual effort to further his career, as information that will help him grow.

To summarize, after you give criticism:

- Follow up on your criticism

APPLYING THE CRITICISM TASK MODEL

Before giving an example of how the model might be applied, there are four points that need to be emphasized. The first two are descriptive — they apply to the model in general. The last two points have relevance in the actual application of the model — when you give criticism.

1. The model's basic function is to help you begin the process of giving criticism productively through applying its several key principles. By learning the model, you naturally begin integrating a strategic thinking style that is part of the Critical Edge. Once the model is mastered, you will be able to delve into the more sophisticated ways of giving productive criticism.

2. The model is directly applicable in two areas — when you criticize the product of the recipient's work, and when you criticize the recipient for something he is doing that affects his work. Included in the first category would be an editor criticizing an author's manuscript, a principal criticizing a teacher's lesson plans, or a head chef criticizing the pastry his trainee prepared. Examples falling into the second category would be an editor criticizing a writer who makes commitments she can't keep, a principal criticizing a teacher for the way he interacts with his students or a fellow teacher, or a head chef criticizing his trainee for not keeping the kitchen in order.

3. In the majority of cases, you probably will not cover all of the components the model lists; some will have little significance for the particular situation. As you develop the Critical Edge, you will develop the skill of knowing when to emphasize some components over others. Furthermore, in our busy work life, it would be naive to think that every time you criticize someone, you will have the time to sit down and go over each of the model's components of prepa-

ration and evaluation. Thus, time in itself becomes a factor in determining whether you deliver the model comprehensively.

4. This last point is most important. When you criticize, it is essential to pay attention to the exact words that you use, that is, the semantics of your delivery. Being aware of and developing the semantics of your delivery permit you to select among degrees of clarity and indirection, to avoid being too vague or too blunt, too obscure or too specific. Each word or phrase that you use projects numerous messages that can increase or decrease the target's receptivity. Making criticism into an art form involves knowing how to use these qualities so that your delivery is apt to increase the recipient's openness. Some semantic rules already described include: Change your "you" messages to "I" messages, change your "should" statements to "could" statements, change your *but*'s to *and*'s, and change *always* and *never* to *sometimes*. These words in particular make a difference when criticizing.

With these points in mind, let's look at how many of the components of the model would work in their most general application by tracing how the criticizer might think through a single sample criticism. Starting off with this criticism in its most counterproductive format — number 1 — note how from line to line the criticism is continually refined by employing the model's principles until a far more productive criticism is attained in number 7.

Situation: Criticizing a researcher's marketing report

1. Your report is sloppy.
2. Your report needs to be improved.
3. I believe your data analysis could be more complete.
4. I would like you to include the Midwest projects in your data analysis.
5. I think the data analysis would be even better if you included the Midwest projects.
6. I think you will be in a better position to get your project approved if you include the Midwest projects in your data analysis.
7. I am impressed with your recommendations and analysis of the situation, and I think that you will be in an even better

position to get your project approved if you include the Mid-west projects in the data analysis, because that will tell our clients that we have been successful on similar ventures. I would imagine that you could do it in two or three days, and then we could go over it again. What do you think?

This last criticism is a far cry from the first. It includes many of the model's components, such as:

- Using the subjective mode — "I am impressed," "I think," "I would imagine"
- Stating the merits — "impressed with your recommendations and analysis"
- Giving the incentive — "get your project approved"
- Offering a solution — "include the Midwest projects in the data analysis"
- Setting a realistic time frame — "two or three days"
- Planning follow-up — "we could go over it again"
- Asking for feedback — "What do you think?"

Although the final criticism would qualify as being productive, there are many other ways of communicating the same information to the recipient. For example, the final delivery might be "I read the report, and I'm wondering if you think the Midwest projects should be included in the data analysis?" The semantics of this delivery take criticism to TASK by inviting the recipient to explore on her own the benefits of including additional information. It is a "softer" pre-sentation in that it does not flatly state that you think the information should be included. In fact, the phrase "I'm wondering" implies that you are not sure of your position (even though you might be), thus increasing the chances that the recipient will not hear the criticism as pointing out a flaw in her work. This delivery also calls for a response; it prompts a dialogue. If the recipient responds by agreeing with you, you complete your task by choosing a time frame for the addition. If the target's response is along the lines of "No, I don't think so. Why do you?" or even a flat "No," you can proceed to mention some of the benefits of this addition, which you think will get the recipient to appraise the criticism positively. Note that in order to respond productively to the recipient's inquiry, you must be familiar with the same information that is contained in the first format, number 7 of the earlier list.

Which format is better? There are no specific guidelines except to consider whom you are criticizing, how they perceive you, and the history of your relationship. If the recipient tends to be defensive, the second delivery might be more effective. If the recipient holds you in high esteem, the first format would be better because it is more authoritative: It gives a concrete recommendation and specific reasons for change. If this is the first time you are criticizing the recipient, you may come up with a different delivery altogether. In the end, it all comes down to knowing what you want to happen, thinking about how the recipient will respond, and figuring out how you can get him to respond productively. That's the TASK of giving criticism.

Chapter 4

Increasing Your Assets

A KNIFE is whistling toward you. It's doubtful that your reaction will be to stand up with your chest protruding so that you are an easy target. This would mean certain death. No! Your first impulse is more likely to be a quick duck to artfully dodge the oncoming threat. But another knife follows, and then still another. You continue to duck and dodge, until your enemy either runs out of knives or until you can get hold of your own dagger to throw back, to defend yourself.

Most people respond to criticism as though it were a knife hurled at them, intended to cut them up. Not wanting to get hurt, they initially deny the criticism or simply ignore it, hoping that the critic will retreat. However, if the critic persists, if he throws more "knives," the recipient is backed into a corner with no choice but to retaliate — to shout back equally damaging remarks to even the score. And the response chosen by those who are unable to duck or throw their own daggers is equally bad. They take the criticism to heart, never thinking about whether it's valid, but just letting it cut them up. So long, self-esteem.

People who take criticism productively do not duck and dodge the critical points thrown at them, because they do not think of them as a military onslaught. Nor do they create interpersonal warfare by retaliating. And they certainly don't just stand there, letting themselves be victimized by a relentless critic.

People who take criticism productively catch the knife. Instead of letting themselves be stabbed, they feel the point and reason, "Gee, this is sharp. But it doesn't have to cut me up. I can use it to carve something better out of myself." They use the criticism as a tool with which to better themselves rather than treating it as a weapon that will destroy them. When you can take the point of criticism and use its sharpness to work for you, you have the Critical Edge.

Learning how to use criticism by responding to it productively will help you be more effective on the job. Your specific job skills will be improved, as well as your effectiveness in your encounters with your boss, peers, subordinates, clients, and customers. In short, you will experience greater professional (and personal) growth. This growth is achieved through a four-step process. The first step is to be receptive to criticism; the second, to appraise it; the third, to acknowledge it; and the fourth, to act on it if it's valid.

BECOMING RECEPTIVE TO CRITICISM

When Ira Berkow, the *New York Times* sportswriter and author, was a student at Yale University, he sent the renowned Red Smith a letter and samples of his writing, asking for Smith's opinion of his work. Smith told Berkow, "I don't want to devalue you. I'd just be giving you criticism. Better you don't ask." But Berkow gamely replied, "Go ahead and ruin my day. I need your criticism." That was Berkow's first contact with Smith. Years later Berkow wound up writing a best-seller — Smith's biography.

This illustrates one of the great paradoxes of criticism: In order to be receptive to it, you must do what makes you uncomfortable — you must befriend the criticism. As a young, hungry journalist-to-be, Berkow was eager for criticism from a man who had made it in his chosen field. Even though it could have been painful, Berkow welcomed the criticism, knowing it could be helpful to him.

It is precisely this attitude that makes some people able to greet criticism with success instead of distress. More than just thinking "Criticism is a fact of life, so I have to learn how to deal with it," the attitude is one of actually wanting criticism, actively seeking it out.

Ira Berkow did. So does the employee at the checkout counter of the Hyatt Regency Waikiki who says to each guest, "Will you fill out this appraisal card so we know how we're doing?" And each year, Bill Marriott sends his five top executives to a retreat. Their sole task: put their criticisms of Marriott in writing. Their president says, "It's always more than I bargained for. It doesn't make me feel good, but I need it." This is actively seeking out criticism and is often the difference between success and failure.

Most people have difficulty in actively seeking out criticism for at least one of two reasons, usually both. The first is that they think negatively about criticism. The second is that criticism hurts.

Negative Thoughts About Criticism

Psychologists working in the Personality–Social Psychology Laboratory at Princeton University conducted a study about how people process information. They had their subjects complete specific sentences whose content dealt with a variety of subjects, including criticism. Their responses were then rated by judges to assess the different ways that people interpret and use such information. The importance of the study here is the finding that as people moved from a rigid interpretative style to a flexible style, they could use the information more productively.

One of the sentences that participants in the study had to complete was "When I'm criticized . . ." Those who responded in what was considered a rigid thinking style answered along these lines. "It means I'm wrong and the other person is right." Viewing criticism in right-or-wrong terms, these people would be destined, when criticized, to end up in a conflict in which they would soon become defensive. Indeed, no one likes to be told that he or she is wrong.

Those who responded in a productive, flexible manner completed the question this way: "When I'm criticized, it doesn't mean I'm right or wrong. It means there's a difference of opinion. . . . You can learn a great deal about the other person from his criticisms. It tells you what is important to him . . . it tells you what his needs are, what his values are. . . . And you can learn a lot about yourself." Their flexible interpretation of criticism allowed them to use it productively.

Holding on to the belief that criticism is a right/wrong issue makes it difficult for you to be receptive to criticism, because if the criticism is valid, it carries the corresponding implication that you are wrong. Once your self-esteem is under attack, your defensive patterns quickly emerge.

However, if you can begin to internalize an alternative thinking pattern, one in which criticism is viewed not as an issue of right or wrong but rather as information that may be helpful, then you will be able to open yourself up to criticism. To be able to do this is always to your advantage. The most immediate way to increase your receptivity to criticism is to remind yourself frequently that criticism is information that can help you grow. Such a restructuring of your thoughts will make you more receptive to the criticisms that are thrown at you, because you will be looking for their potential positive value. It is this way of thinking about criticism that allows you to respond productively, even if the criticism is given destructively.

Restructuring your thoughts about criticism is not an overnight process. As Dick Cavett once said, "It takes a rare person to want to hear what he doesn't want to hear." This is because most people have had years of practice in thinking about criticism as a stiletto. There are, however, several tactics you can use that will facilitate the process. The more you practice them, the faster you will be able to increase your receptivity to criticism.

Listening to Yourself

One of the many ways that our thoughts influence how we feel and behave is through the things we say to ourselves. The conversations we mentally have with ourselves are the mechanisms that allow us to bring to consciousness the appraisals we make and the expectations we have. The statements that we make to ourselves precede, accompany, or follow the things we feel and are directly linked to them. If you believe that criticism is a negative, then it is a sure thing that when you are being criticized, you are talking negatively to yourself.

Self-statements like "This is worse than I thought; when will he be finished? . . . He's going to fire me next" are statements that people frequently make to themselves when they are being criticized. Not only do they reflect a negative concept of criticism, but, more to the point, they make it impossible to be receptive to it. In fact, they make the situation much worse. To counteract this negative trend, you must develop the skill of listening to yourself.

Being able to listen to yourself will allow you to monitor exactly what you are saying to yourself when you are criticized. As you become better and better at listening to yourself, you will be able to pay better attention to your self-statements. You can then examine your thoughts to see if they are helping you or hurting you. You will be able to modify them to help you become more receptive to the criticisms you receive. In effect, you will be able to use your self-statements as productive instructions to guide you through the criticism process.

A good way to practice is to set aside five minutes a day in a quiet environment and sit back and listen to the internal conversation that is currently going on in your mind. Pay attention to how fast your thoughts are and whether you talk in first or third person. You might imagine yourself to be listening to someone else's phone conversation. The key is to familiarize yourself with how you talk to yourself. Listening a few minutes each day for at least a week will be a tremendous boost to your skill in hearing yourself talk. You will soon note that in many situations — while playing sports, listening to your spouse, standing in line at a movie — you are paying attention to your internal thoughts. This awareness is what allows you to use your thoughts productively. Once you have become used to hearing yourself, you can begin to focus on what you say to yourself when someone criticizes you. Chances are, you will find that your internal conversation at such times is filled with destructive messages that not only make the situation worse but also are not true.

These statements — those that you hear yourself saying when you are being criticized — will tend to be habitual. That is, how you talk to yourself when your boss is criticizing you on Monday is apt to be the same as it is when he criticizes you on Friday. As a result of your frequent replaying of this tape, the thoughts come more and more quickly, until they seem to occur without any prior reasoning or reflection. They have become automatic thoughts. Automatic thoughts have the following characteristics:

· They are often irrational. Most people talk to themselves differently from the way they talk to others. When we talk to others, we describe events in a rational manner. But when we talk to ourselves, we are frequently irrational and use horrifying overgeneralizations. Surely an employee who is told that her work needs to improve and thinks "I'm a failure. Nobody will ever love me" is being irrational.
· They are almost always believed by us. Even though many automatic thoughts are irrational, they are almost always accepted as true.

We don't evaluate them or challenge them, nor are their implications logically analyzed.

• They usually are brief in form. Automatic thoughts are frequently abbreviated to one word or a transient visual image. For example, a rising executive may say "Zip" to tell himself that he will not get another top assignment.

• They tend to accumulate alarmingly. Automatic thoughts often act as cues for other thoughts. One depressing thought may trigger a whole chain of depressing thoughts.

Here is an example of an automatic thought that typically arises when a boss criticizes a subordinate:

AUTOMATIC THOUGHT: Blew it.
REALLY MEANS: I screwed up this assignment. My boss thinks I'm stupid. There goes my promotion. What will my family say? They will leave me.

The problem is that these thoughts occur in a split second, and because they seem to be automatic we rarely take the time to acknowledge their destructive content. Instead, we quickly become defensive toward the criticism.

When you can listen to how you talk to yourself, you will be able to pick up the counterproductive thoughts that you have early in the criticism process and use them as a cue: that you need to talk to yourself differently — in a way that helps you listen to the criticism, be more receptive.

The technique to use to get yourself talking differently to yourself is called counterpunching and is based on the idea that your counterproductive critical thoughts are mental punches that you inflict on yourself. Inevitably you become senseless. Counterpunching with the mind is identical to counterpunching in a fight. It is automatically matching every counterproductive statement you make when you are being criticized, or about to be criticized, with a rational comeback, a statement that helps you keep things in perspective so that you are able to act in a more rational and productive manner. For example, if you hear yourself saying "He's out to get me," counterpunch by saying "How do I really know that? He's just telling me how to do better." If you catch yourself saying "I am a failure," counterpunch with "Just because I didn't do something well doesn't mean I am a failure. I will learn so I can do it better." In other words, counterpunching allows you to eliminate the destructive messages that you hear when you are criticized. You then become mentally free to hear the criticism with a more open mind and to decide rationally whether it is actually valid.

A good way to become an excellent counterpuncher is to write down the destructive statements that you hear yourself making when you are criticized. Next to each one, prepare a counterpunch statement that you can use if need be. Knowing your counterpunches in advance will make it easier to talk to yourself rationally, even when the critic is destructive.

Many times, you will find yourself in a situation in which you know you are going to be criticized. In these situations, you can increase your receptivity to criticism by using your self-statements as self-instructions — statements that specifically tell you what to do when you are being criticized. Here are some examples of effective criticism-management statements that you may use, although it is better if you prepare your own:

- "Remember, stick to the issues and don't take it personally."
- "Listen to what he says."
- "I can learn from this situation."
- "Take a deep breath and relax."

Using self-statements like these is effective because they control your emotional arousal, guide your behavior in a productive direction, prevent you from getting sidetracked, and give you confidence that you can cope with the criticism. Many people find it quite useful to write their criticism-management statements on three-by-five cards and put them on their desk as a constant reminder of how they should react. Writing down these statements increases their awareness of them and readiness to actually use them.

As you become a better counterpuncher, you will find that you become more receptive to criticism, because you eliminate your counterproductive thoughts and replace them with a set of thoughts that allows you to befriend the criticism.

Mental Rehearsal

In Chapter 1, it was pointed out that one of the ways we learn to give and take criticism counterproductively is by observing others do it; their counterproductive modes of giving and taking criticism serve as a model for what we are supposed to do when we either give or take criticism. However, modeling is also one of the most effective ways to learn how to perform a new productive behavior. We watch someone else do it successfully and then we imitate them. A shy individual can watch someone initiate a conversation and later be able to do so himself by imitating the model.

Mental rehearsal relies upon this most basic type of learning; we learn, however, not by watching real-life models but by patterning ourselves after the perfect and vivid images we envision. By identifying, refining, and practicing in our minds the necessary steps for successfully reacting to criticism, it becomes easier to be more receptive to criticism in real life. In short, we model the behavior that we have already acted out in our minds.

A good way to apply mental rehearsal is to write down a series of criticisms that you frequently get or the names of the people who frequently criticize you. In a comfortable setting, relax and then visualize yourself being receptive in the face of each criticism and critic. For example, see yourself listening rather than interrupting, asking for specific suggestions for how you can improve, and acknowledging that the critic is making a good point. To get the most out of this procedure:

• Start with the least threatening criticism. Make sure you have a vivid picture of where you are and who is with you. Use your senses of sound and smell to make it sharper. Hear yourself speak as well as see yourself speak.
• Hold on to the criticism scene for at least thirty to forty seconds and be aware of how your body reacts: Notice changes in your heart rate and breathing, particularly the beginning of any muscle tension. Use these responses as cues to take a deep breath and to breathe more slowly. This will enable you to keep focused. In real life, you will be able to relax while you are being criticized, thus increasing the chances that you will be receptive.

• Keep your criticism scene very visual and, at the same time, continue to breathe deeply to help you relax. Occasionally, see yourself losing control and starting to respond defensively. Use the loss of control as a cue to increase your coping efforts. Imagine having the impulse to tell your critic to shut up, then inhibit the impulse by hearing your counterpunch, "Don't interrupt, no need to get defensive, listen to what he's saying and learn something." Visualize your success.

• Stick with the same scene (same criticism and/or critic) until you can think about it without experiencing any feelings of anger or of being threatened. Then go on to the next most threatening criticism or critic and repeat the procedure. As you practice, you will gain important knowledge of how and when your defensiveness builds up. When you are confronted by the real criticism or critic, you will find that you are able to act more receptively.

Mental rehearsal is based on the well-validated theory that imagery can evoke the same response that an individual makes in reality. Consider the research by physiologist Edmund Jacobson, which has shown that when an individual vividly imagines running, there are small but measurable contractions in the muscles, comparable to the changes that occur during actual running. Similarly, by holding a rich, provoking image (being destructively criticized by your boss!) in your mind, you can raise your blood pressure, accelerate your pulse and perspiration rate, and elicit dryness of the mouth — the same physical reactions that accompany a defensive response to criticism.

Mental rehearsal has been found to improve scores of behaviors for all types of people, including children. In the business and sports worlds, its use is now motivating careers and promoting success. In his book *Mind Power,* psychologist Bernie Zilbergeld cites the cases of many business people and athletes, including Jack Nicklaus, Mary Lou Retton, John Sculley, and William Paley, who have used mental rehearsal with success. Conrad Hilton said, "When I was young, I used to envision myself running hotels all over the world. That was my vision." Mental rehearsal will be equally effective in helping you become more receptive to criticism.

Focusing on Your Physical Arousal

When you get defensive, your body speeds itself up as it prepares either to attack or withdraw quickly. Your heart beats faster, you breathe more quickly, and you're apt to perspire, being under the gun. Your blood pressure is zooming, too. As you become more physically aroused, your mental agility is lost and you become more rigid in your views. You automatically lock out the criticism. On the other hand, if you can become sensitive to these physiological responses, you will be able to use them as a cue, a warning that you are starting to become defensive. You can then make a conscious intervention to calm your defensiveness, thus allowing yourself to hear the criticism for what it's worth.

One way to implement this plan is to monitor your physical arousal level in a variety of situations. For example, monitor yourself when you are resting, reading a book, exercising, in a rush to get to work, or being criticized. Train yourself by focusing on your breathing rate and heart rate, getting a feel for how they differ in the different situations. You will soon note that your physical arousal system is much slower at rest than when you are in a rush or becoming angry. After a few days of monitoring, you will become very adept at noticing when your body is speeding up. In a criticism situation, this physical sensitivity will pay off because it will enable you to recognize quickly that you are becoming aroused, and this recognition will serve as a cue to calm yourself. A good physical response may be consciously breathing more slowly. Or you may use your increased physical arousal as a signal that it's time to listen to yourself, since your getting aroused probably means you are thinking counterproductively. You can then counterpunch or use criticism-management statements. Either response will calm you physically, making it easier for you to be receptive to the criticism.

Practicing relaxation on a daily basis also helps you maintain a receptive attitude toward criticism. People who practice relaxation daily are able to develop what Dr. Herbert Benson calls a relaxation response, the ability to quickly calm themselves when they so desire, even in emotionally distressing situations. This relaxation response makes it much easier to keep emotional arousal at a level that allows you to think rationally. In a criticism situation, using a relaxation response is apt to prevent you from getting angry or defensive. You remain mentally flexible and are able to evaluate the criticism more effectively. To develop a relaxation response, first select a relaxation exercise to practice for ten days. One popular relaxation exercise to consider is the tense-relax procedure, which calls for you to tighten and relax the different muscle groups in your body. Start with your calf muscles and proceed to your thighs, stomach, shoulders, neck, and forehead. Tighten each muscle group for approximately thirty seconds and then release it. At the end of the exercise your body will be in a state of physical relaxation. If this does not appeal to you, select another exercise. The key, however, is to practice the relaxation exercise within these parameters:

1. Be in a quiet environment.
2. Be in a comfortable physical position.
3. Have the same mental image, key word, or key phrase in mind as you practice.
4. Have a passive attitude. Don't try to relax — let it happen.

These methods — listening to your thoughts, rehearsing mentally, and monitoring physical arousal — help make you more receptive to criticism because they help you change your old counterproductive cognitive, physical, and behavioral habits to new productive ones. In other words, they help you short-circuit your Pavlovian response. Inevitably, you will find that more often than not you are being receptive to criticism, amenable to it, rather than immediately discounting it.

Criticism Hurts

When CBS News dropped in the ratings during 1987, star anchorman Dan Rather became the target of negative criticism. "I don't like to get knocked down," Rather says. "But if I get knocked down, I get up, dust myself off and come off the ropes swinging. . . . Nobody likes to take a punch, but you learn to take one."

No matter what we do, no matter how hard we insist that our feelings, intellectually speaking, are simply a by-product of our thoughts to be dealt with rationally, criticism still hurts our feelings. This wound is for some people so painful that they shut out all criticism.

Ironically, in their effort to protect their self-esteem, they keep themselves from growing. It is this hurt (along with our negative thoughts about criticism) that you must reckon with if you are to benefit from criticism.

In order to make yourself receptive to criticism and less susceptible to its hurt, you must be willing to make yourself vulnerable and be able to accept that you are not perfect, that you have flaws like everyone else — in short, that you are human.

When you begin to accept yourself and your imperfections, you lose the need always to present yourself as flawless. As a result, you become less defensive. It becomes apparent that the more effective way to protect your self-esteem is not to put a wall around it but to let it be exposed. You become open to the critical information presented to you because no matter how truthful and painful any criticism is, you know you still have worth. And people become sensitive to you because you show your human side; they see you are willing to take a risk to grow. They also come to respect you.

It is this state, that of allowing yourself to risk the hurt for the sake of growth, that gives you a true receptiveness to criticism. But few people like to be vulnerable, so it is a good idea to get some "vulnerability practice" before you experience the real thing. Some actions to take include:

• Try a new activity in which you will be far from perfect. Focus on the enjoyment rather than your performance.
• Express your opinions even if you think they may be criticized.
• Express the positive feelings that you have toward other people. This is a sure way to increase your vulnerability and tolerance for anxiety, a state that frequently accompanies being criticized.

Restructuring your beliefs about yourself and your imperfections and making yourself vulnerable to criticism (each process reinforces the other) increase your receptiveness to criticism because doing so makes you more ready for the exposure of your ego that criticism entails. As a result, you are able to look at yourself more objectively without feeling as though you are inadequate or a downright failure. You can then set yourself free of a defensive posture, one in which you emotionally (and professionally) stagnate.

New York governor Mario Cuomo writes that he, too, has felt

the hurt of criticism: "The first phase is the defensive one. For a short time there is regret, distaste, a desire to return to solitude, separation, the back of the store with partitioned quiet. . . ." But now Governor Cuomo is thought to handle criticism more productively. A staff member says, "He takes criticism far less personally now. He has stopped calling to complain to writers. . . . But anonymous criticism angers him." On this point, Cuomo agrees. "These gutless wonders. They're like shadows. How do you fight them?" Note that the governor no longer reacts negatively to criticism in general but only to a specific type of criticism. One could say he has learned to appraise the criticism, something that is impossible to do if you are not receptive to it in the first place.

APPRAISING THE VALIDITY
OF THE CRITICISM

Criticism can provide valuable information for improving yourself and the work that you produce. That does not mean, however, that you must act on every criticism given to you. After all, it might not be valid. What is required is that you learn how to appraise the criticism accurately so that you can decide if it is in your best interest to act on it.

The process of appraisal is ongoing. Each appraisal that we make, whether it is accurate or distorted, affects the way we respond to our environment from then on. Unfortunately, we cannot and do not always wait around to collect all the information we need to make an accurate appraisal; we do not always spend the time necessary to analyze and assess information and then act accordingly. In this sense, humans are like the rabbit that psychologist Richard Lazarus describes:

> The rabbit cannot stop to contemplate the length of the snake's fangs, the geometry of its markings. If the rabbit is to escape, the action must be undertaken long before . . . the rabbit has fully established and verified that a nearby movement might reveal a snake in all its coiled glory. The decision to run must be made on the basis of minimal cognitive engagement.

We humans often use minimal cognitive engagement when we listen to criticism. Whether we become defensive or simply don't take the time to hear the critic out, our response is based on incomplete information; it is thus impossible for us to appraise accurately the validity of the message. As a consequence, our responses are frequently judged by others to be unfair, to say nothing of the fact that our premature assessment causes us to cast away many potentially helpful criticisms. In these cases, only when we gather more information and reappraise the criticism do we show a change of heart. Thus, an adequate amount of information allows us to appraise the same criticism (event) differently and justly.

Learning how to appraise accurately the validity of criticism prevents your being victimized by decisions based on minimal cognitive engagement. You learn how to gather information and how to use maximum cognitive engagement. As a result, you will be able to accurately assess whether it is in your best interest to follow through on the criticism.

There are several criteria to consider when appraising the validity of criticism, validity in this context implying that it is in your interest to change. (Note that here again we see the influence and integration of the classical and expressive orientations. We are using objective criteria, but it is your evaluation of these criteria that is important.) They are:

1. The importance of the criticism
2. The source of the criticism
3. The emotional context of the criticism
4. The consistency of the criticism
5. The amount of energy required versus the benefits

The Importance of the Criticism

A criticism may be legitimate, but if it is of little importance to you, the chances are slim that you will be motivated to act. The answer to the question "How important is this criticism (piece of information)?" will help you determine whether or not to take action to resolve the criticism.

A salesman, for example, may be criticized by his supervisor for having a messy desk on the grounds that it gives customers a bad impression. However, if the salesman does all of his selling over the phone, he will probably not be motivated to clean house despite the legitimacy of the criticism. On the other hand, if his position changes to one in which his clients are coming into his office, the criticism is likely to gain a greater sense of importance in his mind.

Your ability to appraise the importance of a specific criticism will be facilitated when you take into account the other criteria. What is essential to note is that the importance of criticism is not fixed; rather, it varies depending on your own needs, the needs of others, and the context in which it is given.

The Source of the Criticism

Cary Grant is said to have been rankled by the criticism that he actually played only one role — Cary Grant. "I've often been accused by the critics of being myself on the screen. But being oneself is more difficult than you'd suppose. Anyway, who else would I be? Marlon Brando?"

It's natural to be irritated when you believe the person criticizing you doesn't know what he or she is talking about. Presumably, fellow actors would rarely criticize Cary Grant for playing Cary Grant because of their understanding of the difficulty of their common craft.

One of the criteria that most directly influence how we respond to criticism is the source. To evaluate the source of the criticism, take several factors into account — first, the criticizer's qualifications. Is she qualified to criticize you? How do you know? Remember that just because you like somebody doesn't mean she is qualified to criticize your work. Similarly, the fact that you have negative feelings for someone isn't a good reason to invalidate her criticisms. She can still be qualified to criticize.

Even if the critic is qualified, that doesn't mean you have to agree with him. Perhaps you must temper the criticism on the grounds that, although it is valid, there are other factors to consider that may be unknown to the critic, such as your own goals and your own assessment of your abilities. For example, early in the 1987 season, baseball experts leveled sharp criticism at Boston Red Sox superstar Wade Boggs for not hitting enough home runs. They said he was concerned only with getting singles and doubles. Boggs replied that he was learning to pull the ball for more power but wouldn't try to play beyond his ability. "My goal is to hit the ball as hard and as consistently as I can. Too many players lose it all when they reach for the home run." Boggs's response was well put. At the end of the season, he had won the league batting title, and he broke his season record for home runs. Boggs did not flatly agree with his critics. He tempered their criticism, and his records show that he responded in just the right way.

It's also good policy to assess the motives of the critic. Many times, people criticize out of envy and resentment. While these criticisms may nevertheless have some truth to them, they are usually exaggerated. Understanding the motives of the critic helps us clarify where he is mentally sitting and makes it easier for us to put his criticisms into proper perspective. For example, when Harvey and Marilyn Diamond's book *Living Health* came out, they were besieged with criticism from the American Dieticians Association, which said that their book contained inaccurate and even dangerous information. Not only did the Diamonds refute the ADA's criticism, but Harvey Diamond assessed their motives: "Dieticians who criticize the 'Fit for Life' philosophy are only attempting to protect their own financial interest."

Sometimes it helps to categorize your critics. Wade Boggs, for example, knows that among all the sportswriters in the United States, there will always be a group that criticizes him for not hitting more home runs. Knowing this, Boggs can keep their criticism in perspective, presumably by comparing it with the criticisms he gets from other quarters. Similarly, Woody Allen knows where he stands with a certain group of critics: "I never found myself appreciated by the so-called intellectual critics. The more intellectual the critic, the worse I've done with them over the years. I've never been a favorite of Pauline Kael's or Dwight Macdonald's or Stanley Kauffmann's or John Simon's or those people that you think of as erudite critics." Categorizing your critics is also helpful because evaluating the weight of importance you assign to each group can give you some insight into your own motives.

Sometimes you may hold the critic in high esteem, and she may be well qualified. But you may disagree with the criteria on which she bases her criticisms. Best-selling author Judith Krantz feels that the criterion used to evaluate her work is unfair. "I write the best I can. I know I don't write literature for the ages but I'm criticized for writing entertainment. In twenty languages, the verdict is in — people like my books." After a *New York Times* review called Krantz's *I'll Take Manhattan* "unpleasant," "ridiculous," and "contemptible," Helen Gurley Brown wrote a letter to the *Times* defending Krantz. "She's not trying to be Jane Austen or Joan Didion. She writes this wonderful fiction. It's fantasy because no one is that rich and sexy. People act as if Judy should be Joyce Carol Oates."

Krantz's "pen pal" Jackie Collins also assesses the criteria used by her critics: "My worst critics never read me. The people who really put me down do so because I'm Jackie Collins and I write a supposed kind of book, but they never read them. There's a lot of humor in my books that I think goes right over these critics' heads."

The point, then, is to appraise the source of the criticism from a variety of angles (Aristotle's point): the critic's qualifications, his motives, the criteria used, and any other angle that you think will help you understand his perspective. As you thus familiarize yourself with the individuals who deliver your criticisms, you will be able to respond more appropriately.

The Emotional Context of the Criticism

In 1986, when Joe Namath read press reports saying that ABC didn't want him back as a sportscaster on *Monday Night Football,* his disappointment and anger caused him to say some negative things about ABC to the media. ABC then threatened (probably out of anger and because it was embarrassed by Namath's public criticism) not to fulfill its contractual obligations. Later, Namath admitted to the press, "I may not have handled the criticism right, but they [the reporters] turned it around a bit. . . . What I said was I missed the show. I'm disappointed I'm not back."

To be sure, emotions affect how we give and take criticism. When we are angry or hurt, we often say things that we wouldn't if not for our emotional state. Most of the time, when the emotional context of the criticism is one of distress, the criticisms given have swelled out of proportion. Sometimes they are just outrageously invalid.

These are criticisms that you need to let slip, since responding with your own distress-filled remarks only worsens the situation (to say nothing of your own health).

Therefore, it is important that you be sensitive to the emotional climate when you are being criticized. If your boss is angry or hurt from just being chewed out by his boss, chances are that the criticism you are now receiving is overzealous. You are catching some of his emotional turmoil. Your worst response is to get caught in his mood. If you do, a shouting match may result, with your boss pointing his finger and exclaiming "Look how you're acting." A better strategy is for you to stay calm (use criticism-management statements or your relaxation response) and respond when appropriate. Don't be surprised if later in the day you get an apology.

On the other hand, if the emotional climate of the situation and the mood of the critic seem to be calm and solemn, then you are advised to take your critic seriously.

The Consistency of the Criticism

If you are frequently criticized for the same behavior by a number of different people, it is a strong indication that the criticism is legitimate to the extent that you are in fact "doing" the behavior. The criticism is consistent.

If, conversely, you find that only one person, a co-worker, for example, criticizes you for a particular behavior, then the criticism is inconsistent.

Appraising the consistency of a criticism is important because it helps you decide whether you need to change your own general behavior or whether you have to attempt to change your behavior only in the context of a specific relationship or situation. For instance, suppose your boss criticizes you for continually missing your deadlines. In fact, you have received this same criticism from previous supervisors as well as from co-workers who have worked on projects with you. In this case, it is safe to assume that the best way to resolve the criticism is to make a conscientious effort to change your behavior so that you may meet your deadlines in the future. However, if you have never been criticized for missing deadlines before, if in fact you have always met your deadlines with other supervisors and on other projects, then perhaps it is wise to investigate why you are having trouble in meeting the deadlines that this particular supervisor sets. It might be that her deadlines are unrealistic. Or it might be that the projects she assigns to you are more difficult than others previously assigned to you. It could also be that you and this particular supervisor have difficulty in communicating goals and clarifying expectations. In the last case, the criticism will be resolved most effectively by discussing these points with your supervisor rather than by trying harder. That is, the solution might be your supervisor giving you more time or greater assistance. Similarly, if you are criticized for being late to work, late to meetings, and late for social events, you can assume that the criticism will be resolved by becoming more prompt. If you are late only to work, it is most likely a sign that your efforts need to be put into figuring out what it is about going to work that makes you late, such as not liking your job.

Thus, when criticism is consistent, change yourself. When it is inconsistent, examine the issues that make the criticism unique to the critic and/or situation.

The Amount of Energy Required Versus the Benefits

It takes emotional and/or physical energy to make the changes that criticism sometimes demands. And it may sometimes seem that you are going to be required to expend more energy than the change is worth. Therefore, in appraising a specific criticism you need to do a cost analysis, estimating as accurately as possible just how much energy (or any other type of resources) you will have to put out in order to improve the situation. Of course, your decision as to whether it's too much energy will be directly related to what you see as the potential benefits. If you can see few or no benefits from acting on a specific criticism, then surely any energy expended would be too much. When Steven Spielberg made the movie *Raiders of the Lost Ark,* he made the comment, "For a few more million dollars it could have been a perfect movie, but the only people who would have known it would be the students at U.S.C. Film School." He assessed the bottom line differential to be too much for too few.

It is difficult to judge the potential benefits of a change unless we are prepared to accept the criticism constructively. Being aware of the advantages change may offer is in itself an incentive to positive action and a source of energy. But your ability to recognize those advantages often depends on how the criticism is communicated.

Recall that the Criticism TASK Model cites the importance of offering incentives for change. Many criticizers, unfortunately, fail to do that. In order to do an accurate cost analysis, you need to ask yourself and your critic "What will I gain?" Ask your question in a concerned rather than a hostile manner: "I'm interested in knowing how doing what you suggest will help me" or "Can you share with me how you think this will affect us?" A response like this helps each of you learn the other's motives. Furthermore, by focusing on positives rather than negatives, you will be approaching criticism from an improvement-oriented perspective.

Sometimes your critic will not have any clear benefits in mind, and when this happens, it usually dawns on him that perhaps his criticism isn't valid. Other times, he will be able to explain to you many benefits that will motivate you to resolve the criticism.

Thus, doing a cost analysis is important because it will help you determine if you will receive a significant return on your investment of time and energy.

A final point to remember when you appraise the validity of criticism is that these five appraisal criteria cannot be fully separated from each other. Each of them — importance, source, emotional context, consistency, and energy required versus the benefits — interacts with the others. A "trivial" criticism, for example, may take on great significance if it comes from your boss instead of your coworker, or the opposite. What is most important, though, is that the act of thinking about these criteria in itself slows your appraisal system down, thereby increasing your ability to appraise the criticism accurately. By appraising these factors, you short-circuit your Pavlovian response. (For this reason, a good strategy when giving criticism is to tell the recipient to think about your remarks for a few days before she responds.)

A good way to practice your appraisal skills is to draw and complete a criticism appraisal grid. Select a criticism that you received recently and write it out in as much detail as possible. Then rate it according to each criterion on a scale of 1 to 9, with 9 indicating that it's in your best interest to change. Physically filling out the grid will help you focus your appraisal more than doing it mentally will, and you will also have a visual representation to "show" you what you think. The result is a more accurate appraisal.

ACKNOWLEDGING THE CRITICISM

Whether or not the criticism you receive is valid, once you've appraised it you should let others know how you feel about it.

Often when we are criticized, we ask for time to think about the criticism and say that we will get back to the critic with our response. But what typically happens is that we appraise the criticism as invalid and, consequently, see little need to reconnect with the critic. The problem here is that if you don't express your thoughts to the person who gave you the criticism, she will assume that you ignored her comments, that you have become defensive, or that perhaps you were too defensive in the first place to fairly appraise and react to her criticism.

Some people don't reconnect because they think that the critic will get angry if they disagree. This is usually not the case. What is more likely is that the critic will get angry if you don't respond at all. When you acknowledge someone's criticism, you show respect. You're saying "Your opinion is important to me." You validate their self-esteem by responding, whereas you quickly invalidate it by not acknowledging the criticism. This is what makes them angry.

If the critic asks how you arrived at your decision about the criticism, share your appraisal and you've begun a productive dialogue. You're helping the other person make room for your views.

The experience of one executive for a major retail chain illustrates this point: "My boss gives me a lot of criticism, and quite frankly, much of the time it's not valid. I learned, however, that he doesn't mind if I disagree. But what he does mind is if he doesn't know how I evaluate his criticisms. One time I made the mistake of not directly telling him that I disagreed with his criticism about how I handled a major advertising decision. He knew that I disagreed with him because I didn't change the advertising schedule for the next month. He was furious because by not directly telling him I differed with his opinion, by not letting him know my thoughts, he felt, I robbed him of the opportunity to change my thinking. In the end, his criticism was valid and my actions ended up costing us a great deal of business. Now, when he criticizes me, I usually ask for a few days to assess it and then respond to him face to face when possible, or by letter. Sometimes both."

Sprinter Carl Lewis has a healthy attitude toward acknowledging criticism. He won four gold medals in the 1984 Los Angeles Olympics and has been one of the world's best sprinters and the best long jumper since 1981. As he prepared for the 1987 USA/Mobil outdoor track and field championship, he was subjected to a lot of criticism about whether his athletic skills were still golden. Before the events, Lewis said, "People say Carl can't start and Carl can't finish and Carl is getting old. But I'm relaxed, and the running condition is there. No one has my experience in this meet, no one has ever won more 100s in this meet and no one can. No one else has weathered the storm in sprinting." By acknowledging the criticism, Lewis showed the sportswriters that he had respect for them, even though he felt his track record (as did his later performance in that meet) invalidated their criticism.

And what about when the criticism is valid? After his show *Dynasty* was criticized by its fans for falling down in its story line, producer Aaron Spelling acknowledged, "We let our audience down a little bit, but we're going to fix that. It's not easy to admit you've made a mistake, but if you have, admit it and ask the audience to give you another shot." In other words, show your vulnerability, reassure your critic that you will do your best to improve, and trust that when all is said and done, your critic will want you to stick with it.

ACTING ON THE CRITICISM

A productive response to criticism means accepting it both constructively and effectively. Those words are not synonymous. Constructive acceptance involves appraising a criticism accurately to determine if it is valid. Effective acceptance occurs when you take action to change. Taking criticism productively means combining the two.

Arrival at this stage assumes you have already accepted the criticism constructively as being valid. Your task now is to act on it, to change yourself so that the criticism can be resolved. Of course, many times both people will have to change, but even then you must still act on your part. For example, your overdemanding boss might have to change his expectations of how quickly you can meet your sales quota, but at the same time you still need to increase your sales calls.

For most people, change is hard to achieve, even when desired. Weight-watchers, smokers, and drinkers can attest to this, as well as the employee who frequently runs behind schedule. Changing behavior means breaking old habits and giving up attitudes that we have long held. It also means newness, dealing with the unknown. Some people with self-defeating attitudes also think of change as an admission that they are wrong and end up staying the same to prove they are right.

Your behavior will not change unless you make a concentrated attempt to steer your efforts toward the results you want. Once in a while, we find the criticism we have been given intensely arousing, so that the mere thought of it provides us with the energy and desire to act productively. For example, when Bo Jackson announced in 1987 that he would play football for the Los Angeles Raiders while continuing to play baseball for the Kansas City Royals, he drew strong criticism from sports experts who said that he couldn't play both games well. Jackson responded at a news conference near Auburn University: "I use that type of criticism as fuel for my fire." (Jackson had a very good year with the Raiders.) But such inspirational criticisms generally are not part of our day. Therefore, you must use change strategies that will help you resolve the criticism. Here are three methods for successfully changing your own behavior or that of others.

Signing a Contract

Marriage counselors frequently use contracts to encourage couples to act on the insights they develop in counseling. The contract is a mutual agreement, usually written, in which you commit yourself to making new plans, setting new goals, or adopting a certain kind of new behavior. If you have appraised the criticism as valid, you can make a contract with yourself to act on it.

For a contract to be effective, it cannot be vaguely formulated in your mind. Write terms down; spell out exactly what behavior is involved and how you specifically intend to change it. Follow this framework:

1. Specify the behavioral goal.
2. Determine an accurate measurement for tracking your improvement.
3. Set a reward for reaching the goal. The reward must be meaningful.
4. Set a punishment for not reaching the goal. The punishment cannot be that you don't get the reward, because you wouldn't ever have had the reward in the first place.
5. Choose a realistic time frame. Otherwise you will sabotage your progress by thinking you are making none when in fact you are.
6. Pay off. Deliver the positive or negative consequence, or else your new behavior will not be maintained. If you must give yourself the negative consequence, you will find that receiving the penalty increases your motivation to change the next time you try.

It is important to make sure that the positive and negative consequences that you build into your contract are approximately equal in intensity. If you find that trying to change is hard going, you may decide to throw in the towel, telling yourself that you can live without your reward and, at the same time, that you can live with the punishment you selected. The trick is to make the punishment something that you can't live with; then the chances are less that you will give up your effort. In other words, you must fear the negative as much as you want the positive.

Monitoring Your Behavior and Visually Graphing It

Psychologists have found that monitoring your behavior and visually graphing the results in a particular effort is an extremely effective way of changing your behavior. They give two reasons for its success: 1) the visual feedback shows you that you are improving and thus keeps you motivated; 2) the act of graphing the behavior is reactive — it forces you to be consciously aware of your actions, which enables you to guide yourself more effectively.

To use this strategy:

1. Specify the behavior you will graph.
2. Determine an accurate measure for the behavior and, when the behavior occurs, measure and record it.
3. Put your results on a graph and keep it in plain sight.

Giving Yourself Step-by-Step Tasks and Assignments

The goal here is to prevent yourself from being overwhelmed by what you have to accomplish. You can do this by breaking down the changes being attempted into small, manageable tasks and assignments. As you accomplish each one, you gain momentum and your confidence builds for successfully mastering the next task.

Instead of worrying that you have to rewrite a thirty-page proposal, just focus on rewriting the introduction. Then move on to the next section. After a while, the report is finished. Likewise, the dieter who tells himself that he has to lose fifty pounds is less likely to get started than the one who makes it his goal to lose three pounds. Losing fifty pounds is overwhelming; losing three pounds is very possible.

All of these strategies have one thing in common: You must do them to make them work. You must take action.

GROWING TAKES TIME!

The final point to remember is that learning to take criticism productively is not a process that happens overnight. Restructuring your thoughts and developing new ways of doing things, learning to take risks and be vulnerable, take time and effort, and though techniques help, there is no shortcut. Nobody loses fifty pounds in a week. What is required is for you to go through the process.

But if you actively try, if you begin to explore your reactions to criticism, if you start to expose yourself to it, then you facilitate this

change on a daily basis. The four steps outlined in this chapter —
increasing your receptivity to criticism, appraising the validity of
criticism, acknowledging the criticism, and, when it is valid, acting
on the criticism — will expedite this process. Eventually, the knife
of criticism will become a tool to improve yourself. Jane Fonda puts
it like this: "I welcome criticism, that's how I grow."

deadline approaches, the boss will point out to his subordinate that again he has failed to meet his deadline. However, the deadline has not actually arrived, and, in fact, the subordinate can still meet it. The boss has become overly critical of the subordinate and at the same time has communicated through his premature criticism that he doesn't trust him to succeed. This message is internalized by the subordinate as "I can't do it. Why try?" The irony, then, is that this premature criticism undermines the subordinate's true efforts to improve and causes him to do exactly what the superior wishes to avoid — continue missing his deadlines.

Low expectations that we have about ourselves also affect the criticism process. If you know your boss is going to criticize your most recent report, or if you are getting ready for a performance appraisal, you may be internally expressing negative expectations by thinking "This is going to be terrible. The guy really wants to nail me to the wall." Having these expectations, you lower your ability to handle the criticisms effectively. The first sign of "negativity" from your criticizer becomes a confirmation that your expectations were "correct" — "See, I was right. This guy is putting me down." In effect, your negative expectations trigger your defensiveness. (Note that using criticism-management statements is one way to make expectations work for you because they encourage the mental set that allows you to handle the criticism.)

Part of the Critical Edge is knowing how to use expectations to work for you. For example, the superior must know how to use positive expectations to build a subordinate's confidence. A subordinate needs to know how to change the superior's expectations from "I don't expect my subordinates to criticize me" to "I expect my subordinates to criticize me." And we all need to know how to use our expectations to make taking criticism a more productive process.

For all of these individual uses of expectations, there are three rules that will serve us well:

• Identify your expectations. When you identify your expectations, you give yourself the opportunity to appraise them accurately. Furthermore, you can't communicate your expectations if you don't know what they are. Therefore, identify what you expect of your subordinates, your co-workers, your superiors, and yourself. Writing

PART II

WORKING WITH CRITICISM

THIS SECTION focuses on giving and taking criticism in four specific situations that are found in almost any work environment. Most people find that their job involves them in all four types of encounters, these being: 1) criticizing a subordinate; 2) criticizing a superior; 3) criticizing a co-worker; 4) having their work formally appraised by a superior and/or having to formally appraise a subordinate's work. A chapter is devoted to each of these four kinds of encounters.

In every chapter, issues, concepts, principles, and techniques will be discussed that influence the process of criticism in the work environment. While much of the information is applicable to each of the four exchanges, certain factors take on greater significance than others depending on the organizational relationship (superior-subordinate, co-worker–co-worker) involved. Thus, some information is discussed in one chapter because its importance is best illustrated in the context of that particular relationship, but this information is important in the other chapters as well. For example, while the need to build confidence in a fellow worker is a factor in all relationships, it takes on special meaning in the superior-subordinate relationship since "confidence builder" is thought to be a superior's role more than it is a co-worker's. Similarly, cooperation is important throughout the work environment but is more crucial when criticizing co-workers than when criticizing subordinates, for cooperation is more closely aligned with how co-workers function than with how a superior relates to a subordinate. (A superior is asked to manage or supervise subordinates, not cooperate with them; a co-worker is asked to cooperate with peers, not supervise them.)

What should not be overlooked is that the Critical Edge means being able to integrate all of the concepts, principles, and techniques, since they are all important, rather than trying to master only that which applies to a specific relationship. Thus, the subordinate who knows how to criticize his co-workers will be better able to criticize his superior than the subordinate who focuses exclusively on learning how to criticize upward. Regardless of the theme of each chapter, the information in each is important to all. Furthermore, each chapter in this part will show how the different "forces" — the individual giving the criticism, the superior of the individual, and the organization within which he or she functions — can intervene to facilitate the criticism process. Therefore, each chapter is for everyone in the organization.

CRITICAL CONCEPTS IN THE ORGANIZATION

Two concepts that affect giving and taking criticism and that are inherent in any organizational relationship are work power and expectations. Because these concepts are ubiquitously important to giving and taking criticism at work, they will be discussed now.

Work Power

Although the Criticism TASK Model for giving criticism will help you begin to give criticism on the job effectively, it is not enough to give you the Critical Edge because it does not take into account the concept of work power. In the typical organizational structure, each of us occupies a specific niche with a set of daily tasks to perform. As a result, each of us has a certain fixed amount of work power — the power to influence or to make decisions for other people. If, for example, a head nurse decides to change shift schedules for her hospital ward and there are ten nurses on her staff, her decision will affect all ten. But if the hospital's head of nursing services decides to reorganize the entire nursing staff, scores of nurses will be affected. Clearly, the head of nursing services has greater work power than the head nurse of a single ward. Theoretically, work power increases as one moves up in an organization's structure. Those who have

greater work power than we do are our superiors; those whose work power is less than ours are our subordinates; those whose work power is more or less equal to our own are our peers. Although work responsibilities may change and one's position in the hierarchy may change, one still must function within a superior-peer-subordinate structure of varying work power.

The key point to recognize is that this structure has an effect on how you give criticism on the job; it creates unwritten criticism rules. For example, it is often accepted as a rule that one does not criticize a boss; nor does a boss feel obliged to listen to criticism from a subordinate. A subordinate, on the other hand, is supposed to accept criticism even when he or she feels it is unfair or invalid, in accord with the maxim that subordinates "must" accept criticism (or quit their jobs). Peers usually hesitate to offer even helpful criticism to one another because they reason, "How can I criticize someone who doesn't work for me?"

To get the Critical Edge, one must understand the nuances of work power in organizational relationships and how they create obstacles to giving and taking criticism. Furthermore, one must be able to devise strategies that help one overcome these obstacles, thus making it easier to give criticism effectively.

Expectations

Expectations are the mental bets we make with ourselves about the outcome of events, our behavior, and the behavior of others. They often reflect our goals and standards.

Our expectations are a powerful force in the criticism process. For instance, while high expectations are often desirable, they are also often the cause of our becoming highly critical. When a subordinate's work doesn't meet our expectations, that subordinate frequently fails to get acknowledgment for the good work he or she *has* done.

Sometimes we expect that a person is going to continue the behavior that we criticize; we do not think he or she is going to change. In this case, our expectation may cause us to give premature criticism — as soon as the person approximates the behavior we disapprove of, we criticize. Take, for example, the superior who expects that his subordinate will once again be late with his work. As the

down each expectation is recommended since this will help you clarify them.

• Make sure your expectations are realistic. Your expectations will always work against you if they are unrealistic. One way that you can gauge them is to use similar past experiences as your baseline. If you think your division will triple its outcome in a year, and the best it has ever done in the past is show a 15 percent increase, chances are that you are being unrealistic. What will happen is that you will show a 20 percent increase and define it as a failure because you were expecting much more; you won't feel good about what you have achieved. A second strategy is to ask others what they think. Sometimes it's difficult to be honest with yourself. Sharing the expectations that you have for yourself or others with other people gives you feedback as to whether you are being too hard (or too easy) on yourself or others. Colleagues can help you evaluate these expectations realistically. A third tactic is to assign percentages of likelihood to your expected outcomes. Quantifying chance (60 percent chance, 30 percent chance, 10 percent chance) helps you think clearly about whether you really believe the expectation is going to be met. Once you assign a percentage to your expectation, you can modify it as the situation evolves and, in the process, develop a realistic outlook. This brings up an important point: Expectations will serve you best when they are elastic rather than static. Making expectations realistic does not mean you should not set them high. The perennial track star, a best-selling author, and a movie star all have exceedingly high expectations for themselves — as do their coach, publisher, and producer. Yet their past behavior dictates that these expectations are realistic. But for the average high school star, the first-time author, and the fledgling movie actor, the same expectations would be unrealistic, to say the least.

• Communicate your expectations. Letting other people know what you expect of them is characteristic of the most productive relationships and effective organizations. It also gives employees the opportunity to validate whether your expectation is realistic — whether they think they can meet it. If they think they can't, they are able to explain their viewpoint, and together you can reach a realistic expectation. Communication prevents you from having inappropriately high or low expectations of others and saves you from giving destructive and/or premature criticism. Letting people know what you expect of them also provides them with important information about you — such as what you think is important and what your needs are.

Former football great Don Meredith sums it up when talking about Miami Dolphins coach Don Shula, one of the most successful football coaches in history: "The guys love to play for Don Shula. He sits each player down and tells them very clearly what he expects of them."

Finally, recognize that expectations reflect the criteria upon which our criticisms are based. Thus, identifying your criticism criteria will help you understand what your expectations are all about.

The next four chapters will show, among many other things, how to integrate the concepts of work power and expectations into the four different types of criticism encounters. This will help you use criticism to achieve successful results.

Chapter 5

Making Subordinates Superior

ANDREW GROVE, president of Intel, a superstar company of Silicon Valley, states that one of the most important skills a manager can possess is the ability to criticize his or her subordinates effectively: "Giving feedback — criticizing and praising — is the most important tool of the managing trade. It's through feedback that we'll nudge our employees in the right direction, set and modify their expectations and coax them along toward improved performance. Hard as it may be, we must criticize."

It is essential to criticize your subordinates. You cannot possibly meet your goals if your subordinates fail to achieve theirs. Being able to criticize subordinates productively is a direct way to make them more productive and thus generate what *In Search of Excellence* authors Thomas Peters and Robert Waterman call productivity through the people. Perhaps more important, being able to criticize subordinates productively helps build relationships with them that are characterized by loyalty and trust, two assets that most organizations find indispensable. Criticism is the tool that keeps your subordinates on track, educates them about how to do better, communicates the standards and expectations they are to meet, and makes them feel good about their present and future accomplishments.

Unfortunately, even for the most seasoned superior, what starts out to be a constructive session too often ends up being a destructive confrontation. A case in point is George Steinbrenner, owner of the New York Yankees. After his team lost the World Series in 1981, he publicly criticized them, saying, "I can't find fault with our offense, but I can find fault with our pitchers. The pitching has been lousy. Rick Reuschel was lousy. Ron Davis was lousy. There's no excuse for our pitching. I want to sincerely apologize to fans of the New York Yankees everywhere for the performance of the Yankee team in the World Series. If there's any player who can stand up and say he acquitted himself as a Yankee should, he doesn't belong in the uniform."

It doesn't take a baseball fan to see how humiliating these statements were to the players. And, since they came at the end of the season, all they did was make it a long, cold winter for a team that had almost won the world championship. Nearly ten years later, Steinbrenner has not changed his criticism style. He still publicly berates his team and gives negative criticism to managers, sometimes on a daily basis. His manager in 1987 and most of 1988, Lou Piniella, said, "It tears my heart out." A 1987 article in the *Washington Post* sports section pointed out what many sports experts believe to be true: A significant reason the Yankees have not won a World Series in ten years, despite their superstar talent, is Steinbrenner's constant negative criticism of his managers and team.

Steven Brill, editor of *American Lawyer* magazine, criticizes his subordinates in a style that seems to place him in the same league as George Steinbrenner. Scribbled in red on their stories are such criticisms as "What are you, a moron?" and "Is English your second language?" According to the *Wall Street Journal*, "His reporters often fear his editing." The *Journal* states that his criticisms "are reported to have left the newsroom littered with 'weeping casualties' on more than one occasion." Criticisms such as these can hardly be thought of as productive.

Although most superiors are not quite as destructive as Brill or Steinbrenner in their criticisms of their subordinates, they may not know how to make criticism entirely productive. As Andy Grove points out, when it comes to giving criticism, "most managers are less qualified to handle this part of their job than any other."

This chapter is not going to present a formula or model that will guarantee productive results every time you criticize a subordinate — there isn't any. What it will do is present concepts, help you clarify important issues, and demonstrate techniques that will help you develop the Critical Edge in dealing with subordinates — that is, help you make subordinates superior.

THE SUPERIOR-SUBORDINATE
RELATIONSHIP

The Japanese working world puts a tremendous emphasis on the *Sempai-Kohai* relationship, which roughly corresponds to the mentor-protégé relationship in the West. A Japanese manager from Sony describes its essence: "The Sempai-Kohai relationship is a very honored relationship. The Sempai, who is the senior, has the duty of helping the Kohai develop himself, to help him undergo what is akin to an evolutionary process. In the beginning of the relationship, the Kohai is viewed as a simple insect whose only concern is surviving. The Sempai, through guidance and tutelage, helps the Kohai move up the evolutionary ladder, the next rung being an animal, a pig whose main trait is seen as self-interest. The Sempai continues to develop the Kohai, teaching him the importance of concern for others, and when this lesson is learned, the Kohai finally becomes a human being. The Sempai completes his duty as his experience and wisdom are passed down to the Kohai so that the evolutionary process can be completed; the Kohai becomes an Emperor who is now ready to attach himself to his own Kohai. But what is important to remember is that if the Kohai fails to evolve, so does the Sempai."

Thus, the Sempai (the senior) educates the Kohai (the junior) in the nuances and subtleties of moving up the organization — not by teaching technical competence but by bonding himself to the Kohai in an emotional and functional manner. Senior and junior are seen as inescapably linked; one's failure or success necessarily affects the other's. The relationship, then, is not something that must be endured but rather something that is desired, something of mutual benefit — a force that binds.

The concept of the Sempai-Kohai relationship is important here because it draws attention to what is frequently ignored in the American conceptualization of the boss-subordinate relationship, that is, the quality of the relationship. The typical Sempai-Kohai pairing is both closer and more supportive than the typical boss-subordinate relationship. It is this quality in the relationship that many Japanese management experts say makes the subordinate want to perform rather than have to perform. The Japanese have made the relationship in itself a force that improves the quality of work and those who produce it.

Part of the Critical Edge is being able to make the quality of your relationships with your subordinates a factor that facilitates the criticism process. For example, say that by chance you slip and deliver a caustically critical remark; chances are, if you have a good relationship, your subordinate will still respond productively. The positive quality of his past experiences with you will dictate that he be receptive to and tolerant of your criticisms, even if they are on the negative side, and also, the solidity of your relationship will be such that the subordinate doesn't hold your negative remarks against you. The "goodness" of the relationship will override the negative moment. While there are specific criticism techniques, they are secondary to the quality of the relationship. If you have poor relationships with your subordinates, it makes it much more difficult for you to criticize them. But good relationships with your subordinates facilitate the transmission of such information.

One way to develop such a quality relationship with your subordinate is to help each subordinate wear a COTE of armor: a sense of Confidence, Optimism, Tenacity, and Enthusiasm.

The COTE of Armor

"Some people call it luck, but I call it psychology, which in our business is largely a matter of building and maintaining confidence — upon his ability, a manager has to build morale and confidence. And when a fellow is dealing with 20 or more types and temperaments [among his subordinates] this is not the simplest thing in the world."

These are the words of Miller Huggins, who had the formidable task of criticizing Babe Ruth and Lou Gehrig. Imagine having to make Ruth and Gehrig play better! Huggins was successful because, as his words suggest, he used the recommended basic philosophy for criticizing subordinates; he helped them put on the COTE of armor.

Getting your subordinates to wear their COTE of armor makes subordinates superior because it protects them against destructive criticism; it does this by giving them a strong sense of themselves. Instead of being shattered by the criticism, they will be sure of their ability, regardless of how negative the criticism, to deal with the criticism effectively. They will be confident enough to take on any challenge, tenacious enough to try again when necessary. In other words, the COTE of armor will make your subordinates more resilient in the face of criticism.

Moreover, the process of building your subordinate's COTE of armor helps you develop a strong relationship with her, which of course, as has been noted, facilitates the criticism process. (And reciprocally, as the criticism process improves, so does the way you interact with your subordinates.)

Let's now look at how you can build your subordinate's COTE of armor.

Building and Polishing Your Subordinate's COTE of Armor

The key to building your subordinate's COTE of armor is to recognize that people who are able to ask questions about their performance — and to act on answers that are sometimes difficult to accept — will inevitably give performances superior to those of people who are unable to do the same. The attribute required is called ego strength and is the result of wearing the COTE of armor.

The term "ego" has its roots in psychoanalytic theory and refers to the executive agency of the personality, the director of actions. As such, it is the part of ourselves that decides what aspects of the environment we respond to and how we can meet our needs. The ego is a normal and necessary part of the human personality, and it is a mistake to equate a strong ego with such traits as narcissism or authoritarianism.

Andy Grove acknowledges the ego strength of some of his subordinates when he describes high-achieving employees at Intel as micro CEOs. Their ability to take charge, to be effective in any surroundings, exemplifies the COTE of armor. No matter where he or she is in the hierarchy, the micro CEO who possesses a strong ego feels capable of perceiving things accurately and making effective decisions. This feeling is internalized as self-confidence.

The COTE of armor also often shows up in business and elsewhere as hardiness: the energy to sustain long hours of work and the flexibility to adapt to change. Hardiness comes from a strong sense of being on course (recall that one of the functions of productive criticism is to keep people on course). Co-workers who are less confident spend huge amounts of their energy hiding behind pronouncements of policy and "higher authority" — maneuvering aimed at protecting their fragile armor, which, in spite of their efforts, usually cracks.

Perhaps the best example in recent years of a subordinate's having a strong COTE of armor was Lee Iacocca's well-documented response to his boss's firing him after years of hard work at Ford. His COTE of armor certainly did not ward off the blow, but it did allow him to act successfully on his own behalf once his armor had been shelled. Although he does recount in his best-selling autobiography a temporary increase in drinking and some tremors in his hands, Iacocca did not come unglued. Instead, he made his distressing experience a launching pad for greater accomplishment. What is important to note here is that Iacocca was not born with this hardiness. He credits other people, including his father, with helping him to develop it.

In a similar vein, the subordinate is not born with his COTE of armor, nor should a superior think that he will develop it on his own (although this is certainly possible). Superiors who have the Critical Edge actively build their subordinate's COTE of armor and then polish it frequently. These superiors become Sempais — they develop their subordinates. There are seven tactics that a superior can use to help a subordinate develop this necessary ego strength. They are:

1. Create Successful Experiences. Nothing builds confidence like successful experiences. When a subordinate has a success, she experiences a sense of achievement and gains the "I can do it" attitude. And she knows she can do it again.

The mistake that most managers and supervisors make is waiting for their subordinates to have a success, which may be a long time coming. More important, the "wait till she succeeds" attitude places the superior in a passive role; he thereby ceases to be a positive force in the development of the subordinate. What is called for here is to be an active force by creating a successful experience. By doing this, you, the supervisor, facilitate your subordinate's development and set the stage for her being able to create her own successes.

One way you can create a successful experience is by first giving a subordinate an assignment you know she can handle and then increasing the level of difficulty with each succeeding assignment.

Each success that she experiences gives her confidence and a positive attitude about trying the next task. Since you have work power, you can give her the assignments you think will be appropriate.

A similar method is to break down one specific assignment into small, manageable tasks, making the first step a guaranteed success. (This is an example of how a technique discussed in the previous chapter — breaking criticism down into smaller steps so change becomes easier — can be used in working with others.) As the subordinate succeeds on each step, she gets the "yes" momentum going and thus becomes confident she can successfully tackle the next step. University of Kansas professor Richard Rundquist used this method to help his students successfully get through the dissertation process. Instead of thinking of a dissertation as a singular, monumental effort, his students were instructed by him to concentrate on one section at a time. With the completion of each section, the students gained the confidence to continue.

Breaking down an assignment into manageable increments prevents the subordinate from being overwhelmed by the possibility that she may not be able to do it. The subordinate develops a sense of self-efficacy — a belief in her ability to cope with the task at hand. Feeling in control, she approaches the task uninhibited by fear.

Once you create and take note of a successful experience, you can use it as part of a new criticism technique. The strategy here is to link past positive successes (ones you have helped create) to the task at hand, reminding the subordinate that if she did it once, she can do it again. Pat Riley, coach of the 1987 and 1988 National Basketball Association champions, the Los Angeles Lakers, frequently uses this technique. He tells his players, "Make a pass like the one you made last week" or "Run the same way you did against the Celtics." Both statements contain a reference to a past successful experience, thus setting off positive associations in the player's mind. Thinking about past success, the player (and team) is more likely to have the confidence to duplicate or exceed his previous efforts (assuming his talent is the same). Even more artful is the coach who huddles with his players and says, "Gee, I hope we play today as well as we did in last year's playoffs." The semantics of this delivery also refers to a past success. However, the information is presented as a subjective desire, in contrast to the more demanding tone of "Play the same way you did last year." The latter entails the risk of creating pressure, even though it refers to a successful experience. The former delivery, though, calls for a good sense of timing, since the coach has to wait for the right time to move up to his team and make his play. The drawback here is that the coach has to assume that his player(s) will capture the point — play like "you" did last year! These intricacies of communication are what the art of criticism is all about.

A case similar to Coach Riley's is that of a vice president at Shearson Lehmann Brothers. He observed a young broker making several sales presentations over the phone. In some of the early calls, the VP noted, the broker did not have his facts organized and pressured the prospect to make a decision on the spot. Yet the VP withheld his criticism. Eventually, the VP observed a job well done: The broker had assessed the financial rating of his prospect, presented his information, asked for questions, and did not pressure the prospect to buy. Before the broker made his next call, the VP spoke to him: "Make the same type of sales presentation you did with the last client." Less skilled superiors would probably have voiced the same criticisms in the negative: "Don't take shots like you did last week" or "You are making most of your presentations all wrong."

2. Give Responsibility. You can give your subordinates an explicit vote of confidence by giving them responsibility. Letting them be in charge of their work communicates that you trust them to succeed. Seeing that you believe in them makes it easier for them to believe in themselves. A manager at Hughes Aircraft evaluated one of his subordinates as having excellent ability but felt it was undermined by a lack of confidence. The subordinate hesitated to make decisions and to offer his views at meetings and seemed afraid to be in charge. Yet his work was always on target, and he was respected by his peers. Unlike most managers, who wait until the subordinate proves beyond doubt that he is ready for more responsibility, this manager took immediate action and increased the subordinate's responsibility on an important project. His work quickly improved. When the manager asked why, he said: "When I saw that you believed in me, I realized it was foolish for me not to have confidence in myself, that all I had to do was exercise my ability and I would do a good job. That's what's happening now."

3. Express Positive Expectations. To reiterate, it's a well-known psychological fact that what you expect of yourself and others is a strong determinant of the results you get. You can encourage your subordinates to expect the best of themselves by frequently telling them that they "can do better and better." In the early days of Polaroid, for example, Edward Land walked about his company and continually urged his team to "achieve the impossible." Many thought Polaroid had achieved this when it introduced a camera that could develop a picture in a few minutes. Land's compelling positive expectations had convinced his managers that they couldn't fail. That was more than twenty years ago, and today Polaroid cameras are developing pictures even faster.

4. Give Subordinates Fun Work. When Harold Williams left the chairmanship of the Securities and Exchange Commission, his staff gave him a bound copy of his speeches. One of the inscriptions in the inside cover was: "It was all great fun!" Northeast Apparel president Bobby Reisman says, "I tell everyone in the company that they ought to find their work to be fun."

If you want your subordinates to be enthusiastic, you must ensure that they are enjoying their jobs — having fun. People who don't enjoy their work become susceptible to burnout, and their performance suffers dramatically. Several years ago, tennis great John McEnroe lost his dominant stature on the court. Deciding to take a few months off, he cited one of his reasons to the press: "I wasn't having as much fun."

Letting subordinates have fun on the job certainly does not mean work is one big party. It does mean that you must allow your subordinates to do the type of projects that excite and interest them. This type of work energizes them and leads them to ask themselves, "How can I do this better?" At the same time, the balance of fun work gives them the boost needed to do other, less appealing assignments.

5. Institute Goal Checks. Tenacity is a trait that pays off. One way you can instill it in subordinates is to continually point out their progress in achieving goals, no matter how small. These goal checks reinforce the subordinate's perception that he is "getting there." As a result, he keeps going.

6. *Give Permission to Fail.* Subordinates who fear failure are discouraged from taking risks and thus rarely reach their true potential. Giving subordinates permission to fail is important because it repositions failure as an opportunity to learn, allowing them to do better next time. Failure can be rich in lessons essential to success and development. Through failure, you not only can learn a host of useful skills but you also can gain a more realistic perspective on yourself. Experiencing failure allows a person to learn that she can survive failure — to persevere and try again. Most important, knowing she is not expected to be perfect makes her more comfortable with her own vulnerability, which enables her to be more open to criticism. She begins to view criticism as valuable information that will help her improve over time and thus comes to recognize that one failure is not the end of the battle. She becomes tenacious.

Los Angeles mayor Tom Bradley, when asked about being defeated in his 1980 gubernatorial race, said: "Yes, of course I was disappointed with the outcome of the election in view of the close margin by which I lost. But it was not the first experience for me in losing a contest. I always come back . . . I always hang in there."

One way you can give permission to fail is by not severely reprimanding a subordinate who makes a costly mistake. Instead, use the experience to teach appropriate skills and knowledge. Acting in this manner will help make the subordinate more secure, because his fear of being fired or demoted is erased. Thus, he can be more open to learning how he can prevent a recurrence.

7. *Wear Your Own COTE of Armor.* No matter how hard you try to build your subordinate's COTE of armor, your efforts are likely to fail if you don't "model" the behavior you expect of her. Acting confidently, expressing optimism and enthusiasm, set the pattern for your subordinate's actions. If she senses you are insecure or unenthusiastic, she is likely to be the same — and resistant as well. But if your subordinate sees you expressing excitement about a new project, chances are that she will follow suit.

Detroit Tigers manager Sparky Anderson gives a beautiful example of building the COTE of armor. At the 1987 All-Star game, Sparky was having a conversation with two of the game's best hitters, Don Mattingly and Wade Boggs. Matt Nokes, a Tiger rookie, became the subject of their conversation, and both Mattingly and Boggs told Sparky that they thought Nokes would be a great hitter. Sparky told each of them, "[If] you ever notice a problem with his swing, please tell me so I can pass it on at the right time." Sparky asked Mattingly and Boggs to tell him about any problems because he didn't want to risk Mattingly or Boggs shaking Nokes's confidence by criticizing him to his face in the wrong way. By delivering a criticism himself, Sparky presumably reasoned, he could ensure its productiveness, use it to strengthen the COTE of the young player. He protected Nokes because he saw one of his managerial tasks as developing his players.

In his relations with subordinates, Mark Shulman, president of Ann Taylor clothing stores and the youngest president of any Allied Store division, demonstrates the application of some of the seven tactics for building the COTE of armor. When his assistant confided in him that she hated her present job, he took the time to counsel her, even though he was under the intense pressure that accompanied his presidency at that time. His assistant had been in her job for eighteen months and now wanted to become the company's customer relations manager. After a brief discussion, Shulman agreed. She would still assist him, he decided, but she would also develop customer relations policy and travel around the country to teach it to Ann Taylor's saleswomen. He gave her fun projects. For the first time that year, his assistant grew excited about her job. When asked to describe Shulman, she calls him supportive. Shulman says, "I emphasize successes and I like to encourage employees to improve themselves."

Another woman approached him with a similar problem. She was in charge of processing sales and supplier data and felt tied to her computer. Shulman created a position for her as operations manager. He believed that her organizational skills would help Ann Taylor run at maximum efficiency. Her chief responsibility would be to direct construction of all new stores, a critical function during the company's rapid expansion. In the beginning, the woman was not confident of her ability to do the task, but Shulman applied positive expectations, insisting she could handle the job. He says, "Now her performance is outstanding. Even with growth, Ann Taylor hasn't missed a beat." He adds, "There's a pride I get from knowing I've helped people. I remember from my own experience how difficult it was to muster enthusiasm for something I didn't enjoy in retailing, like buying polyester shirts. I wish someone in authority had helped me make my job more fulfilling back then."

In sum, when you help your subordinates develop into confident individuals who are able to accept your criticisms and act productively, you become a positive force in their lives. In the process, they begin to value their relationship with you, since it is one that makes them feel good. As the relationship becomes stronger, it becomes easier for you to have your criticisms accepted. What has happened is that the positive quality of your relationship has allowed the subordinate to experience your criticisms as a tool for growth. Each criticism now polishes the COTE. Once you have built your subordinate's COTE of armor, it is time to turn your attention to other, and perhaps more direct, ways of influencing him or her to improve performance.

A CRITICAL QUESTION: HOW DO YOU MOTIVATE?

How do you think you motivate people? Since one of the goals of criticism is to motivate, your answer is important. Take, for example, the case of the subordinate who is consistently late with his paperwork. How would you motivate him to improve his work? The fact is, your theory of motivation helps you decide how to criticize your subordinates. Thus, as a part of learning to criticize subordinates productively, it will be extremely helpful for you to assess your theory of motivation.

Motivation is the art and science of effecting change in others at the level of thought, feelings, and/or actions. Anytime one individual influences another, whether they are aware of it or not, they both have been involved in a motivational effort.

One of the most popular theories of motivation is Douglas MacGregor's "X-Y" theory, which holds that there are two basic philosophies of motivation, the X and the Y philosophy. The X philosophy claims that people have little or no internal desire for achievement and work output. Therefore, proponents of this philosophy feel, only the "carrot and stick" approach will motivate individuals or groups. The Y philosophy states that people have an inherent need for achievement and that they will work without the "carrot and stick" approach in the proper motivational environment.

A different motivational theory is put forth by Fredrick Herzberg. He thinks that people are not motivated to produce at high levels for rewards that they take for granted. Although many managers believe that people "should" produce effectively when they receive the benefits they have been promised, this is often not the case. Thus, Herzberg says, you must discover what will motivate others in the "real world" instead of watching production sink and pondering a utopian world of what "should" be.

Management consultant Peter Drucker writes that individuals and organizations are effectively motivated and thus productive when they are made responsible and accountable for their results. Without requiring that people experience the results of their actions, motivational efforts can fall apart. Furthermore, he shows us that an environment of participation inspires productivity; individuals who are involved in the process, and are appreciated and recognized for their contributions, tend to be motivated.

"Need" theory represents another way of looking at motivation. The major proponent of this theory is psychologist Abraham Maslow, who proposed that all individuals have needs that can be categorized into five basic groups, with lower-level needs being more potent motivators than higher-level needs. Only when the basic needs, such as food and safety, are satisfied will individuals strive to satisfy higher needs, such as social acceptance and recognition for making a contribution. The key to motivation, according to Maslow, is permitting the right need to be met.

Which of these theories is correct? Obviously all of them have merit to varying degrees, depending on the target of the motivational effort. For example, the X theory is correct inasmuch as "carrots" are usually necessary, since they help create the goals and dreams of the target. But if they are merely external incentives rather than ideological concepts, they will not be as effective. The Y theory is correct insofar as it taps into human creativity; we also know that this sort of inherent motivation elicits labors of love from individuals and groups. And, finally, to support Maslow's theory, we can all testify to the fact that we do many things simply to meet our needs of being accepted or recognized by others.

Let's now return to the case of the subordinate who consistently misses his paperwork deadlines. Superior 1 believes in the X theory and as a result is likely to deliver her criticism like this: "You won't get that raise if you can't meet your deadlines." The superior assumes that her criticism will be effective because the subordinate wants a raise. Superior 2, who adopts the need theory, is apt to give criticism along these lines: "People will really appreciate you if you can get your work in on time." This superior's assumption is that being appreciated by co-workers is important to the recipient and will thus prompt him to achieve the desired results. Who is right? In fact, both superiors might find that their criticisms are ineffective. The key, however, is that managers who have the Critical Edge, in contrast to those who do not, are aware of their motivational assumptions. This grants them the critical factor of flexibility. If they see that one approach is not working, they can switch to another motivational theory and criticize the subordinate differently. Their chances for success have multiplied exponentially.

Their ineffective counterparts, however, not being aware of their motivational assumptions or not seeing the connection between them and how they criticize, continue to criticize in the same way. This not only does not prompt the desired results but also inevitably causes them to feel frustrated, angry, and helpless. In the end, they say, "The guy's a real problem. I've spoken to him a dozen times and he doesn't change." The truth is, it is the superior who perpetuates the problem by not changing his or her own behavior.

To complete the example, then, superior 1 sees that her criticism is not effective. Not having the Critical Edge, she will again approach the subordinate, saying something like "Listen, I want to recommend you for that promotion, but I can't do it if your work isn't on time." When this isn't effective, she tries "I really want to see you move up in the organization. Let's meet those deadlines and get on with it" and on and on and on. Although the semantics are different, the motivational assumption is the same — that getting a promotion is important to the subordinate. Because it isn't, the subordinate's behavior stays the same, and the superior is bewildered and angry, to say the least.

Superior 2, however, sees that his first criticism is ineffective. Instead of coming back with "Gee, the folks here will really welcome you if you can meet your deadlines," he takes another tack: "Listen, if you can get your work in on time, we will be able to give you more responsibility." If this second approach doesn't succeed, superior 2 will try a third way, using a different motivational tactic. He continues to look for the motivator.

To develop the Critical Edge, begin to think about what motivates each of your subordinates. When possible, build these unique and individual motivators into your criticism. If you are not sure what motivates your subordinates, ask them!

Your Managerial Attitude

Your next step should be to study the source of your own motivational assumptions. Your motivational assumptions and techniques are not randomly developed but emerge from a set of managerial attitudes, different philosophies of what makes people tick in the workplace. Productive criticizers tend to have very different managerial attitudes from those who criticize ineffectively.

Ineffective criticizers tend to have these attitudes:

- People work best when they're somewhat scared. If you want results, make your people feel insecure, build on their fears, and keep them moving.
- Give people half a chance and they'll mess things up.
- If you want something done right, do it yourself.
- People should do it my way or else.
- People are lackadaisical about their work. Not much can be done to motivate them; they'll work when they want to.
- No one ought to rock the boat.
- If you wait awhile, things usually take care of themselves.

These attitudes often keep ineffective managers glued to a strict and negative X theory approach — "You better get your work in on time if you want to keep your job." Conversely, these attitudes may inhibit them from giving any criticism at all.

Productive criticizers tend to hold these attitudes:

- People work best when they see how their work can help them achieve their own goals. You are most likely to get good results when employees are actively and intelligently involved in their jobs.
- I don't manage people. I manage individuals.
- Don't turn your back on disagreements; welcome them. Differences generate ideas.
- I want to hear what my subordinate thinks.
- I don't have all the answers.

Criticisms based on these attitudes typically produce commitment, high creativity, low-to-average turnover, and an open, involved, task-oriented climate. The result is consistently high output. Ian McGregor's behavior illustrates the preceding points. When he took over the chairmanship of the British Steel Corporation, his first order of business was to restore the morale of middle management. "I've always worked on the theory that it's very important for the top person in an organization to figure out how to motivate." Although he couldn't offer the salaries customary in money-making companies, he could provide motivation by building his managers' independence and confidence. "People begin to feel they manage a piece of the business, and they have greater opportunity to show their capabilities," he says.

The message is: Think about whether your managerial attitudes are getting you the results you desire. Chances are, if your attitudes coincide with those of the first list, you are consistently criticizing ineffectively and falling short of your goals. If this is the case, you can begin to get the Critical Edge by realigning your attitudes with those of productive criticizers. Changing attitudes will result in changed behavior; thus, being aware of your attitudes and their effects is a good first step toward changing your behavior.

CRITICISM COMMUNICATES?

A recent study indicated that 84 percent of M.B.A. graduates value communication skills more than any other for being a means to success. Criticism is an interpersonal communication skill. As if its TASK — successfully presenting negative information in a way that positively influences others — isn't hard enough, it must also contend with all the pitfalls that plague good communication. The purpose of this section is to highlight some of the important principles that effective communicators know about and make use of in their critical encounters to circumvent these obstacles to communication. As your communication skills increase, you will communicate, generally, better with your subordinates, making it easier, specifically, to criticize them successfully. The better your communication skills, the better your criticism skills.

The following principles are essential to improving communication.

Principle 1: The message sent is not always the message received.

People often assume that any failure to understand or comply with a message they have delivered is the fault of the other person. Understanding that the message sent is not necessarily the message received is important, because you can then focus on clarifying your communications rather than automatically casting blame when problems arise. Instead of your seeing a personality problem, the emphasis is shifted properly to the communication process itself.

Messages are misexpressed or misheard owing to what sociologist Irving Gottman and others term the filtering process. What the speaker intends to communicate may not be what he actually expresses after the message passes through his filter of thoughts and feelings. For example, if your boss is distressed or preoccupied about something that happened between her and her own boss, her criticism may sound harsh to you. This may happen without intention or even awareness on her part.

Likewise, the message must also pass through the listener's filter, where additional distortions may occur. If the listener expects her boss to be angry, she may hear even helpful, gentle suggestions as put-downs.

In criticizing subordinates, keep in mind that they may not hear your criticisms in the way you intended them. Here are some possibilities to consider:

• The subordinate may not hear you at all. He may tune you out. If you're threatening or boring him, if your criticism is overwhelmingly negative, if you are saying something he doesn't understand, or if his mind is on something else, he literally may not hear you. In fact, a few minutes after you have criticized him, he may not even recall that you said something you considered important. When you bring up the criticism again a few days later, he says, "I don't remember you saying anything," and he is being honest — he doesn't recall it.

• The subordinate may exaggerate what you say. This often happens when your subordinate has a strong need for approval or reassurance. If your beginning criticism of such a subordinate's research project is "It needs more work," he hears "I need to make total revisions." Or you may say "It's pretty good," and he hears "It's terrific."

• The subordinate may "level down" what you say; that is, he judges your ideas to be less important than you intended. For example:

SUPERIOR: Jack, I think it's most important that you let the client know a realistic time frame immediately so that he can make other plans if it's not acceptable.

SUBORDINATE: I'll give them a call after I get some things off my desk.

Why do subordinates level down? They may disagree with you. Instead of voicing their disagreement, they de-emphasize what you say. Another possibility: They believe their own priorities are more important. A third reason might be that they hear your criticism as threatening and therefore level down to cope with the threat.

The only way to be certain that the message you send is the message received is to ask your subordinate to give you feedback about your criticism.

Principle 2: You are constantly communicating, whether verbally or non-verbally.

The employee who is passed over for promotions, not given key assignments, or given the cold shoulder after a presentation assumes her job performance is unsatisfactory, even if she is not told this in so many words. Both verbal and nonverbal communications work well to convey positive messages (a touch or a look can be effective in a positive sense), but nonverbal communication of critical messages can too easily lead to an avoidance of responsibility. The superior who glares at a subordinate can insist that the subordinate is mistaken — nothing is wrong — thus robbing the subordinate of the opportunity to improve her behavior or work. Similarly, the subordinate can easily shirk responsibility by ignoring the nonverbal negative communication: "You never said anything."

The key to making principle 2 work for you is to put negative reactions into words; they are thus expressed responsibly instead of irresponsibly.

Principle 3: Every message has both content and process.

The content of a message is the information that would be conveyed if the message were converted into print — it is the "what you say" part of the message. The process component is "how you say it." When "what you say" is contradictory to "how you say it," communication is faulty. The listener cannot simultaneously respond appropriately to both components because responding appropriately to one component would be inappropriate in the context of the other. This creates a double bind and, again, is a hallmark of ineffective communication. For example, the superior who smiles (thus conveying approval) when she criticizes a subordinate for his sarcastic comment to a client is putting the subordinate in a double bind: responding to the approval in the smile would be an inappropriate response to the seriousness of the content. Responding seriously to the content could also seem inappropriate, since it would mean changing a behavior that ostensibly gets your superior's approval.

Significantly, research demonstrates that whenever there is a discrepancy between the content and the process of a message, the process component — the nonverbal clues — is given more weight by the listener.

Principle 3 works for you when you make the content of your criticism congruent with the process. Your message is clear, focused, and understandable.

Principle 4: When verbally communicating, you must use the right words.

The words you choose when criticizing your subordinate can either make him listen or not. Words tell him how you are feeling, what you think, and what he can expect to happen to him. When you begin a criticism, your subordinate is usually thinking along these lines: "Am I in trouble?" "Will I lose my job?" "How important is this?" Everything you say is interpreted by the subordinate in the context of his needs, hopes, and concerns about his job. Make sure you say what you mean.

Many times, a slight alteration of your words can make a great difference in the response of the subordinate. For example, criticizing your subordinate by saying "Your work is below our standards" will probably evoke a more defensive response than "Your work is not quite up to our standards." The first statement declares that the subordinate is doing poor work, while the second statement suggests he is close to doing satisfactory work.

Your words are also authoritative; they carry extra weight because you are the boss. Even if your subordinate refutes your criticism, you can still back up your words with action. You may, for instance, tell your subordinate, "Your work is way below our standards." He might think, or say, "No way — you're wrong." Wrong or right, however, you have work power; you can act on your criticism and fire him or take some other punitive action. What you say does matter.

One way you can begin to make principle 4 work for you is to avoid emotionally loaded negative words. Recall that productive criticism is based on getting your recipient to be receptive to you. Using emotionally loaded negative words reduces receptivity. Your assistant may be rash, but telling her that she's impulsive, careless, or doesn't think things through is not going to awaken her receptivity.

Criticism Communication Techniques

In the preceding section, communication problems and pitfalls were discussed. But what about when you actually have to deliver the criticism? This section presents some communication techniques that effective superiors use to criticize their subordinates productively.

Criticize in the Language of the Subordinate

When Lee Iacocca spoke to future Chrysler employees who were graduating from Michigan State University, he concluded his speech by saying "Rev up your engines and burn up the road." It's a safe bet that his words were intentionally chosen, on the assumption that the automobile-oriented students would instantly relate to them — much more than they would have if he had said "Let's all get ready to do a great job and be the number-one company."

Talk in the subordinate's language; present information in a way that harmonizes with how the subordinate perceives the world. When you do this, you make your criticism more meaningful because you are putting it in terms that are already familiar to the recipient. Talking in his language allows you to move the information into his frame of reference. There are two specific techniques that you can use to get into the subordinate's "world" — matching sensory modes and using metaphors. Both techniques illustrate and help you implement the principle of choosing the right words.

Match Sensory Modes

We have five senses: sight, hearing, touch, smell, and taste. During the last few years, researchers in the area of neurolinguistic programming, including in particular pioneers John Grinder and Richard Bandler, have discovered that individuals tend to have a preference for processing information through one of their senses. Which one? Listen to them talk; this preference is exhibited in their language. For example, here is how a manager using each sensory mode, in turn, might explain a new project to her staff:

Sight, Visual: "I see this project as a big opportunity. We need to be clear on our goals. It looks like we can do it in a few weeks, which would really be out of sight. The key is not to blind ourselves to any of the data we see. Let's look right through it all so we get the big picture."

Hearing, Auditory: "This project sounds great to me. If you have any questions, speak up and I will listen. I want to hear from everyone. This is our chance to make a lot of noise around here. I know we can bang this out in a few weeks."

Touch, Tactile: "If we get a good grip on it from the beginning, then we can just hold on and run with it. I really feel good about this and know that we can do a solid job. I expect things to go smooth as silk. If there is a problem, we will put our fingers on it right away."

Smell, Olfactory: "This project smells pretty good to me. I want everyone to sniff through the data. Let me know if anything rotten comes up."

Taste, Gustatory: "This is a really sweet project. I think we will be able to taste success very quickly, especially if we can avoid any sour bites."

The last two sensory modes, smell and taste, are used less frequently than the first three. Although everyone uses all of the sensory modes at different times, again, most tend to use one more than the others.

Phrasing your communication to match the sensory mode of your recipient can result in the kind of closed and clear expression often described as *tuned in, clicking with each other, on the same wavelength, empathetic*. You truly do speak the same language. Let's look at what clashes and what resonates.

SUPERIOR: I read your proposal and I am not sure what you want to communicate. Maybe it needs a different tone. The first two sections make a lot of noise. If you move the middle sections up, you will ring the alarm faster. How does that sound to you?

SUBORDINATE: I'm not quite clear on your points. I guess I see it differently.

In this exchange, the superior is using the auditory sensory mode, which clashes with the subordinate's visual mode. The growing body of research in this area indicates that poor communication would be the result. A better exchange:

SUPERIOR: My view of your proposal is that it is a little out of focus. Maybe it will be clearer to the reader if you let him see your suggestions immediately.

SUBORDINATE: Yes. I see your point. The reader will get the whole picture much faster and be clearer on the project's direction.

It would be ludicrous to suggest that using sensory-mode matching is an ironclad guarantee that your subordinates will be receptive to your criticisms. Furthermore, it is advised that in an extended encounter you use the technique with discretion and subtlety. Otherwise you run the risk of making your listener feel that you are somehow mimicking him. However, when used properly, sensory-mode matching is a powerful way to increase your target's receptiveness to your input. It helps in making him believe that you are an understanding and empathetic person and that you are easy to talk to. Defensiveness drops.

Practice by listening to yourself and to your co-workers. First, find out what your own sensory mode is by paying attention to the words you use. Next, practice identifying the preferred sensory mode of the people you work with by listening to their language. Finally, practice translating sentences from one sensory mode to another.

Your clues to identifying sensory modes lie mostly in the verbs, adverbs, and adjectives used. Some examples of each:

Sight, Visual: look, see, observe, notice, watch, appear, resemble, be clear, be transparent, be invisible, be foggy, be murky, have not even a shadow of a doubt, clear everything up, have an eagle eye.

Hearing, Auditory: listen, pay attention to what he's saying, full of static, just a lot of noise, sounds fine, be unable to make out what he is saying, talk it to death.

Touch, Tactile: feel, touch, grasp, handle, hold on to, be solid, get a grip on.

Smell, Olfactory: sniff, stink, be rotten, be nosy, smells sweet, smells right.

Taste, Gustatory: gobble, be sweet, tip of the tongue, make you nauseated, make you sick, went sour.

Another way of using sensory modes as a criticism technique is called switching sensory modes. It is especially useful when your subordinate is resistant to your criticism. Let's suppose, for example, that he has the dominant sensory mode of hearing. He keeps responding to your criticism by saying "It doesn't sound good to me" or "I've heard it before and I disagree." The strategy to use here is not to match your criticism to his sensory mode. Get him to think differently by switching sensory modes. You may say "I know it doesn't sound good to you, but could you see yourself trying it for a couple of weeks?" Or "I know you don't like what you are hearing, but how do you feel about giving it another chance?" This causes him to process the information differently, which often triggers a more receptive response. For example, he may respond, "Well, it still doesn't sound good, but I'll give it a try and see what happens."

Note that this technique allows the recipient to disagree in one sensory mode (and thus protect his self-esteem) while simultaneously encouraging change by using another sensory mode.

A key principle that deserves elaboration here is that it is often good practice to get the recipient to slow down in giving a response to your criticism. His initial reaction, like most people's, is apt to be defensive. By lengthening the recipient's response time, you short-circuit the Pavlovian defensive reaction, thus enabling the recipient to think through the criticism in a more productive manner. Switching sensory modes capitalizes on this principle because it causes the recipient to take more time in processing the information. Another implementation of the "slow down" principle would be "Listen, don't respond now, take a day or two to mull it over. Then we'll talk." Similarly, a recipient of criticism is wise to respond, "Let me think about it," thereby giving himself some extra time to short-circuit his own defensive reaction and thus increase his chances for appraising the validity of the criticism accurately.

To reiterate, using sensory modes does not guarantee success when criticizing subordinates, but being aware of them and using them strategically does contribute to having the Critical Edge.

Use Metaphors

An administrator in a Southern California hospital complained to a consultant that one of her assistants was having difficulty getting along with the researchers, who in this particular hospital were well-known names in the field. The assistant was slow in getting paperwork to the researchers, argued continually with them, and frequently ignored their requests to recruit experimental subjects. Her position was that the researchers were a pain in the neck — they constantly made demands, gave little thanks, and were arrogant to boot. The administrator confirmed that her assistant's perceptions were in fact quite accurate. Nevertheless, the way she interacted with the researchers was unprofessional and unacceptable.

The administrator had intervened several times in constructive ways. She had arranged structured meetings to discuss the problem. She had asked the assistant what she thought could be done to make things better. She had asked what she could do to help. She had explained the importance of getting along with the researchers. She had even used an occasional threat — all to no avail.

After listening to the administrator's complaint, the consultant asked, "What does the assistant like? Does she have a hobby? What is important to her?" A few days later, when the time was appropriate, the administrator spoke to her assistant once again: "You know, these researchers are very special. They are just like your plants and flowers. They need a lot of care. They have to be watered daily, given some sunshine, and you need to talk to them. When you do that, they will bloom and become stronger and prettier. And it will be easier for you to take care of them." By the end of the following week, the administrator noticed that her assistant's attitude and behavior toward the researchers had improved markedly.

What the administrator said might sound hokey and contrived, but the fact is, it helped her finally get the results she wanted. She used a metaphor to get into her assistant's world — she talked about the researchers in a manner that enabled the assistant to relate to them in a familiar and enjoyable way.

Metaphor is a rich and revealing way of communicating, and being able to use metaphors is one of the most important skills for managers to master. Dr. Milton Erickson, the late renowned hypnotherapist, who is considered by many to have been a genius in the area of influential communication, wrote that "metaphors are the gateway to a person's subconscious because they allow you to enter his world in a way that is meaningful to him. In short, metaphors can be a tool that lets you put 'your' picture in his frame." How can you use a metaphor effectively in your criticisms?

· Choose the right metaphor. It's silly to use a sports metaphor if your subordinate isn't a sports fan. Listen to what your subordinates talk about. What are their hobbies? What do they do on vacations?

Somebody who loves classical music and has trouble getting along with his co-workers would undoubtedly relate to the importance of "each musician harmonizing with the others." A subordinate who tends to be impulsive when working on his projects and goes fishing on his vacations will probably be receptive to "This project is like going after Jaws. Go slowly, wait until you are sure that you have it, and then carefully reel it in."

· Know the special language of the metaphor. Whatever metaphor you select, make sure you know its rules. For example, a baseball fan who is frequently late to meetings is likely to laugh if you say, "You're the pitcher on this team, and it's hard for us to play well if you're not here *at kickoff time*." You should say *"for the first inning."* What he has heard is that you don't know what you are talking about. Do your homework. Learn the rules and the terminology.

Like using sensory modes, using metaphors is not a guarantee that your target will be receptive to your criticism, but it does tip the scales in your favor.

Employ Criticism by Question

Psychotherapist Fritz Perls has said that if you turn a question mark on its side it becomes a hook, and that when you ask critical questions you may be "hooking" the other person into defensive behavior. Example:

SUPERIOR: Where did you get this sloppy data from?
SUBORDINATE: From Jack. I thought —
SUPERIOR: You should have asked me before you asked Jack.

Such questions are hooks because the superior knows in advance that the answer is likely to be defensive. Furthermore, the superior knows that regardless of what the subordinate says, the answer will not be acceptable. The subordinate, instead of profiting from the criticism, experiences a sense of helplessness, failure, and loss of self-esteem.

Constructive questions, however, boost the productivity of your criticizing. Asking constructive questions means questioning in the Socratic style (this was how Socrates criticized Plato) as a way of stimulating the recipient to generate his or her own answers. Power struggles are defused, the subordinate is involved, and self-esteem is protected.

A vintage Clark Gable movie, *Teacher's Pet,* masterfully illustrates criticism through question. Gable plays a tough New York City newspaper editor who is helping a high school dropout learn newspaper writing. The youngster presents his work, and Gable reads it quickly. Looking displeased and about to give his usual "This stinks," he catches himself and uses criticism by question instead. The dialogue went:

GABLE: Did you hear about that murder?
REPORTER: What murder?
GABLE: The one that came in on the wire service.
REPORTER: Who got murdered?
GABLE: Jack Smith.
REPORTER: How did it happen?
GABLE: He got shot.
REPORTER: Where did it happen?
GABLE: At his house.
REPORTER: When did it happen?
GABLE: This morning.
REPORTER: Why?
GABLE: You just asked the six most important questions in newspaper writing: who, what, where, when, how, and why. Go rewrite this and put that information in your lead!

The youngster hurries back to his typewriter with a big smile on his face because he came up with the answer. By asking one strategic question, the editor spurred the reporter to ask a series of questions, and these questioning responses provided the information that the editor wanted the reporter to hear. Gable's interaction with the youngster stimulated his thinking and protected his self-esteem. The reporter consequently felt good about making his work better.

Criticism by question is effective because it transmits the information in a way that does not elicit defensive behavior. At the same time, it calls for a response from the recipient — it productively forces interaction. Furthermore, criticism by question allows you to get the recipient to come up with her own solution. When this happens, the recipient's self-esteem is enhanced because she satisfies what Harvard psychologist Jerome Brunner calls the competency motive — a need to feel competent and master your environment. By coming up with the solution, the subordinate gains a sense of competency.

An additional benefit of criticism by question is that it allows you to reinforce previous criticisms without sounding as if you're hounding the person. For example, when former CEO of the Monsanto Company John Hanley wanted to make sure that his subordinates were implementing his directive that they teach people a couple of levels down, he would approach them with questions like "Did you help him realize afterward that it was a lousy presentation, and did you help him make it better?" Not "I've told you dozens of times to help your people." Executives could answer affirmatively only by responding productively.

Here are a few guidelines that will help you employ criticism by question:

1. Devise a question or series of questions whose answers lead the recipient to the critical information: "How do you think the sales division will react to your marketing report?" rather than "You should have checked with the sales division for their reaction"; "What effect will this have on your deadline if you wait another week to collect data?" rather than "You are not leaving yourself enough time to meet your deadline."

2. Do not ask the question in a condescending manner, a manner that implies "See if you can guess the answer." Thought-stimulating phrasing, such as "What if . . .," is recommended. Do say: "What if you were to change the marketing plan and implement it in the Southeast first? What effects might that have on your first-quarter sales?" instead of "You are not thinking through the effect of the marketing plan on our first-quarter sales. Revise it."

3. If the recipient comes up with the "wrong" answer, state your views as another possibility: "That may be true. It may also be that . . ."

4. If you feel as though you may appear to be manipulative or playing games, be straight and openly implement criticism by question: "Let me ask you a few questions, and then I will share my thoughts, and we can come up with some answers together."

Criticism by question enables you to elicit information in a way that is nonthreatening and applies the concept that the criticism process should be two-way, participatory, educational, and developmental.

All three of the preceding techniques for communicating criticism — using sensory modes, metaphors, and criticism by question — will help you execute the criticism instead of your subordinate.

Use Behavioral Interventions — When All Else Fails

A psychiatric head nurse at the Brentwood, California, Veterans Administration Hospital explained her criticism situation:

"It's very important that each day, staff members record their therapeutic sessions on the patients' charts so the evening staff knows what happened on the day shift. Rarely is the staff negligent about this procedure. One exception was a psychology intern. He had a habit of sometimes leaving work before he made his progress notes. The first few times this happened, I mentioned it, reiterating the importance of the procedure. He agreed, and said that he would make sure it wouldn't happen again. But it did. In fact, it happened on a regular basis. Every time he was criticized, he agreed and said it wouldn't happen again. But his behavior never changed."

Almost every manager and supervisor can relate to some derivation of the above. A subordinate is continually criticized for behavior (in contrast to being criticized for a presentation or report, which is usually a one-shot criticism) and continually agrees to change but doesn't. In these situations, verbal criticism is more often than not a waste of breath. What is needed is for the superior to intervene in a behavioral manner; that is, he or she must do something rather than say something.

The head nurse described how she dealt with the problem. "Finally, I decided that talking to him was not going to help so I had better do something else. I came up with a plan. I knew he left the hospital about three-thirty every day. So, at about two forty-five, I went down to his office with one of my co-workers and said, 'Could you please come up and do your progress notes?' We did this every day for two and a half weeks. A couple of times he said he'd be up in a minute, but, rather than risk him not coming, we said we'd wait for him. One day, at twenty to three, as we were about to go and get him, he walked into the nursing office and said, 'I thought I would save you the trip.' From that day on, he always came to the nursing office at two-thirty to make his progress notes. We changed his behavior by changing ours."

Behavioral interventions are based on the premise that if you change your behavior, it sometimes forces the other person to change how he or she responds. Such interventions do require your time and energy, but they might be less expensive in terms of time, energy, and emotion in the long run than continually giving verbal criticism and getting no productive response.

To develop your skill at behavioral interventions:

1. Pinpoint the criticisms you give your subordinates repeatedly and to no avail.
2. Decide on an intervening behavior that may force change: literally, spend five minutes a day with your subordinate checking to see if she has put files back where they belong; call your subordinate daily to remind him to keep his co-workers informed of his schedule; give your subordinate a nonverbal signal (scratching your head) every time he interrupts a co-worker in a meeting. All of these behaviors help the subordinate develop a new behavioral pattern of response in the criticism situation — i.e., she will make sure her files are put away correctly; he will make sure to keep his co-workers informed of his schedule changes; he will make sure to let his co-workers speak without interruption.
3. Be consistent with your intervention.
4. If the problem continues, devise a second behavioral intervention.

Work Together: The Co-op Plan

This last method of criticism calls for the superior and subordinate to cooperate; to sit down together and formulate a plan that will help the subordinate respond productively to the criticism(s). It is especially useful for problems that take time to remedy.

For example, consider the case of the Minneapolis computer programmer who was considered very talented but a pain in the neck. He would demean the intelligence of others, criticize their every comment, and talk to people as if they were computers. His supervisor helped him change his alienating behavior by meeting with him and developing a plan. Together, they wrote out a series of goals; the programmer would, for instance, forever substitute the word "customer" or "client" for "user" (the idea was to get him to view himself as a business person supplying a service to customers rather than as a programmer interfacing with a user). He also agreed to "ask more and tell less" at meetings so he could get the design information he needed. He agreed to be more polite.

Although implementing the plan wasn't easy, his supervisor recalled that "the upshot was that over a period of time, he definitely improved to the point where he had changed his perceptions of internal clients. Complaints fell off and cooperation increased." Instead of putting the responsibility of change solely on the subordinate, the superior cooperated by helping the subordinate develop a concrete — and ultimately effective — plan to resolve the criticism.

The co-op intervention is usually successful because it lets the subordinate know he or she is not alone in the change process. To use this sort of intervention effectively, cover the following points when devising the plan:

1. Emphasize the importance of the subordinate's job. A person who believes her work is valuable is likely to respond in a positive way. Make sure you state why her job is important; otherwise you will be giving a pep talk.

2. Seek out her evaluation of the behavior or situation you are criticizing. This shows you respect her opinions and that you expect her to take part in resolving the criticism. It also indicates that your own ideas are not fixed, that you are willing to learn from others. She is likely to respond with explanations and suggestions for improvement rather than with denials or excuses.

3. State clearly how resolving the criticism will benefit the subordinate.

4. Enlist the subordinate's aid. The new plan of action must make sense to the employee if she is to be motivated by it and committed to it. Ask the subordinate how the criticism can be dealt with, then involve her in formulating the specific implementation of that plan.

5. Ask the subordinate how you can help her implement the plan and how you can be supportive. This is the most important part of the co-op plan because it directly involves you, the superior, in the implementation of the change process. It drives home the point to the subordinate that you are going to cooperate in and share the responsibility for the change process.

6. Do your share of the plan and help the subordinate do hers.

A final point to remember is that nobody is perfect. If you recognize that part of your job as a superior is to develop your subordinates, then you will begin to approach them with a more realistic attitude, acknowledging that better performance is a process. Your task is to help your subordinates continually improve their performance. When you do this, you are making your subordinates superior, and you have the Critical Edge.

THE ROLE OF THE SUBORDINATE

As a subordinate, you can also take an active role in helping your superiors criticize you effectively. One step is to expect that you will be criticized and to prepare for it by learning the skills of taking criticism. This will enable you to handle your superior's criticism more productively, even if it is presented improperly.

Subordinates can also help their cause by telling their superiors that they want their criticisms. Not only does this communicate respect for the superior, but also it helps define the criticism process as a positive mode of feedback. It lets the superior know that through criticism the subordinate expects to learn and to improve his results. Asking for criticism sessions lets your superior know that your desire for criticism is genuine, gives him the message that you expect him to criticize you, and increases the chances that he will do it productively because he will anticipate little resistance or defensiveness. The fact that you are asking for criticism may even increase his awareness of how he communicates it to you, which will perhaps lead to his making a concerted effort to criticize productively.

Finally, subordinates can help their superiors by teaching them how to give criticism. If your boss constantly focuses on the negatives, ask her for her thoughts on what you are doing well. She will be prompted to think about and appreciate your assets, and, in the process, may come to understand that focusing on the positives is part of the criticism process, too. If she is vague, ask for specific examples, telling her you appreciate being told about specific ways to improve. She will become clearer in her thinking and will be able to teach you more effectively. If she uses timing inappropriately, explain to her that you prefer her criticisms to be given in private. In other words, you can help your superior help you by productively criticizing how she gives you criticism.

THE ORGANIZATION'S ROLE

Organizations can help their subordinates become superior in several ways. First, they can implement criticism training for both superiors and subordinates. Criticism training aids each person in developing skills for giving and taking productive criticism. Sharen Wago, director of human resources of Hyatt Resorts, Hawaii, has implemented criticism training on a yearly basis for her hotels' staffs. It is thus not surprising that the employee at the front desk of each Hawaii Hyatt will ask customers to fill out a hotel evaluation card upon checking out. Numerous Fortune 500 companies and government agencies have also provided criticism training to their employees, including Hughes Aircraft, AT&T, IBM, Warner-Lambert, Digital, Sheraton, McDonald's, Fireman's Fund, the U.S. Treasury Department, and the U.S. Labor Department, to name just a few. Additionally, business schools and graduate schools of management, such as UCLA, have worked criticism training into their curricula.

When an organization implements criticism training, it also sends out a message that it values criticism and wants people to present and receive productively. Both superiors and subordinates are implicitly instructed that criticism is a positive and necessary process and that they should focus on doing it right.

A second way that organizations can help is to put a high premium on communication in general. Encouraging employees to talk to each other in itself creates greater chances for productive criticism because it causes people to interact more with each other. The more people communicate, the easier it becomes, especially when communicating negatives. People become more comfortable with bringing up delicate and sometimes embarrassing issues. Giving criticism becomes more permissible.

As a final note, to reiterate Andy Grove's words, every superior must give criticism to subordinates. Doing it well not only betters the subordinates' performance but also improves the superior's. It is a sure way to move up the organization.

Chapter 6

"Executive Sweet" Criticism

LEE IACOCCA has described the imposing presence of his former boss, Henry Ford II:

> The Glass House was a palace, and Henry reigned supreme. Whenever he entered the building, the word would go out: The King has arrived. Executives would linger in the halls, hoping to run into him. If they were lucky, Mr. Ford might notice them and say hello. At times he might even deign to speak to them.
>
> Each time Henry walked into a meeting, the atmosphere changed abruptly. He held the power of life and death over all of us. He could suddenly say 'Off with his head' — and he often did. Without a fair hearing, one more promising career at Ford would bite the dust.

Imagine criticizing a person who has this aura of power. Not very likely. We tend not to criticize the behavior of powerful people, and when someone is our boss, we usually perceive him or her as being powerful.

Why is it so difficult to criticize your boss? Some common answers:

- "Criticize my boss? I don't have the right to."
- "I'd get fired."
- "It's his company, not mine. He doesn't want to hear what I have to say."

Most of us hold on to these beliefs despite the fact that truly top-notch executives actually often want criticism from their subordinates. Walking about United Airlines, CEO Ed Carlson would solicit criticism, both as a source of information and as a way of conveying respect to middle managers. John Sculley helped turn Apple Computers around by soliciting criticism from such clients as Du Pont, General Electric, and Eastman Kodak. His purpose was to find out how Apple's products could be improved.

At ITT, Harold Geneen was well known for the way he bawled out subordinates, but he also structured the organization to encourage criticism of superiors, including himself. "Every manager had a direct line to top management at headquarters. We cut through layers of fat in our management ranks by putting all the people in one room so they could talk with one another, face to face, regardless of rank, and an honest assessment of any situation could be based upon the facts which emerged. . . . People could disagree with me or with anyone else; they could criticize me or anyone else, and no one would suffer as a consequence. I tried to welcome criticism. Naturally, no one likes to be criticized . . . but being open to criticism usually pays unexpected dividends." Geneen felt that criticism of superiors would enable problems to surface more quickly, making them easy to nip in the bud.

Unfortunately, not everyone has the good fortune to work in such companies. According to the *Wall Street Journal,* Walter S. Taylor, grandson of the founder of Taylor Wine, was sacked as executive vice president "for openly criticizing the company." George Steinbrenner is said to have once given Yankees manager Billy Martin a contract specifically prohibiting him from criticizing superiors.

Clearly, criticizing upward — criticism of executives and our bosses — is a paradoxical issue. On the one hand, criticism is essential if superiors are to function effectively. On the other, the subordinate frequently experiences negative consequences for delivering it. The issue becomes even more confounding when one considers these observations:

• An executive in a retail company says, "At our senior level of management, there is very little feedback about how we are doing our jobs."
• A middle manager in the auto industry complains, "I found it much easier to find out what was going on when I was lower in the

hierarchy. As I moved up, I found fewer people willing to give me straight talk about problems in our company, especially if I was involved in the problem."

• An executive at a hospital says, "I've been in this place for five years, and I've never felt that any of my colleagues have leveled with me about how I do my job."

These representative comments from executives and managers strongly suggest that superiors — top executives, middle managers, or line supervisors — do not get much criticism (productive or otherwise) from those beneath them. Given most subordinates' reluctance to criticize their bosses, most superiors, especially executives, get no criticism, even when they want it, making it difficult for them to develop their professional competency and equally difficult for them to help their subordinates excel. From the subordinate's perspective, a failure to criticize a superior at the very least makes him or her subject to an overdemanding and sometimes insufferable boss, to say nothing of making the actual job harder to perform. Perhaps most important, the lack of criticism of executives impedes the effectiveness of the organization by ruling out the early detection by key personnel of problems that inevitably surface despite any company fail-safe system. The space shuttle catastrophe exemplifies this point.

The emphasis in this chapter is on the roles that the superior, subordinate, and organization can play in facilitating the transmission of criticism upward in a productive manner, something that is essential to the subordinate's, boss's, and organization's performance. Specifically, the superior will learn what he or she does that impedes criticism from subordinates and how to elicit useful criticism from a staff without making them feel fearful or embarrassed. The subordinate will learn how to gauge if his or her boss reacts well to criticism, when it's appropriate to criticize the boss, and techniques for how to do it. This chapter will also show what the organization can do to encourage and enhance criticism of executives. Although much of the discussion will be focused on the issue of criticizing executives, it will also be applicable to almost any situation in which subordinates wish to criticize superiors.

HOW THE EXECUTIVE'S WORK POWER INHIBITS CRITICISM

Most people attribute the fact that bosses receive little criticism to the subordinate's fear of experiencing dreadful consequences if he criticizes a superior, or to the subordinate's belief that it simply isn't in the line of duty to criticize one's boss. But there is a growing body of research that indicates that certain attributes of executives, independent of the subordinates' beliefs or actions, inhibit executive criticism. Robert Kaplan's research at the Center for Creative Leadership has isolated several such executive attributes. All are manifestations of the power inherent in the boss's position. The attributes are specific types of demeanor typical of superiors and the boss's exaggerated impact, isolation, and relative autonomy.

The Executive's Demeanor

Demeanor is one's outward behavior, one's behavior toward others. Executive development specialists have identified several types of executive demeanor that especially seem to block criticism. One is a domineering demeanor exemplified by the tendency to monopolize conversation. The executive takes over the conversation in such a manner that it becomes a challenge for the subordinate to regain control even of a conversation that she initially started. Monologues discourage criticism for the simple reason that others have trouble getting air time. In effect, a superior who exhibits this behavior is limiting interaction with subordinates, thereby losing the opportunity to gather important information that can help him or her and the organization.

Abrasiveness can also get an executive in trouble. In a 1983 study called "Why and How Successful Executives Get Derailed," authors Michael Lombardo and Morgan McCall, Jr., found that abrasiveness was the most common reason for executives to derail — to be fired or asked to resign. Abrasiveness in executives typically involves using one's power and position to remind subordinates of their shortcomings or mistakes. One manager at an insurance company said his abrasive superior told him, "This project is too big for you. No way you have the ability to handle it." Such "zinging" usually destroys any instinct on the part of subordinates to help the executive with problems, to offer productive criticism, or to be a confidant. In this case the manager backed off and let his boss commit a blunder just to "teach him a lesson." An abrasive executive may also stifle criticism in less obvious ways; he may deliver an implied threat of using his position to a subordinate's disadvantage, which adds fear and resentment to the reasons that lead people to withhold criticism.

To one degree or another, then, executives' demeanor, which derives from who they are and what they do, affects the willingness of the people around them to criticize their managerial behavior and character. For executives whose demeanor is plainly hostile, domineering, or abrasive, criticism is almost impossible to get. Yet their work power often allows them to act this way.

The Executive's Impact

A second factor that may inhibit an executive's getting criticism from subordinates arises from the relationship between an executive and subordinates. This lack of criticism is not caused solely by the executive's behavior, nor is it simply a matter of the executive's commanding behavior reducing subordinates to spineless mutes. Rather, criticism can be impeded because executives become embodiments of the organizations they lead. The criteria for determining when it is acceptable to criticize one's boss become more restrictive as people sense that they will be criticizing not just the individual executive but the organization he or she represents as well, since employees have a stake in the well-being of the organization. The subordinates of a top executive are thus unlikely to criticize this boss unless they have a very good reason. In this sense, how people react to the executive's presence, what he or she embodies in their minds, are as important as the nature of that presence. The reaction of people to the executive is called his or her impact.

A significant quality of the executive's impact is that it frequently becomes exaggerated. That is, what the executive does or says takes on a far greater meaning than is really intended. In his research, Robert Kaplan cites a university president who reported, "If you're chief executive, people not only take you seriously but spread things around that you have simply sent up as a trial balloon. You're really

saying, 'I want to talk about this,' and BANGO it's all over the lot."
This tendency toward exaggeration may be attributed to the increased
sensitivity people have to an executive's words. A casual comment
can reverberate with significance. Another one of Kaplan's executive
subjects told the story of seeing a picture on a subordinate's office
wall and casually saying to the subordinate, "Why do you have that
picture?" His comment was only conversational, or so he thought.
When he returned to the subordinate's office the next day, he noticed
that the picture had been taken away. People hang on every word.
Comments become commands; statements become injunctions. This
again illustrates the importance of semantics and delivery — words
can and do make a difference. The executive's impact can become so
pronounced that some must guard even their expression. "If I don't
smile," one executive says, "my staff thinks business is bad."

An exaggerated impact creates problems because it makes some
executives reluctant to speak out at all. They voice no opinions until
they are ready to make a firm decision. Having found out later that
their subordinates attached greater meaning to their words than they
had intended, many executives become hesitant to engage in casual
conversations. Although keeping one's counsel may have some benefits, it does add distance to the relationships that the executive has
by excluding others from involvement (in particular from decision-
making processes). The resultingly cooler relationship causes people
to feel less free to offer criticism.

On the other hand, there are insiders, those people with whom
the executive feels free to explore ideas. While these people are probably a good source of critical feedback for some executives, they can
also create problems if they, too, succumb to their boss's impact.
When this happens, they begin to act as "cheerleaders." Cheerleaders
retard the flow of critical information because they tell the executive
what he or she wants to hear and omit what they do not want him
or her to hear, including news of problems that might reflect badly
on them. These subordinates often have their own interests at heart
when, as one writer puts it, they "display to [the executive] . . . the
precise responses, hints and clues which will give him the kind of
assurance about himself and his conduct which they think he needs
at the moment."

Cheerleaders perform a disservice to executives by responding to their willingness to be open with them with what is essentially a defensive posture — their foremost thought being "When I deal with you I better protect myself." Executives are robbed of an important source of information about themselves.

The Executive's Isolation

It's not just the executive's demeanor or presence that impedes criticism. Nor is it only a matter of those around the executive reducing the flow of information that reaches him or her. The organization, by its very nature, also plays an important part.

Most organizations have a pyramidal structure, which dictates that as you go up the organization, you come in contact with fewer and fewer people. Were this not so, people at the top would not be able to play their coordinating and integrating role. In one sense, they must deal with fewer people so that they can attend to the needs of the whole organization; otherwise they would be burdened with a myriad of details. Yet because of this structure and although many executives have taken to "managing by wandering about," it seems that only an immense effort allows top executives to genuinely make contact with a significant portion of the organization. For most, the act of wandering about is usually more symbolic than substantive.

In the majority of organizations, people at the top end up spending most of their time with employees who work at approximately the same level. And these employees tend to be high-level executives who are also isolated.

Besides this structural isolation, executives are also isolated as a result of the organization's attempt to protect them from some of the indignities of everyday life. This process is called insulation, and Robert Townsend, former president of Avis, offers a vivid description of how it occurs.

> Let's say you've just become the Big Guy. You arrive at work in a limo, you climb out of the car in the company garage and get into your private elevator, which takes you to your suite of offices. Your three secretaries are waiting to protect you from any unpleasantness. In your private dining room for lunch, you meet with satisfied customers and senior

officers only. Anything controversial has to be written up, predigested, and sugar-coated before it gets to you. Your calendar is loaded with outside board and committee meetings and social engagements with your powerful new friends outside the company. After a few months of this, you've lost touch with all the colleagues who helped you get the top job and you have no idea what's going on in the company.

Isolation affects criticism of executives because a lack of contact guarantees the absence of information, especially of sensitive information. Furthermore, when communication does occur, it usually happens in the executive suite, complete with the symbols of power that tend to make subordinates uncomfortable about disclosing their thoughts.

The effects of isolation are then paradoxical. On one hand, isolation protects the executive from being exposed to thousands of irrelevant, and relevant, interruptions that would make it impossible to do the job. On the other hand, isolation impedes criticism that an executive could use in trying to develop and perform his or her role even more effectively.

The Executive's Autonomy

For an executive to function effectively, he or she must be able to function in an autonomous manner. However, the degree to which superiors are granted autonomy ranges from the extreme of the executive who is only a figurehead and has no absolute edict to the top person whose power is unchecked. When autonomy approaches the latter extreme, it becomes an important factor in preventing criticism of the executive's modus operandi.

There are several ways in which autonomy may grant a superior — whether a CEO, a school principal, or a manager of a fast food franchise — immunity to criticism. For one thing, executives who have the power to hire whomever they please can (and many do) use that power to hire people in their own image, people whose values, background, and life philosophy are compatible with their own. Executives who follow this practice are not likely to end up with subordinates who will be critical of the boss. In effect, they hire cheerleaders. Why some executives do this is questionable. Perhaps some are insecure and need constant encouragement from their staff. The resultant praise and the perception that the boss's actions and thoughts are always correct serve to satisfy the executive's ego needs. Whatever their motivation for such hiring practices, executives do not often get criticism about their behavior by turning to such "mirrors."

A second way in which executives' autonomy can prevent them from being criticized is their ability to declare themselves not subject to the standard evaluations applicable to others lower on the organizational scale. Performance appraisal is a case in point. In a review of performance appraisal systems in various organizations, it was found that formal appraisals thin out at high levels. Apparently, executives take the position that formal evaluation systems are necessary only for their subordinates. They may further assume that they are able to assess their own progress in an objective manner. Who but the top person is to say otherwise? A personnel director in charge of the system is not usually empowered to define the system as including the top levels or, more important, to enforce it if the executive levels merely go through the motions. Organizations that grant such total autonomy to their executives are in effect allowing their executives to give themselves an immunity to being appraised.

The executive's power to disseminate information as he or she sees fit is a third way in which autonomy can interfere with criticism by subordinates. Consequently, executives may relay their plans only at a late stage, thus robbing themselves and their staffs of the opportunity to evaluate the plans' effectiveness and consider the possibility of changing them so they follow a more productive course. Any plan is denied the benefit of early and/or critical criticism. In contrast, most subordinates are required to present their plans and news of their progress early on, usually at a moment's notice.

EXECUTIVE CRITICISM — THE SUPERIOR'S ROLE

Executives, managers, and other superiors, then, are in a contradictory position. They need their authoritative demeanor, impact, isolation, and autonomy to execute their functions productively. But these same factors that so well serve executives also make it difficult for them to do their job productively, because they interfere with the flow of critical information that may improve results. Furthermore, the lack of criticism prevents executives from developing as individuals. The paradox is resolved when executives learn to elicit productive criticism of themselves.

Perhaps the most important factor here is the executive's attitude about being criticized. Those who believe that they should always know what to do, that to ask for guidance is a sign of weakness and incompetency, or who view criticism as meaning that they are doing something wrong are apt to use their power actively to inhibit their subordinates and co-workers from criticizing them. These executives set up systems intended to make the flow of negative information upward minimal. For example, they limit staff meetings or face-to-face encounters with subordinates, which makes it difficult to have good communication, let alone the opportunity to discuss negative information. Consequently, the best decisions are frequently not made.

The roots of such negative attitudes toward criticism from subordinates are numerous, but one of them is certainly feelings of insecurity. Executives who are insecure about their competency or their job status tend to take a defensive posture to ward off criticism, since any acknowledgment of criticism reinforces their feelings of insecurity. The irony is that their defensiveness inevitably reveals the flaws they wish to cover. In short, the insecure executive perceives criticism as a threat. While much could be said about why some executives are insecure, it is best here just to recommend that any executives who are not getting criticism or who act defensively when criticized would benefit from some introspection, from an examination of their attitudes toward being criticized and their feelings about themselves and their performance on the job.

For those executives, or any boss, who want criticism — and again, research indicates that with it they would be more effective in their jobs — the first task is to increase the amount of interaction between themselves and their sources-to-be. As the executive interacts more frequently with the staff, he or she is able to increase the amount of communication that takes place. As was noted in the last chapter, this increase in communication is important because as communication increases, the chances grow that more and more diverse types of information will be communicated.

Most communication that takes place between superior and subordinates is well defined and takes the form of the subordinate's filling in the boss about the progress that is being made on the subordinate's assignments. Rarely does the information exchange call for a subordinate to tell the superior anything negative. By interacting more, the boss is able to pull more and more information from subordinates, some of which may be criticism of the boss. He or she is thus allowing for an increase in the type of information, not just the quantity of information. Furthermore, greater interaction between a superior and a subordinate that is initiated by the superior is frequently interpreted by the subordinate as an unspoken statement that it is now permissible to say things to the superior that previously were thought taboo. In other words, the growth in interaction and communication helps the subordinate feel more comfortable with his superior, making him less hesitant to express his criticisms of his boss. Increasing interaction (and communication) is one way that productive bosses can take responsibility for and promote the (upward) criticism process.

A concrete way in which executives can increase the amount of interaction they have with their subordinates and, specifically, multiply their chances of hearing critical information is to practice the "open door" policy. The open door policy allows subordinates to talk to their boss about any issues or concerns that they are not normally given the time or opportunity to address. Many managers and companies purport to practice the open door policy, but whether they actually do so is difficult to determine. One procedure a boss might effectively follow is to announce to subordinates and other staff members that he will set aside a specific amount of time each week (or month) for the sole purpose of hearing his people's concerns. If a subordinate comes to his office during that time and sees that his boss's office door is open, he is free to walk in and speak his mind. If the door is closed, then the subordinate is to assume that a conversation is already in progress, but he should not be discouraged, because each interaction is limited to approximately twenty minutes. He knows that his chance will come at any minute. When that time has elapsed, the boss will open his door to check if others are waiting. If they are, the boss will end the conversation that is in progress by setting up a continuance on the next available date. The next subordinate then enters, and the process is repeated. If no one is waiting, the boss can resume the conversation that's in progress. Although this procedure is far from perfect, it has its benefits.

By structuring the length of the interaction, the executive accomplishes several things. First, she forces her subordinates to clarify their thoughts before they see her. Thoughts that are too vague will take too much time to express and thereby prevent the subordinate from making his points. Second, by limiting the time, the executive gives herself a graceful way to minimize the chance that a subordinate will take up too much time and, in the process, rob the executive of time that she needs to do her job. More bluntly, time limitation gives the boss a way to end conversations that aren't going anywhere. Some may object to this, on the basis that shortened and interrupted conversations can be destructive to the boss-subordinate relationship, but this seems to be the case only when the conversations are not followed up on. In fact, the continuity of the conversations when follow-up occurs, the further exploration of the subject, the consistent time that is being spent together, are all factors that actually promote the superior-subordinate relationship, which in turn facilitates the criticism process.

At a more sophisticated level, the open door policy helps the executive elicit criticism by giving formal permission to the subordinate to express critical thoughts. Furthermore, this formal permission may become a more general implied permission to give spontaneous criticism when appropriate. It is a way of helping subordinates, as well as the executive, develop the Critical Edge. A word of caution: If you preach the open door policy, you must practice it. Otherwise, you will accomplish the opposite of your objectives.

If you as a superior decide to be more direct, you can demand that your subordinates criticize you. The best way to implement this strategy is to explain to your subordinates that you need criticism to do your job effectively. In elaborating, you might say that in order to do your job effectively, you need to know how your subordinates and staff think you could be doing a better job. Or that you are unable to do your job effectively if your subordinates and staff do not offer you their thoughts on how you could be doing better. You could even take the approach of letting your subordinates know that one of the measures you evaluate them on is whether they give you criticism. The key is for the superior to build into the subordinate's job the responsibility of criticizing his boss, so if he isn't doing that, then he is not doing his job. A second cautionary note: If you ask for criticism, be sure to thank the source when he gives it to you.

Some executives have found role playing to be an effective instrument for eliciting criticism of themselves. The value of this approach is that in contrast to communicating in abstractions and guarded statements, the subordinate expresses what he might actually do in a specific situation. When role playing is at its best, the boss is able to gain a much better understanding of how the subordinate appraises a certain situation and, in the process, frequently gains new ways of looking at his own plan. While there are many variations on this technique, the basic idea is to have the boss choose a situation about which he wants to know his subordinate's opinion: if he appraises the situation in the same way the boss does or if he concurs with his actions. The boss simply asks the subordinate how he would respond to the situation if he were the boss. Discrepancies between what the subordinate would do, how he would handle the situation, and the boss's actual plan of action give the boss an indication of how critical the subordinate is of the boss's plan. If the subordinate comes up with proposals similar to the boss's, this means he agrees with the strategy. By then reversing roles with the subordinate, the boss can communicate to him how he himself would handle the situation. This, of course, is also a way to educate the subordinate.

Superiors who like to get their subordinates to role-play their criticisms should be warned of what social psychologists call demand characteristics. Crucial to role playing is the context in which it takes place; particularly critical is the relationship between the role players. A father and son role-playing a professor-student exchange are still, in reality, having a father-son exchange. The subordinate who with his boss role-plays a subordinate's presentation to an advertising executive is still, in reality, a subordinate making a presentation to his boss. The principal and teacher role-playing a parent-teacher conference are, in reality, having a principal-teacher conference. The nature of the real-life relationship itself demands that each role player

act in a certain direction, whether this is overtly or covertly acknowledged. In other words, the son will tell the father what he thinks
Dad wants to hear. The same is true for the teacher, and the subordinate. Each subordinate role player, because of his relationship
to his superior counterpart, will tend to act in a way that he thinks
will please his counterpart. At worst, executives who fancy role playing may be creating a squad of cheerleaders. To correct for this
limitation, make sure you elicit your subordinate's response to the
particular situation before you demonstrate your response. Without
having your response to model, the subordinate is more apt to do
and say what he thinks. When you demonstrate your thoughts first,
you give the subordinate role player a framework that he knows he
will be measured against, and therefore he frequently tries to duplicate
the response seen without critiquing it.

One consultant tells a story about being in a car with the president
of a company and three district managers. As part of the conversation,
the president gave the consultant his interpretation of why his company was not functioning at a more productive level. He then instructed the district managers to give their views. They all, more or
less, gave the same analysis. Later on, the consultant met with the
district managers individually, only to hear very different interpre-
tations of what they had earlier agreed to. Apparently, their boss's
technique of inquiry "demanded" that they respond with a certain
perspective.

Rewarding subordinates who dare to criticize them is another way
that executives can elicit criticism. Whether you use an actual thank-
you note, a gold star, or some type of financial remuneration, the
message is the same. By rewarding those who speak out, the superior
is, in effect, changing the assumption from "It is inappropriate to
criticize the boss" to "It is very appropriate to criticize the boss." If
the superior rewards subordinates who criticize her, she not only
hears information that may have been previously — and consciously — omitted but also presents a model of how to respond to
criticism productively.

Bosses who have used this strategy have found that while the
reward is initially important in eliciting the criticism, it eventually
becomes less important. Apparently, the experience of being able to
have a critical give-and-take with one's superior becomes rewarding

in itself. The subordinate and the executive become more comfortable with one another, and criticism of the boss becomes more spontaneous. Nevertheless, in the early stages it is wise for the executive to reward her subordinates in effective ways.

A final point is that superiors have to appreciate how difficult it is to get reactions to themselves and their work. It is easy for them to labor under the illusion that they know where they stand with others. One researcher made a practice of asking executives whether they knew what their subordinates thought of them. They would say yes, they did know. Then he would ask them whether their own superiors knew what they, the executives, thought of them. And the executives would say no. The point has been made: Executives get this kind of information only if they go after it.

EXECUTIVE CRITICISM — THE SUBORDINATE'S ROLE

If you were to review the literature on superior-subordinate relations, especially recent management books, you would find that most of the time the focus is on what the boss does wrong, could do differently, and should do better. The subject is usually broached from the standpoint of the superior. Other books adopt a variation on this top-down view and point out how organizations create a climate that either helps or hinders employees as they try to play their roles. The underlying assumption is that influence flows downward.

Nevertheless, most of us will quickly agree that a large part of job effectiveness is being able to manage upward. Clearly, communication is an interaction; for superior and subordinate to communicate and thus work effectively together, information must flow both ways. And as communication flows, so does influence.

Criticizing upward is especially important when one considers that recent surveys in the United States by the American Management Association have concluded that middle managers regard two out of three of their bosses as inadequate. Some common failings: *spotlighter, underdelegator, crisis maker, overcontroller,* and *stoic.* In such unsatisfactory situations, the ability to criticize upward productively is not only an invaluable aid to your own job success and sanity, but it also is necessary to your organization's welfare. And every day, there are numerous situations in which you have to "communicate to change" your boss. Peter Drucker sums it up: "You don't have to like and admire your boss, nor do you have to hate him. You do have to manage [which implies criticize] him, however, so that he becomes your resource for achievement, accomplishment, and personal success as well."

Criticizing Upward

Criticizing a superior is, as we have seen, difficult to do for many reasons, but one of the most pressing is that the top-down structure carries with it the assumption that it is not the subordinate's role to tell the superior how to do his job. In contrast to criticizing downward, the power of the chain of command is not something that can be relied upon if push comes to shove. The subordinate must win the executive over by maneuvering subtly.

How one goes about criticizing one's boss varies with the situation, but a head start can be achieved by gauging the appropriateness of the criticism and whether the boss has a track record of being receptive to criticism.

Gauging Appropriateness

To determine the appropriateness of the criticism, you must evaluate it on the basis of several criteria (Aristotle revisited). In the context of organizational relationships and top-down theory, the most important criteria seem to be whether the boss you are criticizing is your immediate supervisor, whether the behavior you are criticizing affects your work, and whether you know what you are talking about.

A subordinate criticizing a superior who isn't his immediate boss runs a strong risk of getting in trouble. For one thing, the superior might not even know the subordinate, in which case the subordinate is likely to be embarrassed. He may also be told directly that he is out of line. He may even lose his job, depending on the superior. At the very least, he will be told to discuss the problem with his immediate supervisor.

What if the subordinate has already discussed the matter with his supervisor? At best, the subordinate is allowed by his supervisor's supervisor to drop the issue and return to his work. What is more than likely is that he will be met by his immediate supervisor, who is irate and determined to punish him not only for going over her head but for embarrassing her in front of her own superior. And what about the case in which the subordinate goes over his boss's head without even discussing the matter with her, or stating his intent? A subordinate practicing this maneuver should know that his relationship with his immediate supervisor will never be the same. Anger, hurt, a sense of betrayal, are all common reactions of the supervisor who has been leapfrogged, and these reactions linger for a long time. Violating the so-called immediate-supervisor criterion — that of notifying your own supervisor before tackling another one — is a cardinal sin because it shows disrespect for a cultural rule dictated by the top-down philosophy: Respect the chain of command. When this criterion is ignored, the consequences tend to be negative, regardless of the validity of the criticism. In short, the organizational philosophy and structure justify the superior's negative reaction.

Many subordinates find it difficult always to apply the immediate-supervisor criterion because they find that their immediate superior stonewalls their criticism. Whether it's a matter of the superior's simply not wanting to listen or of poorly evaluating the subordinate's criticism, the result is the same — the problematic situation continues. Are these subordinates not justified in going over their boss's head with the aim of getting some productive action? Yes, they are. Their success depends upon how they do it.

The most reliable method is for the subordinate to inform his superior that since his criticism is still alive and the two of them cannot resolve it, he has decided to go to the next highest level, to superior 2. The subordinate invites his superior to go with him so that she can present her own views. The superior may refuse, but she was at least asked and therefore cannot accuse the subordinate of going over her head. If the subordinate's superior attends, then she can hear how superior 2 responds to criticism in general and can hear his comments as to how the particular criticism may be resolved. Furthermore, superior 2 is given the opportunity to see how the junior superior responds to criticism as well as to hear the type of criticism she receives. Subordinates who adopt this course of action are able to go one step higher because their invitation to their immediate boss indicates that they respect the chain of command and, therefore, the organization's rules.

The second criterion, whether you are criticizing your boss for problems that affect your work, often requires the ability to exploit ambiguity. It requires that the subordinate be capable of effectively demonstrating that any action his boss takes, whether it involves him directly or indirectly, affects his work if for no other reason than that they are both members of the same organization. To do so, the subordinate must have a good understanding of how his organization works. This being the case, he is able to generate better and more diverse criticisms. For example, although you may not be involved in implementing a new marketing plan, its success or failure will still have an impact on your job. Therefore, you are entitled to criticize your superior for his marketing plan — even though you have not been asked for input.

A sales rep for a cosmetic firm made use of this point when she criticized her boss's marketing plan for a new product. Although she had not been asked for her opinion, she approached her boss and said, "I read the new marketing plan and I noticed that the product was going to be targeted to my territory. As you know, my major clients buy products that cost fifteen dollars or less. This product costs twenty-five dollars. Also, my clients tend to go for hand creams and basic shampoos rather than glamour products, so besides the money issue, I'm not quite sure that the need will be there. If you want me to try to market it, I'll do my best, but I'm not sure we will be successful." Her boss, after reviewing the demographics of the sales rep's territory, agreed with her and changed her marketing plan in reference to the targeted area. Note, however, that although the sales rep disagreed with her boss's plan, she indicated that she would still give it her best effort. It is important to communicate to your boss that you will still follow the course he sets to your best ability even if you disagree.

The third criterion of appropriateness, whether you know what you are talking about, can never be ignored. It must be remembered that in most cases, the superior does not expect to be criticized by a subordinate. This is a tough expectation to combat, and therefore it is essential that as a subordinate you validate your criticism. Otherwise, the superior will not only dismiss it but may also begin to perceive you in a negative light, which no doubt will affect your job and your future ability to criticize your boss. While Harold Geneen took criticism, he did not suffer fools. He demanded that his people have what he called unshakeable facts. His position was that his time was too valuable for him to listen to invalid criticism. Ways for you the subordinate to validate your criticism include collecting and analyzing data (if available); accurately documenting how your boss's actions affect your work; and, if possible, consulting with other people.

Gauging Receptiveness

Along with gauging appropriateness of one's criticism, it is important for the subordinate to assess how receptive she thinks a boss will be to criticism. If the boss's receptivity is thought to be very low, it can be a warning to the subordinate that she is wasting her time and that any criticism, no matter how strategically presented, could ruffle the boss's feathers. In these situations the best bet may be for the subordinate to accept the current situation and do her best. If this is not possible, then the subordinate can use her boss's low receptivity as a starting point, with her goal being to increase the boss's receptivity before she delivers the criticism.

Having a boss who is from the start receptive to criticism is a plus to any subordinate, if for no other reason than that it lets subordinates know that if their criticism is valid, it will probably be acted upon. The message to the subordinate is "You count," and the subordinate is empowered to influence.

There are several indicators as to how receptive your superior is to criticism. If he interacts with you outside structured meetings, and if he is flexible enough to make changes in organizational policy from time to time, he probably tends to see criticism as a source of information rather than as a personal attack. If your boss keeps to himself and seldom encourages change, criticism will probably not be welcome, despite its constructive intent, and you may be seen as a complainer. Since most superiors block criticism, a good practice is to assume low "superior receptivity." This will cause you to develop your criticism carefully to the point at which you believe it will be most effective. You can tailor it from there to your superior's response. If you're successful — if your points are well made and effectively put, and if they show that you know what you are talking about — you will find that over time, your boss will become more and more receptive to your criticisms.

Techniques for Criticizing Superiors

Given that he has determined that it's appropriate to criticize and has evaluated the boss's receptivity as adequate, the subordinate now has the formidable task of executing his criticism. There are many ways to go about this, but one principle always applies — avoid a power struggle.

Therefore, the subordinate must be careful that the way he presents the criticism does not threaten the boss's self-esteem or his job security. When this happens, the superior is apt to become defensive. The problem is that once a subordinate and superior lock horns, the superior almost always comes out on top. The top-down philosophy allows the superior to use her work power to win her point. The result is that the criticism is rejected; the status quo is maintained. Thus, any strategy for criticizing a superior must protect the superior's self-esteem and acknowledge, implicitly or explicitly, that she is the superior.

Using the Two-sided Solution

One of the most effective ways for a subordinate to present criticism to a superior is to use what social psychologists term the two-sided solution.

The two-sided solution calls for the subordinate mentally to acknowledge that his superior has attained his position because he deserves it. Consequently, he is adept at his job and will tend to be a tough critic of any criticism. The criticism needs to be persuasive for the superior to act on it. Subordinates who fail to take these points into account usually make the mistake of presenting their criticism "one-sidedly" — they emphasize the benefits of their suggestions, thinking that upon hearing them, their superior will quickly agree with them and take the appropriate action. However, it has been demonstrated that the more sophisticated the listener, the more negative his response to a one-sided criticism will be. This is because the sophisticated listener conducts a silent debate with the criticizer. He mentally evaluates the criticism presented and then devises reasons for the criticism being not valid or reasons for maintaining the status quo. The subordinate who uses the two-sided solution counteracts his superior's mental defense system by integrating the significant objections his superior may have into the actual presentation of the criticism. Therefore, there is less need for the superior mentally to criticize the criticism or to defend his own position; the subordinate is doing it for him. It becomes easier for the superior to listen, to evaluate the criticism accurately. An effective implementation of the two-sided solution can be accomplished in three steps.

First, rather than criticizing the superior for something that he personally is doing or not doing, the subordinate presents the criticism of his superior by describing the "current situation." In so doing, the subordinate has depersonalized the criticism and protected the superior's ego because he has not explicitly stated that the superior is doing something wrong. Not feeling threatened, the superior is free to listen, and a power struggle is avoided.

In describing the current situation, which is in essence the criticism of the superior, the subordinate is wise to begin with the positives. Then he goes on to the negatives of the current situation. There is still little reason for the superior to become defensive or to argue mentally, because the subordinate is not pointing the finger at him, and the subordinate has presented both sides of the situation. In effect, the subordinate has presented the boss's position. How well this is accomplished is up to the subordinate. Abraham Lincoln was said to be a great attorney because he could argue his opponent's case better than his opponent could. The same strategy is recommended for the subordinate. The better both sides are presented, the less resistant the superior becomes, since there is little left for him to say; his views have been fairly represented.

As an example, take the case of a junior advertising executive criticizing his boss for the fact that deadlines are set without fully consulting the employee who is actually going to have to handle the project:

"Boss, the way you set deadlines is causing a lot of problems. You don't even ask us what we think when you do it. It is really making it tough to work here. A lot of the other guys feel the same way. In fact, we think your unrealistic deadlines are the reason our division is doing so poorly."

This presentation will be ineffective for numerous reasons, among them: It places fault on the boss, it does not explain why the deadlines are causing a problem, and the reference to other employees feeling the same way indicates to the boss that people are complaining behind his back. Many bosses react to this last point as though the subordinate who is doing the criticizing is organizing a conspiracy.

Better results can be achieved with the two-sided solution:

"Boss, I'd like to describe to you what I see happening in reference to how deadlines are set in our division. It seems the projects come to you, you decide whether we want them and then let the client know when we can have something for him. It is certainly helpful that you can screen everything to see if it suits our division and whether or not it will be a profitable project. I also think that it is important to let our clients know when we can have our work to them as soon as possible. We are certainly doing that. I also like the fact that we have short deadlines for most of our projects. That seems to allow us to have a faster turnover of projects, and we can handle more work. But I find that when deadlines for my projects are set without your getting my input, there are some negative consequences. For one, it seems to me that some of the deadlines that are set become unrealistic because they don't take into account my other responsibilities. This makes it hard for me to give the client my best work because I feel pressured not only to meet his deadline but also those of my other projects. Then when I do a rush job, it's not what they wanted, so they want me to do it over. Although it hasn't happened yet, the client might even want another company to handle his work. I certainly don't want to lose a project on the grounds that I didn't meet an unrealistic deadline. Of course, I am speaking for myself. I'm not sure how the other guys feel, but you might want to check it out, since I think some of them may be feeling extra pressure, which might be impeding their creative juices, too."

In this presentation, the subordinate specifically notes the importance of having short deadlines. He then goes on to cite the problems of the current situation but notes that he speaks only for himself, though he suggests that others might feel the same. Most important, the boss is not told that he is at fault.

The second step in implementing the two-sided solution is for the subordinate to present what he thinks is the answer to the criticism. Once again, the subordinate is to present the negative aspects as well as the positives. However, the key feature in this step is that the subordinate does not call his solution "my idea" but presents it as an alternative response to the current situation. In so doing, the subordinate does not lay claim to having a better idea than his boss. Such a claim typically causes the boss to defend his turf, since surrendering to his subordinate's idea could easily be interpreted as an admission that the subordinate knows best, a point that is usually difficult for a superior to acknowledge. In short, the subordinate's presentation of his solution in the form of an alternative response serves as a safeguard against the superior's initiating a "my idea" versus "your idea" thinking pattern, which typically ends up with the superior keeping his idea.

To continue our example, an ineffective implementation of the second step would be: "Boss, here's the way I would do it." Anything after this statement will probably not be heard because the initial statement raises the boss's defensiveness by implying that the subordinate knows a better way to set deadlines.

An effective implementation of step 2 would be: "Perhaps it would be possible to set up a staff meeting where we could all go over any possible new projects that you are considering. I know the drawback to having such a meeting would be the time that it takes, and also it would slow down how quickly you can respond to the client. But you might find it very useful. One positive aspect would be that you would get a feel for how long it would realistically take to complete the project because we could all quickly review our work schedules. This would prevent us from giving unrealistic deadlines to our client or having to turn in work that we know isn't our best. I think, in the long run, this would improve the reputation of our firm. Also, you could see if anybody was especially interested in the project, or if anybody had any great ideas off the cuff. I know this procedure would work well for me, and perhaps the others, too."

There are, in addition, several principles that can be used to add extra effectiveness to the first two steps (and these are demonstrated in the preceding example of effective implementation). The first has to do with the order in which the positives and negatives are presented in each step and how they are brought together. The principle to be applied is that the latter part of a message is the part that tends to be better remembered. Thus, in describing the current situation, the subordinate would start with the positives and end up on the negatives, the rationale being that the subordinate wants to leave the superior thinking about the negatives. In contrast, when the alternative response is presented, the subordinate would reverse the order so that the superior is left thinking about the positives.

A second tip is to link the positives and negatives together with the word "but." Recall that when people hear the word "but," they tend to discredit the information that preceded it. More important, they increase their attention to what comes after the "but." Since the subordinate wants his superior to think less of the current situation, he should sequence his criticism like this:

Positives — BUT — Negatives

On the other hand, the subordinate wants his superior to dwell on the positives of his idea, the alternative response. Therefore, he needs to sequence this part of the criticism like this:

Negatives — BUT — Positives

In each case, the subordinate is using sequence and the word "but" to help him accomplish his TASK.

A third point to remember is that the exact words, or semantics, play a significant part in giving criticism. Here the subordinate is advised to use the word "negatives" when referring to the problems of the current situation and the word "drawbacks" when referring to the problems of the alternative response. "Negative" is an attention-grabbing word, one that influences us to exaggerate the negativity of the situation. "Drawbacks" has just the opposite effect — it minimizes the negativity of the situation. The subordinate wants to maximize implicitly the negativity of the current situation and minimize the negativity of the alternative response.

The two-sided solution's last step is simply for the subordinate to acknowledge to his boss that he is "just bringing some information to your attention." This gives the implicit message that it is clearly up to the superior to do what she thinks best. In other words, the subordinate acknowledges to his superior that he indeed is the subordinate. The boss's self-esteem is protected, a power struggle is avoided, and the chance that change will occur is increased. In our example: "Boss, I just wanted to bring this to your attention. You may want to consider it. Thanks for the time." The middle part of this statement, "You may want to consider it," is a good example of using implied communication that reflects the subtleties of criticizing upward. A subordinate cannot openly tell his boss that she has to consider his criticism, since the organizational hierarchy dictates that it is not his job to tell his boss what to think about, to say nothing of the fact that his boss is apt to respond, "Don't tell me what I should think about." However, the addition of the word "may" allows the subordinate to tell the boss to consider his input without infringing on her turf, for he is telling her only that she may want to consider his criticism. Communication research makes the key point that when an individual processes the message that he "may want to consider," he is most likely to drop the "may" and thus hear that he does want to think about it. In effect, the subordinate has explicitly stated that the superior may want to consider his input, but he has also implicitly communicated that his superior definitely wants to consider the message. Other examples of this subtlety are "You might want to think about," "Maybe you would want to take this into consideration," "Perhaps you want to mull this over," or any phrase that buffers the direct statement of "Think this over."

When used effectively, the two-sided solution accomplishes many things. For one, it gets the situation changed to a more productive one. For another, the superior ends up feeling pretty good because she has used her power to change a situation for the better. Her self-esteem is enhanced. The superior-subordinate relationship wins, too. Since the subordinate has proved himself a good source of information, the superior is more apt to interact with him in the future. Their relationship evolves, and future criticism will be more easily accepted. And the organization benefits, too, simply because a better system is now in place. The subordinate feels good for all of the above reasons, not the least being that he has probably made his own job easier.

Some subordinates find it difficult to practice the two-sided solution because successfully using it means letting the boss take the credit for the alternative response. These subordinates are experiencing a bad case of egoism; they feel a need to be acknowledged for everything they do. Subordinates like these find it almost impossible to let their boss take credit for their ideas. Yet, for the sake of success in the long run, it is best that these subordinates practice self-restraint and realize that when criticizing a superior their sole goal should be to get the situation changed, not to win recognition and credit for a good idea so that they can move up in the organization. Skillful subordinates recognize that nothing facilitates harmony, and thereby accomplishment, so much as not being regarded as a serious contender for power or credit. Those who adopt a low profile are often better able to accomplish things than are their more nakedly competitive colleagues. Besides, subordinates who give their boss credit facilitate their relationship with the person who has the power to promote them.

Emphasizing the Validity of the Criticism

Many subordinates have found that another effective way to present criticism to their superior is to emphasize the validity of the criticism per se. The point here is not to present yourself as a valid source of criticism but to present your information as valid, maximizing the significance of the information rather than taking the position that you the subordinate know best, which, again, can lead to a disruptive power struggle. Instead of coming on as a critic, you present yourself as sharing valuable data that relate to both your jobs. The superior, instead of having to accept or reject a criticism, is now in the face-saving position of merely having to evaluate the information supplied by the subordinate. If the information is valid, there is an excellent chance the superior will take action. Some ways you can build up the validity of your criticism are: citing authoritative sources, submitting supportive data, showing reference material to your superior.

A data analyst for Control Data used this technique in criticizing her department head for the computer system she was considering. Instead of telling her boss that she was choosing the wrong system or that she knew which one she should buy, the data analyst gave her several current reports that indicated another system would be more responsive to their needs. Her boss, after reading the articles, changed her choice and thanked her subordinate for supplying her with "invaluable information."

Requesting Help

A third way a subordinate can get a superior to be receptive to criticism is to present the criticism as a request for help. In other words, instead of pointing out what the superior is not doing right, the subordinate explains that he is having a problem that he doesn't know how to solve. From the subordinate's point of view, the problem exists because of the superior's behavior and can only be resolved by the superior's changing his behavior. Yet expressing the information that directly can too often sound like accusations or blame, factors that precipitate defensiveness and then the inevitable power struggle (to say nothing of the fact that it's inappropriate for a subordinate to address a superior in that manner). Therefore, the subordinate uses the strategy of saying merely that he has a problem and wants the superior to help him solve it. The assumption is that the superior will recognize that the only way to help the subordinate is to change his own behavior. On the other hand, if the superior is able to help the subordinate solve his problem without changing his behavior, the subordinate still probably comes out a winner because the situation has been changed.

A secretary at Hughes Aircraft used this technique with her boss. Her boss had a habit of keeping her in the dark about his schedule, which made it difficult for her to set up appointments for him with his other subordinates and co-workers. Out of frustration, these people were continually pressuring her to get them in to see the boss or at least to tell them when he was available. Her replying that she didn't know only intensified their anger. Furthermore, she had several times previously asked her boss for his daily schedule in advance and was rebuffed each time with "I will let you know my schedule when I want to." At her wit's end, she approached her boss, stating that she had a problem and was wondering if he might be able to help her solve it. He became quite receptive, and she went on: "I don't know what to tell your co-workers and clients when they ask me when you are available. When I keep saying I don't know, they get frustrated and angry and take it out on me. I don't know how to handle it. Do you have any suggestions?" After thinking about it, her boss replied that the only answer he could come up with was for him to let her know of his availability. However, he could let her know only two days in advance. The secretary acknowledged that even knowing his availability a day in advance would be helpful and thanked him for helping her solve her problem. Although this was not the perfect solution, it was a significant improvement over the previous situation. In effect, she changed her boss's behavior by getting him to "help" her.

As another example, suppose your superior is chronically late in providing you with data you need to function effectively. You can say "I'm having trouble running my department on those days when I don't yet have the weekly productive figures. Can you give me some suggestions for improving this situation?" If your criticism is valid, chances are your superior will solve the problem — and resolve the criticism — by meeting her deadlines more promptly.

Subordinates who take this approach can expect good results for a few reasons. The first is that people tend to be more receptive and responsive to information when they hear it as a request rather than a demand. Criticism presented as a demand usually threatens the recipient's self-esteem. It is as if the criticizer is saying that he is superior and that his concerns are more valid. Defensiveness comes into play.

Asking for help instead allows the subordinate simultaneously to communicate several messages that increase the superior's receptivity. First, the subordinate communicates that he respects his superior, because he is asking instead of telling. As respect is communicated, the superior's receptivity is increased. Next, and more cunning, is that the subordinate increases his superior's self-esteem (and thus her receptivity) by voluntarily taking the "one-down position" of asking for help. The subordinate is implying that he can't do something on his own as he says outright that he needs his boss's help. This is a "put-up" message that confirms to the superior that she is still superior. More important, there's a good chance that this ego boost will motivate the superior to take productive action. Asking for help not only lets the superior know that she is needed but also that her subordinate believes she has the ability to achieve results. To phrase this more elaborately, when the subordinate explicitly asks his superior for help, he implicitly taps into the superior's need to be needed and need to achieve. Satisfying these needs is for most people a powerful incentive to action, and when the subordinate arouses them, he is almost guaranteed that the superior will try to satisfy them by involving herself in the problem and generating a solution. Given these implicit messages, taking the one-down position requires self-restraint on the part of the subordinate, but the payoff is worth the price.

Asking for help also reaps good results because it allows the subordinate to show his superior that he feels comfortable in coming to her when he has a problem. The superior can take pride in the fact that her subordinates feel this way about her. She feels good and consequently is only too happy to help. The superior will probably see the entire process as a request for help rather than a criticism, but what matters is that the problem is effectively resolved.

Impossible Bosses

What about the impossible bosses? For such bosses, subordinates must create and develop different criticism strategies, trying each until successful. Some possible solutions: When a stoic boss doesn't tell you where you stand, bring up the organization's goals as a basis for determining specific criteria for next year's performance rating, so "we" can monitor our performance accordingly. If the boss is a crisis maker, develop a strong network of relationships with co-workers that will help you get the information you need to decide whether each crisis is real or manufactured. When the boss is over-controlling, work out of the office a lot if possible, exaggerate procedural obstacles, and frequently reassure the boss that you are on target. If the boss is truly impossible, if he has a short temper or never listens, then attempt to offer criticism only if you can be clever and creative. Gear your strategy to answering the fundamental question: "How can I communicate this information so that my superior perceives it as useful?"

What is most important is for the subordinate to recognize that the techniques for criticizing upward do not rely on direct, overt communication. The chain of command prohibits a subordinate from telling a superior that he's an idiot or that he made another foolish mistake even if the superior says such things to the subordinate daily. Instead, to criticize upward, to create change at her superior's level, the subordinate must rely on informal relationships, timing, ambiguity, self-restraint, and implicit communication. These are not skills, however, that usually come to young managers without the benefit of education and experience. And there are few formal opportunities to learn the skill of benign guerrilla warfare. For these subordinates, their ally is their organization.

EXECUTIVE CRITICISM — THE ORGANIZATION'S ROLE

Organizations can do a lot to increase executive suite criticism. One step an organization can take is to de-emphasize power differences. This seems to make subordinates feel that their superiors are more approachable and thus increases the likelihood that they will give criticism. A procedure growing in popularity that implements this tactic is making executive offices less impressive and locating them close to those of others. Organizations such as Honda, Northeast Apparel, and Technology Concepts all have their executives working in offices that are easily accessible to those whom they manage. Furthermore, these companies have no separate dining area for executives. Contrast this with the usual practice of segregating executives by means of separate dining quarters and exercise rooms. For example, at Ford, there is the Glass House, where only top management is allowed to eat. While this certainly is nice for the executives, it reinforces the perception of subordinates that they are a breed apart, making them less likely to offer criticism, even when they think it would be beneficial. If organizations segregate executives less and take away some of the symbols of power and isolation, then the executive becomes more approachable.

A second strategy that organizations can use is to give an overt message that it is appropriate to criticize and, in fact, that it is expected. One way to give such a message is to have and to give high visibility to criticism boxes whose labels say that anybody is welcome to submit criticisms. These boxes foster productive criticism in general but upward criticism especially, since criticizing the organization is by definition criticizing upward.

Many organizations think they do the same thing by having suggestion boxes and would not make a distinction between a criticism box and a suggestion box. Yet there is a world of difference between the two. First, the word "suggestion" provides only an implied invitation to criticize rather than a direct request. Consequently, the organization is not actually saying that it is okay to criticize. The organization's members need to see and hear the direct message that it is okay to criticize. Second, many organizations that use suggestion boxes feel that asking members to offer their criticisms would result in a barrage of negatives and would create an atmosphere of dissatisfaction and low morale. So instead they ask for suggestions because this focuses on the positive. While there is some validity to this focus, the argument against criticism boxes misses the point.

What is the point? First, if people do have a lot of negative things to say about their organization, it is in the organization's best interest to know it. In contrast, if you ask only for suggestions, you put individuals in the position of being able to respond only if they can think of how to improve something. If unable to do so, they make no suggestion, even when their criticisms are valid. In other words, subordinates are told implicitly to keep their negative perceptions to themselves. This suppresses one of the positive uses of criticism: to alert an individual or an organization to a negative. More important, employees need to have the experience — offered by criticism boxes — of voicing their negative thoughts so that they can learn to communicate them in the most effective way. With experience, the chances increase that they will learn to criticize productively.

In order to make criticism boxes most effective, it is important for the organization's members to see that their criticisms are recognized. Ways of doing this include printing all of the criticisms in an organization newsletter; giving special recognition to the best criticism; and, most important, responding to specific criticisms by changing. Criticism boxes thus provide organizations with a means of announcing that it is okay to criticize and also with a means of training their members in how to give productive criticism.

Another possible organizational intervention is to create mechanisms that specifically generate productive criticism of executives. Standard practices, such as performance appraisals, are available; the issue is whether they are applied to executives. Probably the most significant factor is whether the chief executive believes in the system to the extent of using it himself. For example, Lee Iacocca periodically sits down with each of his top executives to discuss in detail their current performance and future plans and goals.

Another mechanism an organization can use to encourage criticism at high levels is to set up criticism teams whose task is to go into a specific area of the organization and productively criticize the people in charge. At Northeast Apparel, for instance, it is common practice for a team of district managers to visit another of the company's regions with the purpose of productively criticizing their counterparts on how they run their operation. This type of intervention sets in motion the exchange of criticism among executives and simultaneously serves as a model to lower employees that top management is open to being criticized. Employing criticism teams does more than communicate the message that criticism is important and permissible, though; it also facilitates productive communication because the team gets practice in giving productive criticism and the recipients of their criticism get practice in taking it.

Using outside consultants offers organizations another means for encouraging criticism and getting it to executives. Here, the outside consultant acts as an ombudsman. His or her job is to keep an ear to the ground and elicit criticism from various organizational members. He or she then passes the criticism on to upper levels. The key factor here is to make sure the consultant is well versed in eliciting criticism and has the skill to pass it on in such a way that executives can accurately appraise and use it.

Nobody expresses the importance of executive suite criticism better than former president Jimmy Carter. When he was at one time faced with a domestic policy crisis, he summoned dozens of businessmen, government officials, labor leaders, and clergymen to a summit meeting at which he asked for their "bluntest possible" criticism of his ideas and leadership qualities. After the meeting, Carter said, "I'm not the kind of person who responds easily to criticism. I hate to admit that I have defects and that I have made errors. But over a period of a few days I began to see how constructive and helpful this could be to me as President."

Chapter 7

Developing Peership

THE YEAR 1890 is officially accepted by historians as the end of the rapid settlement of the American West. Just as our land frontier was conquered, so the era of the rugged individualist in business has petered out. Most of us now find ourselves in a work environment that is dominated by the "organization man," the "gamesman," and David Riesman's other-directed "lonely crowd." In short, most of us are no longer individualistic entrepreneurs. We're part of a team. Even people who work on individualized tasks require the cooperation and goodwill of others in the organization to do their jobs well.

Today, men and women who cannot easily get along with their co-workers find themselves ostracized. Although these people work conscientiously, they never seem to be offered the remuneration — promotion, better assignment, an increase in salary — that their efforts deserve. They watch in anguish as the office politicians, the yes-men, and the other group favorites surge ahead. Being banished to the role of outsider, they are not privy to the office grapevine and thereby miss hearing critical pieces of information that could alert them to pitfalls or promotion opportunities. The conclusion is obvious: When there's friction between co-workers — let's say between you and a co-worker — you and your work suffer.

Sometimes the friction is highly noticeable. Reports, memos, phone messages, are often "forgotten," misplaced, or delivered hours late. Favors that could help you resolve a crisis are withheld. Other times, it's a matter of covert sabotage in which your antagonists contrive to drag their heels on any cooperative effort or otherwise make every daily contact difficult.

On the other hand, if you get along well with your peers, you ease your daily work life. You transform possible enemies into allies. Your phone messages and memos are remembered instead of forgotten. Whatever relevant information your co-workers have passes regularly to your in-box and ears. When you need reasonable help, you get it.

One way to ensure that you reap the benefits of good peer relationships is to be able to criticize peers productively. For the organization, productive criticism among peers is a significant factor in the establishment of an esprit de corps; the extent to which such criticism is productive helps determine how well co-workers can work together. It has also been found that productive criticism among peers is one of the best ways to foster innovativeness. More important to most people, however, is that being able to criticize your peers productively is essential to your own job success and satisfaction. After all, if you can't get your co-workers to be receptive to your ideas, your work suffers, inevitably creating feelings of frustration, anger, and apathy.

This chapter identifies the key issues that make it difficult to criticize co-workers productively and offers some practical strategies for resolving them so productive peer criticism can occur.

OBSTACLES TO PEER CRITICISM

The Organizational Structure

To reiterate, peers are co-workers placed at more or less the same functional job level in the company hierarchy. It is assumed that peers are at approximately the same level of competence and have approximately the same status and that they have the same amount of work power. Boundaries in the sense of who has power over whom are foggy. Therefore, peers are not officially sanctioned to criticize each other. As a result, an individual may hesitate to criticize a peer, even when he or she thinks it would be extremely helpful, because he or she feels, "How can I criticize someone who doesn't work for me? I am not his boss." A co-worker can refuse a peer's criticism on the same grounds: "You are not my boss. Do not tell me how to do my job." Thus, the organizational structure becomes an obstacle to peer criticism; peers' sense of rigid hierarchical roles inhibits them from criticizing each other and, at the same time, provides a convenient rationale for defensiveness as a response to criticism even when the criticism is valid.

Competitiveness

Advocates of competition base their case on the assumption that competition brings out the best in people. Without competition, even minimal productivity, to say nothing of excellence, would disappear. A noncompetitive society would represent, in Spiro Agnew's assorted metaphors, "a bland experience . . . a waveless sea of non-achievers . . . the psychological retreat of a person . . . into a cocoon of false security and self-satisfied mediocrity."

However, the fact is that the competition often arising among co-workers is the major obstacle to peer criticism because it means a cultural norm of watching out only for yourself. Criticism comes across in the form of put-downs, one-upmanship, and other ploys that are intended to make one look better than one's co-workers. It is also not uncommon for a peer intentionally to pull back criticism because the information that would be communicated would improve the co-worker's standing. Thus, competition often makes people suspicious and hostile toward one another and actively discourages each from helping the other. Consequently, when criticism comes out of competition, it loses the quality of the helping spirit and stops being improvement-oriented because the criticizer is more concerned about making himself look better with his criticism than about genuinely helping the recipient do better. Competition is why criticism among peers so often comes across as a put-down.

It is not simply the competitiveness of an individual that undermines productive criticism and the associated achievement. A structure that demands competition tends to have the same effect. The traditional organizational hierarchy, for example, implicitly communicates that the way to get financial remuneration, receive recognition, and move up the organization is to do better than your co-workers. Consequently, the internalized attitude becomes "To be successful, I must be better than my co-workers." This sets up what social psychologists call a zero sum situation, an environment in which the winner takes all and the loser gains nothing. A zero sum situation often causes individuals to be self-serving, even at the expense of their co-workers, their organization, and the people they serve.

To promote productive criticism among peers, it is necessary to establish a cooperative environment, a sense of peership, which "forces" co-workers to give and take criticism in a way that benefits all. In fact, recent research in the behavioral sciences suggests that a cooperative style of interacting is much more productive for the organization generally than a competitive one. Alfie Kohn, psychologist and author of *No Contest,* reviewed all of the literature comparing competitive and cooperative environments and found that virtually every experiment indicated better results from cooperation than from competition. Why? Author Kohn provides some clues: "Success often depends on sharing resources efficiently, and this is nearly impossible when people have to work against each other. Cooperation takes advantage of all the skills represented in a group as well as the mysterious process by which that group becomes more than the sum of its parts." Thus, when criticism in particular comes out of a cooperative spirit, it becomes productive because the attitude of both the criticizer and the recipient becomes "This can help all of us." The "you-me" attitude becomes a "we" attitude. The emphasis shifts from wondering whether you have the right to criticize a co-worker to wanting to help — and be helped by — a co-worker. Boundaries become less rigid, and criticism flows more readily and productively as its intent becomes to "put up" instead of put down.

Let us now look at what individual co-workers can do, what their boss can do, and what their organization can do so that peer criticism can achieve its TASK.

THE ROLE OF THE CO-WORKER

There are two steps that you can take to increase your ability to criticize your peers effectively. The first is actively to develop peership, which, as we shall soon see, forces the criticisms that are given to be productive. The second is to learn how to present the criticism in a way that allows one's co-workers to hear it productively. Each course of action reinforces the other. Since most of the working world is usually in a rush, the second step, which can be more quickly implemented, will be discussed first.

Making Criticism Sound Good

Since, as Samuel Butler said, "He that complies against his will / Is of his own opinion still," co-workers need to phrase their criticisms of each other in a way that avoids starting arguments. The first way to accomplish this is to use some generally applicable techniques that reflect, as we shall see, the qualities of peership.

Techniques for criticizing peers are based on the assumption that you do not have the organizational authority to tell your co-workers what to do. This is in marked contrast to the superior-subordinate relationship, in which the superior is granted organizational power to, if necessary, make the subordinate respond to the criticism (even if the subordinate disagrees) or experience negative consequences. Although it is not an uncommon occurrence for subordinates to argue with their superiors when they believe a criticism is not justified, the result is usually compliance, at least overtly. True, the argument may silently persist for several months or longer, but it is silent because the organizational rule is "Don't argue with the boss. He can hurt you." In most cases, though, the arguments are short-lived.

Peers, on the other hand, have equal work power, making arguments not only permissible but expected in critical encounters. The problem here is that, as is well known in psychological circles, when an argument between two people intensifies, each person becomes more and more ego-entrenched in his or her position, with self-esteem potentially threatened. This makes it difficult to resolve the disagreement, because to each person, "giving in" carries with it a loss of self-esteem. This is one of the reasons that power struggles are so common among peers and that a compromise is the standard solution — each needs to have his or her self-esteem protected. Thus, any criticism of co-workers that has the potential to cause an argument has little chance of being productive since the co-workers will protect their self-esteem by defending their behavior, and their equal work power will justify their right to do so.

Moreover, it is not unlikely that when you criticize a co-worker, your criticism will be met with anger simply because your peer perceives you as overstepping your boundaries or thinks that you are criticizing her out of a competitive need, a desire to show her up.

General Techniques for Criticizing Co-workers

The following set of techniques for peer criticism are general guidelines that can help you defuse sensitive situations and protect self-esteem. In the majority of criticism situations, these strategies will help your criticisms sound good.

Create the Perception of a Common Goal. Delivering your criticism in terms of a common goal unites you and your co-worker. It immediately helps you create for your co-worker the perception that you have a common ground on which to relate and thus minimizes the possibility of an argument. From your peer's point of view, a common goal means that you are both in the same boat, going in the same direction. There is little reason to resist. Having this perception, she feels less threatened; her need to compete to protect herself changes to a desire to help herself by cooperating with you.

The best way to implement this strategy is to use words and phrases that stress cooperation rather than competitiveness or blame. For example, "We can get our report done quickly if you firm up the statistical data while I edit the text" is bound to be more effective than "Unless you get moving faster on the statistics, I won't be able to finish the report on time" or "You are not doing the statistics section fast enough." Emphasizing the common goal and using words like "we" and "our," which imply a sharing of credit for a job well done, reduce the harmful sense of competition and the chance of starting a nonproductive argument. Movie writer Jack Epps, Jr., whose credits include *Top Gun,* endorses this strategy. "It's never 'my idea' or 'your idea,' " he says, referring to working with his partner, Jim Cash. "It's always 'our idea.' " Similarly, according to former Harvard Business School professor Anthony Athos, now a consultant, erstwhile United Airlines CEO Ed Carlson used "we" instead of "I" in all his letters and meetings, which resulted in a "far more cooperative spirit than in other companies."

It is especially important to remember to use cooperative words when things go wrong. After his team lost the second game of the 1983 World Series, Pete Rose, then with the Philadelphia Phillies, commented, "We just didn't get the big hit when we needed it. We need to do better to win." Using a cooperative vocabulary in a losing, or criticism, situation has the effect of building cohesiveness and support among peers because nobody is blamed. Dissension is avoided and criticisms are resolved.

Show How a Peer's Performance Affects Both of You. To be able to criticize a fellow worker productively, it is important to convince him or her that you are not intruding on his or her territory. Even though your criticism may be intended as helpful, the other person may think you are sticking your nose into something that is none of your business — that you are playing boss. Therefore, a good strategy is to show your co-worker that the behavior you are criticizing has an effect on both of you. (This is derived from the affective orientation, in which criticizing is done on the basis of how the work / co-worker affects the reader / you.) Since you are both affected by the behavior in question, since you both stand to gain if the criticism is resolved (or suffer negative consequences if it isn't), it becomes easier for your peer to hear the criticism as an offer to cooperate rather than as an order; in essence, he or she sees it as "some of your business" rather than "none of your business."

This strategy is particularly useful when two persons frequently work together. For example, let's say your co-worker is constantly late for sales presentations, leaving you to stumble through your presentation alone without all the pertinent facts. The habitual criticism would be "You're never on time and it makes me look like a fool." A more effective phrasing would be something like "It's important for both of us to be at the sales meetings on time. If one of us is late, it creates a bad impression and we both suffer." When you show your peer how his actions affect you (and vice versa), you are showing how both of you can benefit if he acts upon your criticism. This increases the chances that the criticism will be productive because you have forestalled the argument that you don't have a right to criticize. Also, your highlighting the fact that he will benefit as well as you indicates that your criticism is not (solely) coming out of self-interest. Thus, your co-worker is more likely to respond co-operatively.

*Agree with or Support a Peer's Behavior but Refer to Significant Others —
People More Important Than Yourself — Who Probably Won't.* Underlying this strategy is the fact that a common and unproductive facet of communication between peers is the expression of blame. How often have you heard someone, if not yourself, say, "I would have had the report in on time, but Bob didn't get me the statistics on time." Perhaps your co-worker didn't carry out his part of the assignment on schedule, but putting all of the blame on him merely sets up a destructive accusation-defense situation. Bob is hardly likely to accept the criticism, for if he does he is implicitly accepting responsibility for the breakdown of the entire project. The only way he can protect his position (and his self-image) is to reject the criticism out of hand.

Although it is not very often that we can agree with or support the "wrong" idea, attitude, or behavior of a co-worker, when we can pretend to, it removes any implication of blame and provides a bridge with which to make your point in opposition to the behavior. It has the advantage of putting you on his side. This, in fact, is exactly the purpose of the aforementioned strategy.

A research librarian noticed that her co-worker did not return reference cards to their appropriate places until the end of the day or until she had a dozen so that she could save time by returning them all at once. Although she did not want to play boss, she knew and wanted to let her co-worker know that their boss wanted these cards put back immediately. She got her criticism across by agreeing with her co-worker: "I've noticed that you put the cards back at the end of the day. I agree that's easier and just as accurate. I used to do the same thing until I learned that the boss gets very annoyed if the cards aren't returned immediately. I think you'll save yourself a lot of trouble if you take my suggestion." This comment made the criticizer an ally of the recipient. If her co-worker was going to argue about the matter, she would have to do so with the boss. The beauty of this technique is that you usually end up being thanked for saving your co-worker from the negative consequences you have tactfully pointed out.

A derivation of this procedure is to claim agreement in the past with your co-worker's position. Blame is never implied if you stress that you once felt the same way, until some clear or overwhelming evidence changed your opinion. This means that you have put yourself on her side of the argument in the past and that you only gave up the position she now holds after learning better. Actually, you are just dating your agreement to a prior time when you knew less about the subject or situation. Helpful phrases to use are "That's how it looked to me, too, until . . ." or "I used to do it that way, too, but . . ."

Ask for "Permission" to Criticize. If a person has given us permission to present an idea, he is more receptive than if the idea is presented without such permission. The mere fact of your having asked permission not only protects his self-esteem in all cases but also builds it up when the technique is used skillfully. Asking for permission serves to increase your peer's self-esteem because it communicates that you respect him. All of these axioms apply when the "idea" you are asking permission to present happens to be criticism, though you should ask explicitly for permission to present criticism.

Asking for permission to criticize is especially effective with co-workers because it makes irrelevant the issue of whether you have the right to criticize — if you are granted permission, you gain the right. Ways of initiating this strategy are: "May I talk to you about something?" "May I make a suggestion?" "Do you have a few minutes to talk to me?" and "May I show you an easier way to do it?" Many individuals have found this strategy to be extremely effective with defensive co-workers, since the act of giving permission commits the co-worker to listening to what you are saying. Occasionally, a co-worker will respond along these lines: "No, I don't have time" or "I am not interested in what you think." When this occurs, the best response seems to be "Is there a specific time when we can talk?" or "It's just a thought, you don't have to agree with me if you don't want to." If this doesn't move you closer to success, go back to the drawing board and be creative.

All of the aforementioned strategies have a common denominator: They avoid competitive patterns of relating, minimize the chance of arguments, and build cooperation. These are the general guidelines for criticizing peers.

Specific Techniques for Criticizing Co-workers: The Power Principle

A second way to facilitate comfortable criticism between peers is to use strategies that recent research in social psychology show can allow you to gain and use power over your co-worker even though you are on the same organizational level. (Unlike the preceding techniques, these can be used only in specific situations.)

To repeat, work power is the ability to influence or to make decisions for other people, even if they are opposed to your decisions. Although you are not granted formal organizational work power over your co-workers, there are times when you have more power over them than you think. According to the research of social psychologists John French and Bertram Raven, who wrote the article "The Base of Social Power," these situations arise either when you possess some attribute that can influence your co-workers, such as technical knowledge of how to do a specific task, or when they perceive that you have the ability somehow to influence their future success. Knowing what these attributes and abilities are, when and how much you have of them, when your co-workers are likely to perceive that you have them, and being able to integrate them into your criticisms are known collectively as the power principle. Applying the power principle is a way for you to manufacture work power over your peers — when in reality you don't have any — and thus increase the likelihood that your criticisms will be effective.

The Four Types of Power. Four types of power have been identified that can be used to influence your co-workers. Note, however, that with each type, your hierarchical position in relationship to your co-worker remains the same. Here is a brief description of each:

1. Legitimate Power. You have legitimate power when you have a position of authority. Examples include being a team leader or heading a project. But in each case the other participants are at the same functional level. It is important to recognize that while you do have legitimate power, it is not actual work power, because if push comes to shove you cannot fire your co-workers. For example, a nurse who is a group leader cannot fire her co-worker for coming late to a staff meeting or for failing to make a notation on a patient's chart. That power belongs to the nurse supervisor.

2. Expert Power. You have expert power when you are more competent or knowledgeable than your co-worker in a specific situation or in a specific skill. Two computer scientists may be co-workers, but one may be far more knowledgeable in developing software programs. Although he would have expert power in this area, he still couldn't fire his co-worker for making too many mistakes, so he would not have work power. An experienced teacher has expert power in writing lesson plans, but she still can't have a first-year teacher transferred to another school.

3. Reward Power. You have reward power when you can indirectly but significantly affect the course of a co-worker's job and career. (Work power is the power to officially and directly affect the course of someone's career.) A staff editor who can influence the senior editor's choice of who should be given a specific book to edit has reward power over her co-workers, since she can help a specific editor get a specific book. If you have a good reputation, reward power will frequently come to you, because your opinion, suggestions, and recommendations will be sought by your superiors. However, there are other factors besides a good reputation that will give you reward power. For instance, if you are the boss's son or best friends with your boss, you probably will have reward power over your co-workers. You can also develop reward power. This is accomplished by establishing good relationships with your superiors, for the better your relationships with them, the more receptive they will become to your recommendations (and, if you recall, your criticisms).

4. Attractive Power. You have attractive power if you are physically attractive, have good interpersonal skills, have good communication skills — including a good vocabulary and a pleasant voice — and have a positive attitude. Attractive power has the effect of pulling people toward you; they want to work with you.

It is important to note that all four types of power — legitimate, expert, reward, and attractive — are attributes that you possess. (Legitimate power is assigned, but once it is assigned, you possess it until it is taken away.) Obviously, the type of power you possess will vary over time, with the situation, and with the particular co-worker you are criticizing. Therefore, the first step in using the power principle is to assess your power base.

Assessing Your Power Base.   You can begin to assess your power base for a particular criticism situation by asking yourself four questions:

1. Have I been given some formal authority that hasn't been given to my co-workers? (A "yes" indicates legitimate power.)
2. Do I know more than my co-worker? (A "yes" indicates expert power.)
3. Can I help my co-worker advance (or can I deter) his career? (A "yes" indicates reward power.)
4. Does my co-worker like being with me? (A "yes" indicates attractive power.)

A good way to gain a more accurate assessment of your power base is to place your answers to each question on a scale of 1 (Absolute No) to 9 (Absolute Yes). The higher your rating, the more of a particular type of power you possess. Sometimes you will have a lot of power across the board, but there will also be many times when your power among the four types ranges from high to low. For example, a junior accountant may have expert power over his co-worker but little or no attractive power. Once you assess your power base, you will know what type of power you have and what type you need to develop. You are then ready to integrate the power principle into your criticisms.

Power Plays.   You must next decide what type of power you think will facilitate the criticism process. For example, if you are criticizing your co-worker for consistently being late to meetings that you are in charge of, then you might want to play up your legitimate power as the basis for your criticism. If you are criticizing a co-worker for how she analyzed some statistical data, expert power would probably be more useful. Obviously, it is always best to use as much power as you have, but for the standard situation, one type of power should usually predominate.

Once you know what type of power will be most useful, you can begin to determine how best to apply it. You can also assess whether you have an adequate amount of the power to be effective. If not, you may be able to develop it. For instance, if expert power is needed, you can read a particular article or get some extra training. If the situation calls for attractive power, a change in dress and diction might help. There will also be times when you'll want to play up some types of power and play down others. A balding, middle-aged attorney with bad breath would probably want to play up his expert power and minimize the effect of attractive power, since the lack of the latter would be likely to undermine his effectiveness when he criticizes his partners.

Powerless to Powerful. Your power is useless unless you know how to use it. Therefore, the next stage is to integrate it into the actual delivery of the criticism. What is important to note is that while you are using power to effect change, your primary goal is still to get your co-worker to cooperate. You are using power to increase the chance that your co-worker will cooperate with you. Here are some strategies for using each type of power as a means to get your co-workers to cooperate with you and, thus, resolve the criticism in question.

Legitimate Power: The preferred way of integrating legitimate power into your criticism is by phrasing the criticism as a declarative statement, an assertion of what you want. For example, if you are criticizing your co-worker for continually being late to sales presentations that you are in charge of and you have one coming up, you could criticize by simply saying "I'd appreciate it if you would get to the meeting by 10 A.M." (Note how this delivery differs from the criticism of the same behavior mentioned in the section on showing how your co-worker's behavior affects you. In that situation, you had no legitimate power, so a different approach was taken.) When you put your criticism in the form of a declarative statement, you are implying that you expect your co-worker to comply. The fact that you actually have legitimate power increases the chances that this will be the outcome, for a refusal of your "criticism" would be a challenge to authority that most people in the work environment try to avoid issuing. Since you have legitimate power, there is no need to ask for cooperation, which entails the risk of your co-worker's refusing, for whatever reason. The use of a declarative statement exaggerates your legitimate power in the eyes of your co-workers by letting them know that you have the power.

When you use a declarative statement to apply your legitimate power, it is good policy to soften the criticism in the context of the words you use so that the criticism is not heard as a demand. After all, despite your legitimate power, you are still not your co-worker's boss, and if he perceives you as too demanding, as playing boss, he might refuse to comply. Thus, telling your co-worker that "I want you to get there on time" will probably not be as effective as "I'd appreciate it if you would get there on time."

A second and less effective (but sometimes necessary) way to use legitimate power in your criticisms is to state explicitly that you have the power. For example, you might say, "Well, since I've been asked to run the presentation, I'd like to start at 10 A.M., so please be there on time." Note that in this delivery, even though you definitively state that you have the power, you soften your words by acknowledging that the power has been given to you by someone else rather than implying that you have absolute power over your co-worker. At times, though, it may be necessary to exaggerate legitimate power, because nothing else is working. The criticism would then come across like this: "Listen, I'm in charge, so I want you there by 10 A.M." While this approach may be effective, it is apt to create bad feelings that will negatively affect future encounters with this particular co-worker. Furthermore, using this power play might create an impression that you are on a power trip. A rule, then, is that if you explicitly acknowledge your legitimate power, point out that it has been given to you by your superior or your organization.

Expert Power: Using expert power is especially helpful when you criticize a co-worker for something she is doing that does not necessarily involve her cooperating with you; for example, how she is handling a particular project on her own. Your criticism here comes from a desire to help her (and your organization) meet goals more effectively. Expert power, of course, is also useful in those situations in which you are directly involved.

One way you can integrate expert power into your criticism is by referring to specific information that demonstrates your point. A psychologist working on a psychiatric ward, for example, criticized a colleague for the way he was conducting therapy with a patient. Instead of telling him how to do therapy, he pointed out that "research demonstrates that this type of patient will respond best to a supportive therapy rather than a confrontational approach. I have several recent articles on this subject if you'd like to see them."

Using expert power is similar to building up the validity of the criticism, a technique used in criticizing your boss. The difference is that when you criticize your boss, you do not want him to see you as an expert, because this perception can threaten his authority and decision-making power; thus, you want to emphasize the information you provide. Here, you want your co-worker to perceive you as an expert, since this gives you the leverage you need to force the change, something that you cannot do with your superior. Another difference between the two methods is that building up the validity of the criticism usually involves a one-shot criticism situation; expert power is an attribute that will serve you over time and be useful in other criticisms, such as the psychologist's criticizing his co-worker's group therapy skills, diagnostic skills, and psychological testing skills.

Expert power can also be integrated into your criticisms by explicitly mentioning your past accomplishments. "When I used to work at the Menninger Foundation, I did a tremendous amount of work with these types of patients." The pitfall to avoid here is coming across as a braggart, which will decrease your attractive power, which in turn will make it more difficult for you to use your expert power. This is a good illustration of how the types of power play off each other.

Reward Power: Using reward power when you criticize a co-worker is tricky because if you fail to advance (or hinder) your co-worker's career after you use it, it quickly diminishes, making it unlikely that it will be an effective power source a second time around. On the other hand, if you deliver the reward, your power increases, making it easier for you to criticize your co-worker in the future.

Take the case of an experienced television staff writer who criticizes his co-worker's script by saying, "I think if you make the first scene shorter and introduce the main character sooner, you will make it a much stronger script. By the way, I'm having lunch with the boss and I plan to let him know what a good job you are doing. I'm going

to recommend that he give you another story to develop." Dissecting
the criticism, we can see that the power play is based on the assumption that the co-worker wants another story to develop and
that he perceives that the experienced staff writer is in a position to
help him get it if he makes the suggested changes. What is crucial
is for the experienced staff writer actually to have his recommendation
accepted.

If, shortly after the criticism situation, the co-worker is granted
another assignment, he will probably be more receptive to future
criticisms by the experienced staff writer because he will perceive him
as being able to influence his job success — he acknowledges the
reward power of the experienced writer.

However, if the co-worker makes the changes not because he
agrees with them but because he wants another assignment and does
not get another assignment in the near future, he will be less apt to
be responsive to the experienced staff writer's criticism the next time
around. He will believe that his co-worker really has no influence to
get him another assignment and therefore will feel that he is better
off writing a script as he thinks best.

An important point to remember here is the power of semantics
when giving criticism. There is a significant difference between saying
"I'm positive I can get you another assignment" and "I think I can
get you another assignment" and "I'm not sure, but I'll try to get
you another assignment." Using the initial statement creates strong
positive expectations in the recipient. Although this delivery will
increase the power of the criticism, a failure on the part of the critic
to fulfill his commitment is apt to discredit him in future interactions,
to say nothing of the negative feelings that the recipient will have
after being "lied" to. On the other hand, the last delivery, which will
probably be least effective because it minimizes reward power, will
not hurt the critic's reputation if he fails to deliver nor be too up-
setting for the recipient, because he knows the chances for the reward
are slim but has decided to take a chance. The principle is to correlate
your use of semantics with your degree of reward power. Thus, the
art of integrating reward power successfully into your criticisms entails knowing when you can actually influence your co-worker's future
success.

Attractive Power: You integrate attractive power into your criticism on the assumption that your co-worker wants to help you because you display attractive attributes and because it is his self-serving wish to be with or help attractive people. You implement the power by phrasing the criticism in the form of a request. An example of the use of attractive power in criticizing your co-worker's punctuality would be "Could you do me a favor and get to the meeting by 10 A.M.?" Although this is similar to a technique discussed in the chapter on criticizing your boss — asking for help — the rationale is quite different. With your boss, you ask for help on the assumption that she will feel good because she perceives that you are paying homage to her ability to solve "your" problem; thus, you elevate her self-esteem by letting her know that she is superior. With your co-worker, the rationale is that he perceives you as being attractive and thus wants to help you because the act of helping you in itself is pleasurable. If you were to use a declarative statement, and if you had no legitimate power, your criticism could be heard as more demanding, which could diminish your attractive power. Thus, the theory behind attractive power assumes that the recipient wants to help you and that he will choose to help you.

Attractive power is especially useful in those situations in which the only way a criticism can be resolved is through the actions of your co-workers. In these criticism situations, it is essential to get co-workers to cooperate. Using attractive power, if you have it, is often more effective than legitimate power or expert power for the simple reason that it makes your co-worker want to help you.

One of the more interesting ways to use attractive power is to build ongoing cooperation by applying what social psychologists call the foot-in-the-door technique. The strategy is to start off by asking your co-worker for a small favor, one in which she is required to make little effort. After getting your foot in the door, you ask your co-worker for another favor, this one requiring a little more effort. As the weeks go by, you continue the process, each time asking for a favor that not only helps you but also helps her. As time goes by, it becomes second nature for your co-worker to "help you out," or to cooperate with you.

To reiterate, none of these power techniques gives you actual work power over your co-workers. What they do give you is manufactured power — leverage with your co-workers that increases the chances that your criticisms will be more effective. In effect, you have gone from powerless to powerful!

Developing Peership: The Key to Productive Peer Criticism

The basic building block for productive peer criticism is peership, a relationship between co-workers that is characterized by empathy, trust, accurate communication, support, and continuity. The nature of the relationship is cooperative rather than competitive. When co-workers are able to experience this cooperative relationship, criticism is likely to become more productive because the qualities inherent in such a relationship are incompatible with the obstacles to criticism — competition, blame, and a sense of overstepped boundaries — among peers. In general, information between peers flows more readily when peership has been created. Criticism is perceived as information that will benefit all rather than as an attempt to tell a co-worker what to do or to increase one's standing at a peer's expense.

At first glance, peership may seem to be synonymous with teamwork, but the two terms are quite different. A team comes together for a specific time period and to accomplish a specific goal. A film crew, for example, is put together for a few months for the purpose of making a film in accordance with certain production guidelines, such as budget and time frame. When the production is over, each crew member usually goes his or her separate way in search of another project. A task force is called together for a few days to come up with a strategic plan or to solve a company problem. Upon achieving its goal, its members break up and return to their daily functions. Baseball teams play as a team for six months to achieve the goal of winning a championship. At the end of the season, they, too, break up. (Although the baseball team does come back together again for the next season, it is common that if it is not successful, players will be traded before the start of the next season, resulting in a new team.) A successful team, whether it's a film crew, a task force, or a baseball team, is evaluated on whether it meets its goals.

In contrast to the idea of teamwork, "peership" is a broader term. It refers to a certain quality in the daily interactions that take place between co-workers, regardless of whether these co-workers are formally linked by a team goal or only occasionally rely on each other's efforts. As part of peership, work relationships are seen as ongoing and not defined by a temporal boundary. The emphasis is on development rather than outcome. The philosophy behind peership is that if relationships develop productively, teamwork is a natural consequence, not something that has to be called into play in a specific situation for a specific goal. In essence, peership means that members in an organization interact successfully with each other.

As peership develops in an organization, productivity is enhanced (assuming talent stays the same) because a more harmonious environment is created in which each organizational member can reach his or her full potential. The quality of the peer relationship in itself becomes a force that helps each individual do better. It is in this type of environment that the whole becomes greater than the sum of its parts.

Co-workers can thus facilitate productive criticism among their peers by developing peership — cooperative relationships — since cooperation forces people to interact in a generally more productive way, specifically improving the way they criticize each other. Since cooperation implies mutual benefits, the give-and-take of criticism between peers in a cooperative setting becomes defined as a means for helping both parties. Peers consequently begin to welcome criticism rather than dread it or use it destructively.

Building Peership

As Los Angeles Lakers general manager Jerry West aptly describes him, Boston Celtics superstar Larry Bird is someone who embodies the qualities that promote peership. Listen to what West says about Bird's relationship to his co-workers: "What he does is change everybody's perception of what the game is about. . . . But he keeps the emphasis on the team. He plays to make the team play better. He makes wins feel better and losses not hurt so much because no one's pointing any finger. He is such a special player. They just don't get any better than him."

Indeed, Larry Bird exemplifies peership, and it is not surprising that he has won his sport's Most Valuable Player Award three years in a row and has been a leading candidate several other years. As most basketball fans know, this award goes not to the best player in the league but to the one who contributes the most to the welfare of his team. In a similar vein, developing peership not only helps you contribute to the welfare of your organization but also enhances your value to your organization.

Peership can be developed in two ways. The first is by integrating your needs with those of your co-workers. The other involves being able to skillfully create cooperative relationships.

Giving to the Needy. How to build long-term cooperative relationships among co-workers is a question that has long plagued psychologists. The major reason for the difficulty associated with building such relationships can be explained in the context of need theory.

As noted, Abraham Maslow and many others have written that there are some human needs that are common to us all. Two of the most influential in work relationships are the need to succeed and the need to be accepted by others. A major glitch in peer relationships is that these two needs frequently conflict. It's tough to work well with people when you are competing with them for financial remuneration, advancement, and recognition, three things that most of us work for. Furthermore, we know that competition with peers works against us in that it makes us hypercritical of them, hardly a quality of psychological acceptance. Thinking "I will help a co-worker do better" is incompatible with the thought "I need to do better than my co-worker." The latter tends to triumph, and cooperative relationships and the Critical Edge are lost.

Since we know that competitiveness can actually impede our work, as well as sabotage our psychological need to be accepted, it is clearly not in our best interest to continue competing with our co-workers. Yet if we don't compete, how do we get our due respect? What co-workers need to do is learn how to integrate these two needs — the need to succeed and the need to be accepted — in a way that leads to successful behavior for each personally. This paves the way for peership.

One way this integration can be accomplished is through the concepts of celebrity and reputation. All of us are acquainted with celebrity: the big prize that organizational contestants vie for because it says that we did something special and brings us recognition from our organization. If celebrity is managed carefully, it can contribute to one's long-term image. Most people, and almost all co-workers, compete for celebrity, since we see it as a means for helping us move up the organization.

But there is another route to success, that of reputation. Reputation is acquired gradually and is more enduring. You gain a positive reputation from being trustworthy, skilled at making things happen, and able to achieve goals through working well with people. Seeking our opinion, inviting us to participate in a significant meeting, trusting us with confidential information, and thanking us for the role played behind the scenes are ways that people use to tell us we have built a reputation.

People who are effective in working with and through their co-workers tend to focus on building long-term reputation rather than short-term celebrity. Their strategy is to give celebrity to their co-workers — to give them credit, to let them be recognized, to help them stand out in their organization. Most co-workers are inevitably grateful when you help them achieve celebrity, for you are helping them satisfy much of their recognition and acceptance needs. The key point, however, is that while you have helped your co-workers, you have also enhanced your own career because you are increasing your reputation. Your contribution becomes valued, and in effect you, too, achieve greater success. In essence, you satisfy your needs by helping your co-workers do the same.

Most important, when you help your co-workers satisfy their own needs, you create peership and thereby productive criticism. Your helping spirit serves as a binding force that facilitates the flow of information, including criticism. And since your co-workers have already benefited from your efforts, they become more receptive to your future criticisms, which in turn helps you, too.

To implement these points, begin to think of areas in which you can assist your co-workers in achieving success. Look for ways to give them credit and recognition. Say positive things about them when they're not around. When possible, cover up for them. You'll end up being the MVP.

The Daily Task. The second way an employee can build peership is to recognize that co-workers are not fixed entities who "have to be" dealt with on an everyday basis but rather are people like himself or herself who have feelings, thoughts, and varying ways of responding to their environment. Every day, we interact with these individuals, usually not being cognizant of the fact that what we put out affects what we get back. Consequently, when we think about the bad relationships we have with our co-workers, we accept them as coming with the territory. Not having the power to make our co-workers disappear, we scheme about how to avoid them, be one up on them, or simply tolerate them; we practice "antagonistic cooperation," as David Riesman calls it in *The Lonely Crowd*. Furthermore, we almost always explain these relationships' not working by citing the qualities of other individuals. Acknowledging "I don't get along with my peers because I'm a jerk" doesn't seem to be a popular choice. Yet, it is this choice that makes peership possible, because it sparks the realization that we not only significantly contribute to the quality of our peer relationships but also have the power to change them.

We can begin to change the quality of our peer relationships from antagonistically cooperative to genuinely cooperative by building into our daily interactions the interpersonal factors that bring people in working relationships closer together.

One is empathy. Most people think of empathy as the ability to feel what others are feeling, to experience the world as if you are the other person. Here the term takes on a more cognitive connotation, meaning a mental flexibility that enables you to take into consideration the views of others while suspending your own judgment. When caught up in a discussion or a project, this cognitive empathy allows you to see your co-worker's point of view and create compromises or new solutions that integrate his work and move him in the same direction that you are going. That is, being empathic enables you to find the common ground.

Accurate communication is another important factor in bringing people closer together. One of the most disruptive forces in a cooperative relationship is the flow of distorted information. Two particular pitfalls are withholding information for no reason except to be in control and supplying incongruent information.

Many co-workers withhold information on the mistaken assumption that doing so increases their power over their co-workers. What they fail to realize is that when their co-workers find out that they knew something all along, these co-workers become angry and distrustful. These feelings actually minimize the power of the withholder.

Communicating incongruently is no better. When this occurs, co-workers become confused because what they hear is at odds with what they are experiencing. For example, telling a co-worker that you support her efforts and then acting in a way that indicates otherwise sets up a confused and suspicious relationship that is hardly conducive to working well together.

A vice president of a large Ohio hospital once initiated a project to improve the psychiatric department of her hospital. Working closely with another VP, she felt they had the same goals and were in agreement on what actions had to be taken. When push came to shove, though, she was dismayed that her counterpart acted in a way that was contrary to what they had talked about. Her counterpart started to cancel meetings, avoid the consultants involved in the project, and withdraw her department's financial commitment to the project. Consequently, the VP felt betrayed and, more important, found it exceedingly difficult to work with her co-worker on future projects. In recounting the experience, she says, "It was one of the worst moments of my career. I put a tremendous amount of energy into this project all for naught. But the real anguish was that I felt betrayed by my co-worker. She told me for weeks that she would support my efforts, and at the end, when it was do or die, she deserted me. It really hurt."

Without accurate communication, co-workers cannot move in the same direction, because they do not know their co-workers' agendas. The possibility of cooperation increases when information is accurately communicated between co-workers since everybody knows where the other stands. A common ground can then be defined, and options can be created. Here, the key is to continually let your co-workers know what is going on, what you are doing, what you expect of them.

Another factor to take into account is support. Usually thought of as agreeing with your co-worker's views, the term takes on a more humane quality in this context. To be supportive amounts simply to encouraging others to follow through on their goals, to be enthusiastic for them when they are feeling discouraged, to be frustrated along with them when they suffer a setback, and to motivate them to overcome it. This type of support breeds peership because it energizes the environment. When it's absent, you are likely to find an environment similar to the one at Twentieth Century Fox before Barry Diller turned it around. Jonathan Dolgen, a senior VP for Fox, described the situation: "It was like a car where everything is broken at least a little. The attitude was, 'Can't do. It's too hard. Even if we work at it, we won't finish, so why bother?' "

Although these three factors — empathy, accurate communication, and support — are all important in their own right, they have their greatest power when they are connected, when they are all used on a daily basis without interruption. In essence, it is the continuity of the three factors that shapes the quality of the working relationship. Being supportive of a co-worker on Monday is fine, but it will not change the quality of the relationship if the support does not persist. The same is true for being empathic and conveying accurate communication. It is this continuity that most readily promotes peership. And as peership becomes the daily routine, so does productive criticism. Each serves to reinforce the other.

SUPERIOR PEERSHIP

Co-workers are not the only people who can promote productive peer criticism and help develop peership. Their superior can play a big role, too. The first and most obvious way a superior can inspire productive peer criticism among subordinates is to develop peership in his or her own peer relationships. By presenting a model of peership, the superior communicates to the staff how they are expected to act with each other. In effect, this helps the superior set the tone of the environment that he or she wants the staff to develop. When enough superiors at different levels of the organizational hierarchy provide examples of peership, the message becomes clear that cooperative relationships are valued. The results to be expected are better interdepartmental relationships, more collaborative projects, and a greater sense of organizational cohesiveness.

A more direct way that superiors can increase productive peer criticism among their subordinates is to tie individual success to how much each contributes to meeting departmental goals. The key is to design a system that makes each person's success interdependent on his or her co-workers'. In such a system, workers inevitably push for their co-workers because it is in their own best interest for them to succeed. Members of the staff begin to root for each other. The sports industry finds this strategy particularly useful. Each player tends to root for the others because, regardless of his own play, he will still share in World Series or Super Bowl money if his co-workers are successful enough to make it to the championship.

Superiors can also attempt to promote peership among subordinates simply by recognizing it in a positive manner when they see it. It is important to explain what positive action you see and how it contributes to group goals. It is also wise, intermittently, to let the other subordinates know of their co-workers' peership-promoting actions and how they have affected the work of the group. Theoretically, the good feelings the superior expresses to the subordinate in response to such behavior, the sense of being recognized by the boss, and the gratitude the subordinate receives from co-workers will be enough to make each co-worker actively work toward peership.

Finally, superiors can help develop peership by setting up formal systems that promote interaction among peers. Jack Welch, CEO of General Electric, did this. To add a cohesiveness to GE and promote synergy, Welch in 1986 created the Corporate Executive Council. Every quarter it brings together the fourteen business leaders and the heads of the corporate staff departments, plus the CEO team. In pre-Welch times, this group might have seen one another only at an annual GE gala, and then only for chitchat. Now they meet for frank, often heated discussion. Roger Schipke, who heads GE's major-appliance business, describes it like this: "It's open-kimono time. Business plans are held up to scrutiny, and no one is shy about criticizing. Yet everyone is expected to help out, offering suggestions that might work in another part of the company."

ORGANIZING PEERSHIP

What can the organization as an entity do to encourage peership? One option is to sanction it formally by implementing a peer review system. Here, a selected number of co-workers are asked to evaluate each other's work. Through this process, each co-worker learns how his peers perceive the quality of his work and ways in which they think he can improve. Many hospitals, such as Cedar Sinai in Los Angeles, are implementing peer review systems for their nursing staff on the assumptions that they will improve the quality of care and that the exchange of productive criticism will enhance staff relationships.

One specific program for developing peership and facilitating productive criticism among peers is in place at GE's Management Development Center in Croton, New York. Employees who become new GE managers come to "Crotonville" and are given case studies. They work in groups and present their analysis of a "GE problem" to other groups, which then criticize their decisions. Besides passing on methods of cooperation, the course teaches people that they can handle bigger problems than they thought. Participants seem to relish the course. One radar programs manager in GE's aerospace business was part of a team devising ways to expand a service business in GE's power systems group. "It's an 'up' experience," she says. Criticism from her co-workers prompted her to delegate more to the four hundred people she manages.

If a formal system isn't right for your organization, peer criticism can be encouraged more informally. At Northeast Apparel, for example, it is not unusual for managers to be assigned on short notice to evaluate their co-workers' operations. Sometimes they travel two thousand miles to accomplish the TASK. According to President Reisman, this productive exchange of information appears to be leading the company to greater efficiency, profitability, and cohesiveness. Reisman also holds gala week-long bashes for his managers so that they can meet each other and get each other's input on how to run their shops more effectively. Although this is also a time for celebration, he makes sure that ideas are exchanged by having new managers dine with more experienced ones throughout the week.

Whether one uses a formal peer review system or a more relaxed one, the emphasis must be as much on promoting interpersonal relationships as it is on improving each person's performance. Many co-workers forget this, since they tend to focus on what their co-workers are doing wrong or how they themselves are doing it better. As a result, the exchange becomes competitive and destructive. It is the wise organization that continually points out the purpose of peer criticism.

Another way the organization can promote peership is to build it into its value system, with the expectation that the organization's members will internalize the same value. One means of implementing this is to come down hard on those individuals whose behavior has no other purpose than to further their own political ends and to structure the reward system so that people who have good peer relationships are rewarded appropriately. As they go through the peership motions, even if only for the sake of reward at first, they will come to enjoy the value of peership in itself.

In the end, each individual is responsible for developing peership with his or her co-workers. Because the rewards are seldom immediate and because, despite everything, we do want to compete and to shine at work, it is often a monstrous task to develop peership on a day-to-day basis. But those who do have the Critical Edge. To this end, it is good policy for each of us when we go to work to remember Ken Kragen's peership message to the superstars who recorded the song "We Are the World": "Check your egos at the door."

Chapter 8

Performance Appraisal: A Special Kind of Criticism

EVERY YEAR, hundreds of thousands of managers and supervisors sit down with their subordinates, either through choice or edict, to perform what has now become a corporate ritual: performance appraisal. Performance appraisal, or PA, is supposed to be a process by which an organization measures and evaluates an individual employee's behavior and accomplishments over a finite time period. Typically, the appraisal is conducted annually by the employee's immediate manager. The judgments are often used subsequently to make administrative decisions (e.g., regarding promotion or salary) that directly affect the employee.

Performance appraisal is not new. As far back as the third century A.D., emperors of China's Wei dynasty employed an Imperial Rater to evaluate the performance of the official family members. Chinese philosopher Sin You's criticism of this system is in tune with many of the criticisms heard today about PA: "The Imperial Rater of Nine Grades seldom rates men according to their merits but always according to his likes and dislikes."

Robert Owen is credited with first establishing PA in industry. Owner of cotton mills in Scotland in the early 1800s, he hung a cube of wood over each employee's work station. The wood denoted, according to its shade, the different grades for deportment: white for excellent, yellow for good, blue for indifferent, and black for bad.

In the United States, PA probably began in 1813, when army general Lewis Cass submitted to the War Department an evaluation of each of his men, describing them in such colorful terms as "a good-natured man" or "a knave despised by all." Thirty years later, appraisal was implemented and soon became widespread in the U.S. federal government. By the 1950s PA was an accepted procedure in many organizations. Common to most systems were the following characteristics:

1. Top management was exempt from appraisal. PA was often applied only to hourly workers; when management was included at all, it was usually only at the lower levels.
2. Graph rating scales (rating traits) were used.
3. One or two different forms covered all employees involved.

These characteristics are still common to many of today's PA systems.

The passage of the 1964 Civil Rights Act and the 1966 and 1970 Equal Employment Opportunity Commission Guidelines for the regulation of employment selection procedures put strong legal pressure on organizations to structure their PA systems. Representatives of major corporations found themselves in court trying to validate the basis on which salary, promotion, retention, and hiring decisions were made. Since PA ratings were frequently used for such personnel decisions, they became a useful source of information in documenting prima facie evidence of discrimination against protected groups. Other legislation and the women's movement are putting continual pressure on organizations to increase the validity of their PA systems. For example, the United States Supreme Court handed down an opinion in the 1975 case *Albermarle* v. *Moody* that legally required supervisors to use more than vague and subjective criteria in reaching employment decisions.

Although there are many aspects of PA that are the same today as they were several decades ago, some changes in PA practices have been made. Two major trends are the emergence of hybrid systems (PA systems that incorporate features of several different PA approaches) and the increased use of MBO (Management by Objectives). Hybrid systems take advantage of multiple, different PA approaches by integrating the strengths of each approach. MBO changed PA systems by introducing the concept of formally setting goals and then evaluating the employee's performance in relationship to his or her goal achievement. Although some surveys show that MBO is the most frequently used PA system, other studies indicate that essay responses (writing brief descriptions of how an employee functions at a given task) and rating scales (rating sets of employee traits) are more widely used. The research discrepancies are probably due to several factors, including which system an organization thinks is most effective.

How does this affect you? Considering that 95 percent of large businesses, 84 percent of small businesses, and 73 percent of general organizations have a performance appraisal system in place (numbers that will increase), the chances are great that you will soon be giving (and/or receiving) a performance appraisal. If you and your organization are using an inappropriate PA system, you both are legally liable for any inappropriate decisions you make based on the system. Equally important, you are also wasting time and energy (and money) by going through an ineffective process. The result is that you fail to get the improved behavior from subordinates that you need, making it that much more difficult for you to manage your own responsibilities. Similarly, if your superior is not doing PA effectively, your work is not only impaired, but you may be missing out on raises and promotions that you justly deserve. The bottom line is that it pays for you to improve your performance appraisal system. This is especially important in light of the fact that several surveys conducted for this book strongly suggest that more than a third of PA users feel their system is ineffective.

The purpose of this chapter is to help you improve your PA skills and system. First, you can make your PA system better by learning how to criticize it. Second, you can improve your skills by learning a general framework for conducting — and receiving — a productive performance appraisal.

PERFORMANCE APPRAISAL IS ALSO CRITICISM

It is important to recognize from the start that performance appraisal is a form of criticism. This is why giving and taking criticism productively will enhance your PA skills; you are practicing many PA skills every time you give and take criticism productively. True, there are some obvious differences, but these differences are merely a matter of PA's and general criticism's being on different places on a continuum of feedback. For example, there are differences in frequency: Criticism is an everyday occurrence, while PA is usually a once-a-year procedure. Criticism usually relates to a specific task performed at a specific moment, while PA applies to the person's complete performance over a long period. Criticism can be given anywhere, while PA usually takes place in the superior's office. Criticism can usually be given in a short burst of time, while PA is given over an extended block of time, usually one to four hours. As we have seen from the earlier chapters, criticism is exchanged between employees at all job levels, while PA is almost always a top-down procedure. Finally, criticism is usually structured informally, while PA is very formal, to the extent that there is a specific agenda to cover as well as a very specific procedure to follow.

On the other hand, there are other characteristics associated with the feedback continuum that bring criticism and performance appraisal close together. In terms of their most basic nature, both performance appraisal and criticism involve communicating evaluative information. A related and significant similarity, though, is that they are both experienced as a negative event. The information communicated is perceived as a negative; the accompanying feelings are typically negative; the process of communicating is usually marked by anger and defensiveness. These are strong parallels and indicate how equally difficult it is for most people to criticize effectively and to conduct a productive performance appraisal. Basically, despite their differences, criticism and PA are two sides of the same coin. Given this similarity to daily criticism, PA must also be considered a set of communications that one must learn to give and receive productively in order to capture the Critical Edge.

IMPROVING PERFORMANCE APPRAISAL: THE SUPERIOR'S ROLE

As we have seen in other critical encounters, the superior (the individual conducting the appraisal), the subordinate (the receiver of the appraisal), and the organization must all do their part to make a procedure effective, and this naturally applies to PA as well. Let us turn our attention first to the ways in which you the superior can use PA to your own advantage and your subordinate's.

Criticizing Your Appraisal

The first step toward improving your PA skills is to criticize productively the way you currently conduct a performance appraisal; the outcome of your criticism will be that you have a better PA MO: Performance Appraisal Modus Operandi.

Unfortunately, most managers and supervisors do not know how to go about criticizing their current PA MO. The basic reason for this seems to be that they are not educated and trained in the PA process. As a result, it is hard, if not impossible, for them to improve their own PA skills, let alone their organization's system. The idea here is not to suggest a specific procedure for PA — that will come later — but to set forth a series of six questions whose answers will give you productive criticisms of your current PA MO. Taking action on these criticisms then helps you improve. These questions are generic, so exploring the underlying issues will help improve any PA system.

1. What is your philosophy of PA? Your philosophy of PA is important because it shapes your attitudes and actions; it shapes the way that you conduct a PA. A philosophy that advocates collaborative behavior will create different PA skills than a philosophy that includes a belief in winning through intimidation. Posing this question is intended not to initiate an argument about which or whose philosophy is better but rather to draw attention to how important it is for you to think about your own views on PA. Once you have developed and/or recognized your own PA philosophy, you can begin to act in ways that will help implement it. Here are some suggested philosophical PA issues to consider:

- Why are you doing PA? Do you personally want to do it?
- What if your organization's philosophy of PA is different from yours? How do you plan to integrate the differences?
- What is your responsibility to the appraisee?
- What role does confidentiality play? What if an appraisee in a PA session asks you to keep secret certain things that you feel others should know about? What if he or she will give certain information only if you give your word not to repeat it?

· What should the goal of PA be?
· Is PA fair?

The fact that there are countless answers to these questions only serves to reiterate how important it is to have and be clear on your own PA philosophy, since it is your philosophy that gives you the impetus to make your PAs better.

2. What are you going to appraise? A fundamental task in setting up any PA system is to decide what exactly you are going to appraise. More specifically, what is meant by performance? Some people believe that performance is a specific outcome, a matter of results. Thus, the saleswoman is appraised on the basis of how many sales she made; the baseball player is appraised on the basis of his batting average and other statistics; the teacher is appraised on the basis of how well his class did on national testing. Others take the position that performance is a matter of certain personal attributes that a person demonstrates — leadership, responsibility, initiative. These qualities are appraised because they are assumed to have an effect on how well the person does a job. Although there is no correct way to define performance, experts in PA lean toward a definition that encompasses both views: Performance is both the results that people get on the job and whatever qualities they demonstrate that affect those results. Performance, then, is the outcome of actions on the job, and it is also the qualities and actions that produce the outcome. But regardless of how you define performance, it is essential that you give the question of what you intend to appraise some thought. Your answer will help you clarify several things, including:

· What you think is required for success
· Your expectations for each person you appraise
· Whether you think of performance as meaning the same thing for everyone you appraise
· Whether it makes sense to appraise the performance of everyone in the same way

In essence, you begin to think about why you are looking for certain behaviors, and in the process you develop your management and business philosophy, including a knowledge of what you want out of PA. An important point to remember is that people do lots of things on the job that don't affect results. And people also display many characteristics on the job that don't influence the outcome of their work. None of these things should come under the heading of performance. The key question is always: What difference does it make? If someone does something on the job that makes no difference in results, then that behavior shouldn't be discussed in a performance appraisal session.

3. Is your PA system valid? Validity refers to whether your PA is accurately measuring the selected behavior or performance dimensions. For example, if leadership is a criterion for performance on your forms, then you must ask yourself how you go about measuring leadership. Your answer might include considering how frequently people ask the individual for advice or how many times this individual takes responsibility for projects. But are you sure these measures truly reflect leadership? Maybe you are really measuring intelligence.

The question of validity is important because if you are not accurately measuring what you purport to, then the subsequent decisions you make on this basis are unlikely to produce the results you desire. Many times, low validity has led to the wrong person getting the job.

A significant point here is that even if your organization's PA system does not have a high degree of validity, you can increase its validity through your own application of it. A frequent finding about performance appraisal is that many appraisers in the same organization have different ideas concerning how to measure a certain behavior. Ask five principals how they would measure what good teaching is and you are sure to get at least five different answers. The same is true for a board of directors discussing how to measure whether a CEO is a strong leader. The problem that this causes is that you end up with different appraisers in the same organization measuring the same behavior differently. While this is not necessarily bad, it is often perceived by the appraisees as being unfair. One individual gets a raise for showing initiative, while his cohort is overlooked even though he has acted similarly. The bypassed worker is confused because in his mind, he has demonstrated as much initiative as the other fellow. Indeed, he might have. Unfortunately, his manager has a different measure for initiative. Or it might even be that he has the same manager, but this manager uses different criteria to measure initiative in each of her subordinates. Therefore, it is good policy to inform each of your subordinates not only what behaviors or qualities you will be appraising but also how you will measure them. While this does not completely solve the problem, it does help.

Appraisers, then, need to ask themselves: How will I measure the appraised behavior? and Have I selected an accurate way of measuring the behavior in question? As a word of caution, there have been many court decisions in favor of the employee on the grounds that the organization's and/or manager's way of appraising his or her performance has not been valid.

4. Do you involve your subordinate in the PA process? Typically, the role of the appraisee in PA has been and continues to be predominantly passive. When there is appraisee participation, it is usually only during the actual PA session; the appraisee is asked for her evaluation of her performance, or if she has any suggestions on how to improve her behavior for the next year. However, there are many other ways in which an employee can participate in the PA process; goal setting, criteria development, data collection, self-rating, and problem solving are just a few. Getting and keeping subordinates involved in the PA process is important because the PA literature indicates that employee participation increases motivation to improve. One study described by David DeVries and Ann Morrison in their book, *Performance Appraisal on the Line,* shows that individuals who were involved in the goal-setting process set higher goals and had better success in achieving them compared with those who were not involved in the goal-setting process. The same authors cite studies that support the impact of involvement on satisfaction; both managers and employees reported being more satisfied when employees were more involved.

5. How do you know you are a qualified appraiser? Anytime you do a PA, you are giving your own evaluation of how the person is doing. The issues that appraisers need to confront are these: What makes your evaluation accurate? and Are you qualified to judge the person's performance? (Recall Plato's and Aristotle's emphasis on criteria.) For example, what makes a high school principal a qualified appraiser of what constitutes good teaching? What makes a supervising psychologist a qualified appraiser of whether his psychology interns are good therapists? How does a newspaper editor know her assessment of a reporter is accurate?

No doubt almost every manager wants to think of himself or herself as qualified to evaluate a subordinate's performance. Nevertheless, many aren't. And as with day-to-day criticism, if the subject of your evaluation does not see you as a qualified source, there is apt to be resistance. Some people believe that the appraiser should be able to do the job involved better than those whom he or she is appraising. But this is not realistic or even appropriate. The fact is, much more often than not, we look for people who can do a job that we can't do or for a person who can do it much better than we can. Just because we are appraising them doesn't mean we know more about their jobs. And subordinates know this to be true. Therefore, rather than trying to be a know-it-all, the appraiser is better off assessing and substantiating the right to appraise. Ask yourself:

1. What is my familiarity with this person's job?
2. How do I know he is doing good, bad, or adequate work?
3. What are my appraisals based on? What data do I have and where did I get them?

You can follow up on this and enhance your qualifications by continually educating yourself about your subordinate's work. The high school principal who is abreast of educational research will probably be more qualified to evaluate teaching effectiveness than his counterpart who hasn't opened a research periodical in years. As you become a more qualified evaluator, the effectiveness of your PA system improves.

6. What do you do with your results? After a PA, and after decisions are made, many managers and supervisors take their completed forms, put them into the appropriate file, and forget about them until next year's appraisal. Doing so limits the effectiveness of any PA system because its potential for improving future performance has been ignored; it has been used only to assess the past and not to improve the future. Furthermore, the job issues discussed in the PA session are usually not brought up again until the next PA session.

Being cognizant of how you use your PA results will help you improve your PA system and skills. Noting whether and how you use them helps you and the individual in question see the value and the importance of the information, if any. Thus, actively using the results communicates to all involved that PA is a serious process and that the information collected should not be taken lightly. Nor should the person collecting the information be taken lightly.

Furthermore, if you are going to take the time to conduct a PA, you might as well use the evaluation to your own and your appraisee's advantage by following through on the recommendations. For example, one manager in an electronics company received an appraisal that included a recommendation that he work more closely with other companies. During the next six months, his superior frequently asked him whether he was doing so. This gave the appraisee a clear message that the recommendation was important and was to be acted upon.

When people see that PA results will be used in a broader sense than just in making one-time administrative decisions, they become motivated to get involved in the PA process and, equally important, begin to question whether it is a good PA system and how it can be made better.

7. **How do you feel when giving a PA?** Most people find a face-to-face formal evaluation extremely uncomfortable. The common feeling is anxiety, which not only impedes the PA process but also causes defensiveness and anger, thus always derailing the process. Therefore, it is extremely important to get in touch with how you feel about conducting a PA in general and how you feel when you encounter the expected rough moments that surface in most PAs. For example, how do you feel when the appraisee becomes angry, silent, or agrees too readily? How do you feel when you have to confront the unsatisfactory or marginal performer? Until you can feel comfortable in the PA process, it will be difficult to make it productive, because your feelings will create a tense environment, much in the same way that an individual criticism encounter frequently becomes tense. As with giving and taking criticism, you can begin to feel more comfortable in the PA process by recognizing that PA is in your best interest and that to formally evaluate an employee is part of helping him or her to improve.

In sum, any individual can improve his or her own PA skills and PA system by answering these critical questions:

1. What is your philosophy of PA?
2. What are you going to appraise?
3. Is your PA system valid?
4. Do you involve your subordinate in the PA process?
5. How do you know you are a qualified appraiser?
6. What do you do with your results?
7. How do you feel when giving a PA?

Conducting a Performance Appraisal

The second way superiors can improve their PA skills is by learning a general framework for conducting productive performance appraisals. The first step is to define what is actually meant by PA. Although there are many definitions of performance appraisal, we will define it as an ongoing process between a superior and a subordinate, set up with the purpose of discovering how the subordinate is currently performing on the job, why he or she is performing at this level, and how the subordinate can improve performance in the future so that the subordinate, the superior, and the organization all benefit. Note that in this definition, the emphasis is on a process that has as its main goal to improve the performance of the subordinate, not to decide whether he or she is going to get a raise or a promotion. Thus, the presented model is generic to any PA, regardless of how the results are to be used.

The Five Phases of Performance Appraisal

A performance appraisal is composed of five basic phases. First, tasks are established and performance standards are developed and discussed with the subordinate. Second, a work period allows the employee time to accomplish these tasks, while the superior monitors the activities and provides guidance and feedback. Third, the superior informs the subordinate of an upcoming PA interview, and both prepare for it. Fourth, the interview is conducted, terminating with the establishment of the tasks and standards for the next period. Fifth, a follow-up session is conducted to discuss the previous phase and to review the actions that have been deemed necessary for improving performance. The follow-up session also provides both superior and subordinate with an opportunity to air any feelings and thoughts that were not discussed in the PA interview, as well as to appraise the appraisal process for the purpose of improving it.

Phase 1: Assigning Tasks and Setting Performance Standards. Effective task planning and assignment are the key to an effective performance appraisal. Subordinates must know in advance what is expected of them, by when it should be done, and what the criteria for success are. Thus, effective goal setting is critical to the productive handling of this phase.

Goals are crucial to the PA process because they serve as criteria for determining whether the subordinate has achieved an acceptable result. An increase of 20 percent in sales has little meaning if there has been no standard set up in advance. Perhaps the subordinate should have achieved a 40 percent increase or more. Goals give the subordinate, superior, and organization direction, and the degree to which goals are met is an indication of how well people are performing.

Much has been written pertaining to effective goal setting. A survey of the literature indicates that for goals to be effective, they must meet the following criteria:

1. Goals must be realistic and require optimal effort. The principle to adhere to is to make goals neither too easy nor too hard. If goals are too easy, some subordinates will work just hard enough to attain the goal but not a bit more. Thus the subordinate loses because he is not working up to his potential and therefore does not develop himself. Easy goals also may make the subordinate feel bored or feel that his job is not challenging. As a result, he may look for another job. Goals that are easy to accomplish also hurt the organization because if the subordinate does only what is necessary, minimum results are achieved. On the other hand, if goals are too hard, frustration, anxiety, and disappointment are bound to follow. Some people will take the attitude "It's impossible. Why try?" Others will become so anxious that despite their efforts to meet the goals, their performance will actually deteriorate.

The key is to find what Aristotle called the golden mean — the point between two extremes at which everything comes into proper balance. You want to set goals that induce the right amount of stress, urgency, and exertion. Goals should be tough enough to stimulate extra effort but not so out of line that they make people feel hopeless. In other words, goals should be realistically difficult. Goals that are realistically difficult elicit optimal effort. The obvious question is, "How do you determine what is realistically difficult?" and unfortunately, the only answer is, "It depends." It all depends on the factors involved: the job to be done and the person who has to do it. An optimal goal for one person might be too easy for another and too hard for someone else. Thus, an important asset for effective goal setting is a good understanding of the person involved — her strengths and weaknesses, her interests, her ambitions. Last but not least, it is essential that the subordinate also believe that she is capable of achieving the goal.

2. Goals must be specific. The two points to consider here are what you want to achieve and the time allotted for achieving it.

If goals are vague, they cannot produce optimal results because they will not explain what's optimal. Furthermore, if they are global, you set the stage for argument, since while the superior may point out that the goal hasn't been met, the subordinate may say the opposite.

SUPERIOR: Well, George, you didn't meet the production goal.

SUBORDINATE: Of course I did. The goal was to improve production and I did.

SUPERIOR: Yes, George, but you only improved it four percent.

SUBORDINATE: Well, that's an improvement.

In this example, you would improve your goal setting by stating exactly what is meant by improvement, say, increasing production by 6 percent or more. However, by when is this to be accomplished? Next week, next month, or next year?

SUPERIOR: Well, George, you haven't met the goal. You've only increased production by four percent.

SUBORDINATE: That's true, but in a few months, it will be up to six percent.

Always build a deadline into the goal. Otherwise, the implied message is that time is not a factor, and the subordinate may feel within his rights in saying that he is always on target.

3. Goals must be comprehensive. Imagine a subordinate who had a goal of increasing her department's sales quota by 10 percent within six months. At the end of that time, she has increased it 30 percent. On the surface, it looks as if she did a terrific job. However, upon closer examination, you see that the increase in production was actually due to an increase in staff and a bigger advertising budget. In other words, the increase in sales had nothing to do with the subordinate's efforts.

Making goals comprehensive refers to the need to take into account all the conditions that make optimal goal achievement possible, so that when you appraise a subordinate's goal achievement, you can decide whether she met the goal solely as a result of her own actions. In the example above, this is not the case; the addition of staff and a bigger advertising budget increased the sales quota. Without them, the subordinate actually might have achieved a sales quota significantly below her goal.

Failure to set comprehensive goals leads to discussions like this:

SUPERIOR: Well, you increased your quota, but you were lucky.
SUBORDINATE: What do you mean, I was lucky? It went twenty percent higher than expected.
SUPERIOR: You were lucky. The ad budget increased.
SUBORDINATE: So what. I still did it.

In this case, the subordinate would have to prove that the increase in quota was in fact attributable to her own efforts rather than to the budget and staff changes. You can avoid such discussions by simply stipulating that goal achievement be attributable solely to the subordinate's actions.

4. Goals must be understandable. An optimal goal is one that is totally understood by the subordinate. It may be worded in plain English or technical jargon; the only criterion is that the subordinate understand it.

There are several other factors that are important in the goal-setting process. First, as mentioned earlier, goals are more likely to be met when the subordinate is involved in formulating them. Besides allowing the subordinate to help make the goals optimally realistic, involving the subordinate makes them more meaningful to him, since he is able to see the rationale behind them. Without this involvement, the subordinate frequently sees the goal as arbitrary.

Second, you must remember that you and your subordinate rarely have complete freedom in setting goals. For example, the goals you set with your subordinate will be influenced by the goals of your own boss, and your subordinate's, in turn, will influence the goals of his subordinate. Your goals will also be influenced by other departments and your own co-workers. You may find that an optimal goal is an increase of 20 percent in sales, but if the advertising department puts its money into another division's product, your goal may be unachievable, regardless of Herculean efforts. Outside forces such as current economic conditions and competing products will also affect your goals.

There is also the notion of short-term versus long-term goals to keep in mind. Short-term goals basically are to be used as steps to achieve the long-term goals. They keep the subordinate on track and also provide him with encouragement, for achieving each short-term goal is a successful experience and thus serves to motivate him to achieve the next goal. Therefore, it is important to break long-term goals into short-term goals.

All of these factors must be taken into account when you set goals. If they are, and if your goals meet the criteria discussed, you and your subordinate will be in good shape to perform the next phase of a productive PA.

Phase 2: Establishing Work Period and Supervisory Guidance. There is more to this phase than simply waiting for the employee to finish the assigned tasks and to meet her goals. Ongoing monitoring and feedback can assist the individual in attaining the standards established in phase 1. Actions to consider are: notifying the employee of unforeseen problems, discussing periodic budget and expense reports, forewarning her of developing conditions, acknowledging outstanding or unusual achievements, offering productive criticism, notifying her of commendations or complaints received, and, of course, revising objectives or responsibilities when necessary.

The essential criterion of this phase is to allow the subordinate enough time to achieve her goals. Otherwise, you will end up doing a PA session prematurely. (This is another reason realistic expectations are important.)

Phase 3: Preparing. This phase begins approximately two to three weeks before the PA interview. Overall, it is necessary for the simple reason that you cannot do an effective appraisal interview off the cuff. You can do it well only if you have systematically prepared for it.

Preparation helps the PA process in several ways. First, you will be able to arrive at a much more factual appraisal, instead of just relying on a vague estimation of what you and your subordinate think is going on. Most of the data that you need will not be at your fingertips. Records, dates — these are hard data and are usually in files or computers. It takes time to get this information, and if you don't have it and study it before you conduct the appraisal session, your evaluation will probably be based on nothing more than cloudy recollections. Furthermore, without the data, you may spend a lot of time arguing with the subordinate as to who is right about his performance.

SUPERIOR: As I recall, Frank, you only increased orders about five percent.

SUBORDINATE: What are you talking about? It's more like eight or nine percent!

SUPERIOR: No way. I know you didn't improve sales that much.

SUBORDINATE: Oh yeah? Let's go check the files and see who's right.

Exchanges such as these not only take up time, they create tension. They turn the appraisal session into a contest to see who is right and who is wrong.

A second reason that preparation is important is because if you are well organized and have analyzed the data in advance, you are less likely to become emotional in the actual PA session. Angry outbursts on the part of your subordinate will be less frequent because the discussion will be based on facts. This does not mean that the PA session will not be emotional, but at least your preparation will help keep destructive emotions at a minimum.

A third reason for preparation is that it will keep you on track.

Your preparation will help you develop a format that you will be able to follow. Preparing notes will allow you to remember what points you want to cover and, at the same time, will prevent you from forgetting certain information about the subordinate's performance as well as recommendations that you want to make.

In order to reap some of these benefits, during the preparation stage you must fulfill several objectives. You must accurately examine how the subordinate has been performing; analyze the factors that account for his performance; develop action plans that will help you and the subordinate improve his performance; and think of how you can best get the subordinate to cooperate with you during the appraisal session.

It is important to remember that any assessment, or recommendations that you formulate, are tentative; you must reserve final judgment until after the PA session, since your subordinate will have his own evaluation of his performance, and it may affect yours.

Phase 4: Conducting the Performance Appraisal Session. Conducting the PA session is analogous to the "what to do when criticizing" stage in our model for productive criticism; the key difference is that the PA session is much longer. Thus, the PA encounter usually involves much more interaction. The PA session can be conceptualized as a process of several steps. Although the steps are orderly, you will probably find yourself using each step several times in the PA session.

As we go through the model, we will assume that the PA session will be productive, that the appraiser and the appraisee will engage in a worthwhile process that benefits both of them. This will make the model easier to follow. We will deal later with the major obstacles that the appraiser is likely to encounter and see how they can be effectively handled.

The first step is to break the tension and create rapport. A performance appraisal is a formal evaluation, and with its formality comes an air of tension. In order for communication to flow readily and for both parties to be able to objectively appraise the data, a more comfortable psychological climate must be created. Thus, you must build rapport. The time it takes to build rapport will vary with each subordinate, but a good working relationship on a daily basis will facilitate the process. Don't worry if you are spending time on casual conversation, for it is part of the process of getting the sub-ordinate ready to participate. The rule is to make sure your sociability suits the subordinate you are appraising. You might find it helpful to point out that many subordinates find PA stressful, so any feelings of nervousness on her part are appropriate. During this phase, also explain the benefits of the appraisal. As the subordinate begins to see that the appraisal is a helping process, not one in which she needs to feel threatened, rapport is built. To explain the benefits effectively, you must know what the subordinate wants from her job. As in criticism, the proposed benefits must be important to the subordi-nate. The key here is to tie the benefit into the results of the appraisal; emphasize that if the subordinate does what the appraisal will indicate she should, she can expect to get her benefits. (This is similar to the contract technique for changing someone's behavior.)

Assuming you and your subordinate are comfortable, the next step calls for both of you to get down to business; each candidly evaluates the subordinate's performance. It is important to have the subordi-nate evaluate herself because it gives her an opportunity to let the superior know how she assesses her own performance. In effect, she is able to tell the superior where she is mentally sitting. By evaluating herself, she is forced to take a hard look at how she is performing and at what areas she needs to improve upon. Asking the subordinate to evaluate herself also makes her interact with the superior. Fur-thermore, the subordinate's self-evaluation frequently provides the superior with new information.

There are two points to remember. First, your asking the subor-dinate to evaluate her own performance should not come as a surprise to the subordinate; it is not a trap, and you are not trying to catch her off guard. Therefore, your subordinate should be told way in advance that she will be asked to evaluate her own performance so that she can prepare. She, too, needs to collect data, formulate ques-tions, and just get comfortable with the idea that she will have to evaluate herself.

Second, your subordinate's evaluation should precede your own. This ensures that she will have plenty of time to make her presen-tation. Sometimes when the superior presents first, he uses up so much time that either the subordinate is put in a time squeeze to do an adequate presentation or the superior grows impatient with the whole proceeding and cuts the subordinate short. This causes the subordinate to be resistant to the appraisal results because she feels that she has not been listened to in a fair and respectful manner. If she asks for more time to present her evaluation, it sounds like a defensive reaction. On the other hand, if the superior runs out of time, it is easy for him to reschedule another session because he has the work power. It is also important that your subordinate's evaluation precede yours so that her evaluation is less likely to be colored by yours (the same point made earlier about using role playing).

When your subordinate is evaluating her performance, your task is to assess her evaluation. To do this effectively, you must listen carefully. If you have trouble following her or don't understand what she is saying, ask her to clarify. Ask yourself what data she is using to back up her points, and, if the data are accurate, whether her conclusions make sense. When she is finished, acknowledge the points on which you agree. Then begin your evaluation.

Make sure you present only a few points at a time, since this will make it easier for your subordinate to digest what you are saying. Pause between points so the subordinate can ask questions that will clarify her understanding and allow you to find out how she feels about what you are saying. Refer to your data with each point so your subordinate will know how you have arrived at your evaluation. If you have done adequate preparation, this information will be logical and easy to present.

Remember the rules of productive criticism: Use no blaming or accusatory statements. Speak from your reference point. Be calm, for if you become emotional, chances are that your subordinate will follow suit. When you are finished, summarize where you agree and disagree with your subordinate's evaluation. (How to handle disagreement will be discussed later.)

It is at this point of the PA process that many people make a significant mistake: They proceed to working out final goals and recommendations for the next year. While this is important, there is another part of the process that must come first — clearing the air of distressing emotions. When people disagree in a PA, emotions tend to flare up; even if things appear to be calm, there is usually an underlying tension that will impede any productive problem solving, a requirement for the PA process to be effective. Therefore at this point, as you did initially, you want to reduce tension and resolve any disagreements before you proceed. (This is an example of using each step in the PA process several times.)

When this is accomplished, you are ready for the final step: working out the results of the PA. This includes developing goals and action plans that will specifically help the subordinate achieve her new goals. Here it is important to reiterate the benefits to the subordinate and to tie them directly to the goals you have formulated. Check again for your subordinate's understanding of what has been decided. Also assess her commitment to follow through. Finally, schedule a follow-up session. Doing so will remind the subordinate that PA is serious and that you intend to help her meet her goals.

A summary of this stage is:

1. Break the tension and create rapport.
2. Get down to business: present evaluations of the subordinate's performance, subordinate first.
3. Reduce tension, resolve disagreements.
4. Work out the results of the PA.

Phase 5: Conducting the Follow-up Session. The follow-up session should be held approximately four weeks after the appraisal session. This gives you and the subordinate plenty of time to think about what transpired in the PA session. Here, you want to have the subordinate reevaluate the PA session. Does he still agree with the evaluation? Do the goals and action plans still make sense? At this time, you will also find out if the subordinate is having any problems in implementing the results of the PA session. If he is, find out what they are and how you can help resolve them. This stage is extremely important because it gives continuity to the PA session. It helps you both realize that PA is simply a tool that helps you work together so that you can both benefit. Many people find this stage to be the most rewarding aspect of the PA process, since it is usually characterized by a strong sense of mutual support.

Problems You May Encounter

It is unlikely that a PA session will run its course without any hitches. However, this will not be a problem for you if you know how to respond. The major obstacle to a productive PA session is your subordinate's disagreement with your evaluation. It may be disagreement about your evaluation of his performance or disagreement about future goals. Disagreement is what causes negative emotions to enter the PA session, and as long as there is strong disagreement, a productive appraisal will be hard to accomplish. Although disagreements can be handled productively, it would be naive to think that all disagreements will be resolved to the satisfaction of all parties involved.

The first step is to recognize disagreement. Sometimes it will be quite evident from the subordinate's response — "I disagree" — or a sarcastic comment. Other times, it will be more subtly expressed, such as when your subordinate is silent on a key point or makes a noncommittal statement like "Well, maybe that's true." Constant interrupting, a raised voice, and certain facial expressions are additional signs that there is a disagreement.

Once you recognize disagreement, your next task is to acknowledge it. You do this by finding out why the subordinate disagrees. Start by comparing your data with that of your subordinate. This is why it is so important to prepare adequately. If your data are different, find out why. Are numbers correct? Are dates correct? If critical incidents have been cited, are reports documented accurately? Is the subordinate aware of them? Try to find another source who will validate your information or that of your subordinate. When disagreement stems from data discrepancies, it usually can be cleared up very quickly, since most people — superior or subordinate — usually do not argue with facts.

If, however, the data check out, perhaps the disagreement is due to how they are being interpreted. This is a much more common cause for disagreement. Find out how your subordinate thinks. Is he making inferences that are inappropriate? Ask him how he has arrived at his conclusions and explain the same about your conclusions. It is a good strategy to point out at the same time that while your interpretation differs, you are both in agreement about the validity of the data. Acknowledging this point gives you a common ground to which you can always refer as a reminder that you do both agree on something; that is, it changes the issue from total disagreement to partial disagreement, making it easier for you to resolve differences.

Follow this by discussing with your subordinate how to avoid future disagreements over evaluations of the behavior in question, whether it's improving relationships with his co-workers or getting production costs down. This is an important step to take because it moves the disagreement from an argumentative framework to a solution-oriented framework and helps increase the chances that a similar problem can be avoided in future appraisals.

Needless to say, this procedure does not eliminate the problem of your still having to make decisions on the basis of a contested PA. Although your subordinate might be very happy to reduce the possibility of disagreement in the future by taking recommended steps, he will still be upset by the current appraisal. This is why you must allow him to vent his emotions, talk about his feelings and concern. You can reduce some of the tension by remaining calm, guiding the subordinate through his explanation as to why there is a disagreement, and acknowledging that it is okay for him to disagree. It is also important for you to correct any misperceptions that he has about how the PA results will be used. He might think that his current PA will prevent him from getting a promotion or a raise or will cast doubt upon his ability to handle challenging assignments. While in some cases these perceptions are undoubtedly correct, you will find that most subordinates exaggerate the implications of the results. Reduce his anxiety by putting the results in the proper perspective. True, a raise might be out of the question — but only for now. Let him know that if improvement occurs, he will get the benefit. The key here is to be extremely supportive and emphasize that the point of the appraisal is to help him do better in the future. Although this is no guarantee that negative feelings will be alleviated, it is your best bet.

Probing: A Key PA Technique

One additional and general way that you can make your PAs more effective is by using "probing." Probing is a communication technique that is used to investigate or explore a topic. Probing facilitates the PA process because it helps you find out what the subordinate thinks and feels. At the same time, it increases the subordinate's receptivity by communicating to her that you think her thoughts are important, that you are not trying to force your opinions down her throat. Probing makes the appraisal meaningful to the subordinate because she is using her own words to express her own ideas. This in itself reduces negative emotions.

Probes serve additional functions. By demanding a response, they get the subordinate to participate. They can elicit information that the subordinate might have been hesitant to divulge. Also, probes force you to listen to what your subordinate is saying. Each probe calls for an answer, which sets the stage for another probe. In this context, probing is a method for developing discussions in the PA session.

There are several different types of probes. Some of the more effective ones that can be used in a PA session are:

1. Open-ended questions. These help you get an elaborate response to a broad topic. They serve the purpose of getting the subordinate to open up and get involved. The chief characteristic of an open-ended question is that it cannot be answered with a yes-no response. An example would be:

"How do you think the ad budget affected your sales?"
Open-ended questions are very effective with subordinates who tend to be withdrawn in the PA session.

2. Reflective statements. This type of probe indicates that you understand what the subordinate is saying and feeling. Examples would be:

"I can see that you are upset about this."

"It sounds as if you really are proud of your achievements."
Reflective probes are important because they get the subordinate to vent emotions that are inhibiting the PA process. They break the tension and set the stage for a more businesslike exchange.

3. Neutral phrases. These are probes that increase the flow of information (in contrast to open-ended probes, which start the flow). They encourage the subordinate to go deeper into the subject and at the same time let the subordinate know that you are interested in the points that he is making. Examples would be:

"I see."

"Tell me more."

"I'm listening."

"Yes, uh-huh."

4. Closed-ended questions. These are probes that elicit a specific answer to a question. They are extremely useful when you want to get the subordinate to voice his commitment to the plan or gather specific facts. Examples include:

"Do you think this is realistic?"

"Is this deadline appropriate?"

"Whom would you recommend?"

An important function of close-ended questions is that they will keep the subordinate from wandering off track. Thus, because they usually end a discussion and enable you to move on to another point, they will be useful with subordinates who have trouble sticking to pertinent issues.

5. Clarification probes. This type of probe is used when you want to make sure you understand what the appraisee is saying. It helps you get things straight. Examples would be:

"I hear you saying that your own subordinates hurt your performance. Is that right?"

"I'm not sure I understand. Is this what you are saying?"

Clarification probes are most effective when used as soon as confusion arises. They can also be used to let your subordinate know that you get the point and that it's now time to move on.

6. Summary statements. This type of probe is similar to a clarification probe, the difference being that clarification probes cover shorter bits of the conversation. Summary statements are used periodically in a PA session, either when you have covered a lot of ground or are ready to end a discussion. They are useful because they communicate to the subordinate that you have absorbed what she has said, and they help you evaluate whether you have heard her correctly. They also bring the key points into focus. Examples include:

"To sum up . . ."

"So it sounds as if you are saying . . ."

You can use some of the same wording that you use in clarification probes. The most important point to remember is that summary statements serve as a check of what you are hearing from your subordinate, not as a chance to voice your own opinions. Therefore, after a summary statement, use a closed-ended question to see if you have summed up correctly. If there is hesitation, go to an open-ended probe to find out where you are off.

To reiterate, probing is a useful technique because it gets the subordinate involved in the PA process, helps uncover what she is actually thinking, and helps you listen more attentively. All of these factors are necessary for a productive performance appraisal.

It would be hard to imagine a superior who would not benefit from improving his PA systems and PA skills. This is especially true of those on a board of directors, a school board, or any group responsible for putting an individual in charge of an organization. For these superiors, Richard Vancil, a Harvard Business School professor who studied how companies pick new CEOs, offers this framework:

> It [the board of directors] should perform an annual formal appraisal of the CEO's performance and, after discussing this appraisal with him, should go into executive session to discuss its conclusions. The appraisal should range more broadly beyond bonuses and awards to include the CEO's objectives for the coming year and to review his performance against those goals a year later.

Productive PA sessions are a good way for any superior to help give subordinates, whether they are CEOs or otherwise, the Critical Edge.

IMPROVING PERFORMANCE APPRAISAL: THE APPRAISEE'S ROLE

So far, the burden of improving the PA process has been placed only on the appraiser. But the individual being appraised can help, too. Answering the following questions will help make your role as an appraisee a productive one.

1. **Do you ask for PA?** Just as the recipient of criticism must develop an aggressive attitude toward seeking out criticism, so must the appraisee have an aggressive attitude toward getting his perfor-

mance appraised. This attitude will come naturally if you appreciate criticism on a daily basis. Let your superior know that you want to have a formal performance appraisal. If possible, schedule dates far in advance. This serves the purpose of tactfully reminding you and your boss that PA is serious business, something to be prepared for, and at the same time demonstrates your desire to improve.

2. Do you clarify the PA procedure? Ask your superior what aspects of your performance will be appraised, how information will be collected, and how the information will be used. Seeking answers to these questions helps you and your boss clarify criteria (and measurements) to be used. Equally important, your questions will help your boss (if he hasn't done so already) define what PA is all about.

3. Do you prepare for your PA? Being formally appraised can be an anxiety-arousing experience. The more anxious you become, the less likely you are to benefit from it, because your anxiety is apt to trigger a defensive reaction. By actively preparing for the PA session, you can forestall anxiety. Two effective strategies are: mental rehearsal (see the section on taking criticism in Chapter 4), and keeping pertinent records so that when PA time comes, you have the information you need to back up your own sense of your performance without becoming defensive.

4. Do you have a PA goal? It's a mistake to go into PA with the attitude of *Que será, será*. Be clear in your mind as to what you want to get out of your PA session. For example: "I want to know specific ways in which I can improve my performance" and "I want to know what my boss sees as my strengths and weaknesses."

5. Do you ask for time to respond? If the PA process is productively planned and productively executed, there is little chance that you will be given any surprise information. But, unfortunately, proper PA is the exception. It is likely that you will be confronted with some information that clashes with your perceptions. Instead of responding argumentatively or with complacent agreement, feel free to ask for time to respond. There is no rule that says PA must be completed in one day, and if you take a day or two to think about the information your superior has presented, the odds greatly increase that you will react to it in a more objective manner. This will also give you time to think about how you can reasonably refute any information that doesn't match your perception.

6. Do you ask your superior for help? Productive PAs conclude with the development of an action plan, steps that you can take to improve your performance. As you help formulate this plan, think about how your superior can help you achieve your goals. Come up with specific actions that your superior can take to make it easier for you to achieve the desired results. Although she might respond negatively, the chances are better than average that she will be happy to do her part. After all, if you improve your performance, she improves her performance. Asking your superior for help is a way to get your boss to follow through productively on the PA process.

When both superior and subordinate do their PA jobs, the result is a procedure that approximately follows these steps:

1. The PA process is formally discussed as to purpose, goals, and responsibilities of both parties.
2. Dates for the PA are set in advance. Ample time is allotted.
3. The subordinate is told in advance what aspects of his performance will be appraised, what criteria the superior's judgments will be based on, what data will be collected and how.
4. The subordinate is given, in advance, any forms that the superior will be using.
5. The PA session is conducted when scheduled. Besides exchanging the usual information, both appraiser and appraisee let each other know how they assessed the value of that particular PA session and brainstorm on ways to improve it.
6. The actual PA session is characterized by an attitude of mutual support and constructive effort, with emphasis on the manager and employee working together in problem areas.
7. A short, formal follow-up session is conducted approximately two to four weeks after the PA session to go over any additional thoughts and plans.

By using this procedure, you will be improving your individual PA skills, regardless of how your organization conducts PA.

A few more final points about PA and criticism: Performance appraisal is a much more fluid process than criticism because it is a much longer process. This becomes paradoxical. On one hand, the length of the PA process provides greater opportunity for accurate communication to occur, for information to be exchanged. It is the basis for a true dialogue, whereas criticism that is artfully given many times appears to be no more than a passing comment, à la Pat Riley criticizing his players by saying, "Let's play the way we did last week." On the other hand, because PA is an extended communication process, there are more chances that communication will break down and barriers be put up. It is here that we can best see the relationship between criticism and PA, with the former becoming a specific skill that facilitates the latter. In other words, the skills for giving and taking criticism, which are developed and practiced on a daily basis, are used in the PA process; the better your general criticism skills, the smoother the PA. Recognizing this relationship will help you give and take both criticism and PA more effectively.

IMPROVING PERFORMANCE APPRAISAL: THE ORGANIZATION'S ROLE

The role of the organization in PA is much broader than that of the individual appraiser and appraisee. While it is true that the individuals actually are the implementers of the PA system and therefore have the power to make or break it, it is the organization as an entity that is responsible for the PA system that the individuals use. Like the individuals, organizations can improve their PA systems by answering some critical questions. These include:

Who designs the PA system, and are they qualified?
    The people in charge need to assess their skills for designing PA systems and seek consultation when it is needed.

Is the PA system psychometrically sound, a statistically valid system?
    This is important because you are legally liable for having a statistically valid system.

Does your PA system legally protect your organization?
    Many organizations have found that their PA systems did not do their job in the eyes of the court. People in charge should investigate the legalities of their system.

Is your PA system consistent with your organization's management philosophy and practice?

If it isn't, individuals will sense discontinuity between the roles that are required for PA and the roles that characterize everyday business. When this occurs, PA may well be viewed as awkward and manipulative, and its effectiveness is diminished.

Is your PA system accessible to its users?

If it isn't, most users of the system will find it mentally taxing and ineffective. Organizations can help by making the system easy to use, using forms that do not belabor the process and providing training for employees in conducting PAs. Fireman's Fund does both of these things.

Performance appraisal is a valuable tool for superiors, subordinates, and organizations alike. When all of these forces focus on improving their PA skills, the result is not merely an accurate assessment of what someone's performance is worth but rather a method for making it worth more. When you get PA to do and be this, you have the Critical Edge.

PART III

THE ART OF CRITICISM

IT WOULD BE a valid criticism to say that so far this book has overlooked many important, specific criticism situations that often prove to be troublesome and are daily occurrences. These include giving criticism over the phone, handling secondhand criticism, and having to criticize a client or customer (without losing them).

This section will present ways to deal with such situations by demonstrating the art of criticism — the ability to use creatively and effectively all of the principles previously discussed. This art allows you to translate principles into actions that help you change a negative or potentially negative situation into a positive encounter with positive results.

What is usually required is that you be able to combine principles, or to take one component of a technique and integrate it with a component from another technique, in a way that has not previously been described. This is the art, the creative part of making criticism a productive process.

The examples of common, troublesome criticism situations that follow have been identified on the basis of data collected from more than five thousand workers, ranging from CEOs to company chauffeurs. In addition to the data from individuals, difficult criticism situations were identified by having groups of workers cite situations that affected all of them. The surveys and group interviews were conducted at such organizations as AT&T; IBM; Hyatt; Rockwell International; TRW; KraftCO; Hughes Aircraft; Digital; Intel; Control Data; Fireman's Fund; McDonald's; Warner-Lambert;

McDonnell Douglas; University of Michigan Medical Center; University of Alaska; Washington Hospital Center; California, Chicago, and Arizona school systems; the Treasury Department; the Justice Department; the Department of Labor; and dozens of other corporations, hospitals, schools, universities, and government agencies.

Proven, effective solutions — criticism interventions — to each situation will be presented, with each intervention using information previously discussed. It is important to note that there is no one right answer to any situation but rather several interventions that could all be effective.

As you go through this section, your TASK is to criticize the solutions given, thereby making each one more effective. Sometimes your criticism will cause you to handle the situation in an entirely different manner when you run across it in your workplace, one that is more effective. When you do this, you are using the art of criticism, and chances are, you will soon have the Critical Edge.

Chapter 9

Managing the Impossible

ACCORDING TO the more than five thousand workers surveyed, the following are the most common and troublesome criticism issues and situations that you and your fellow workers must manage effectively to gain the Critical Edge in the workplace.

- Giving criticism over the telephone.
- Giving criticism through letters.
- Receiving secondhand criticism.
- Criticizing somebody for behaving in a way that his or her culture sanctions or for not behaving in a way that his or her culture disapproves of.
- Criticizing friends at work.
- Criticizing an individual in a group setting, and criticizing a group of workers.
- Criticizing clients and customers — without losing them.
- Criticizing someone who used to be your co-worker and now is your subordinate or boss.
- Criticizing someone who responds with anger.
- Being criticized by your boss for something your subordinates or peers failed to do or did ineffectively.
- Criticizing the subordinate who almost always makes excuses for his or her results.
- Deciding whether to criticize when it's not your place to do so but when your ethics tell you to.
- Criticizing someone for personal hygiene.
- Criticizing the co-worker or boss who is almost always giving you negative criticism.

Criticism Over the Telephone

TELEVISION PRODUCER IN LOS ANGELES: George! Listen, I got your script the other day. I didn't read it thoroughly, but I gave it a glance. I think there are some problems.

WRITER (cleaning his desk and looking for a pen): I'm listening.

TELEVISION PRODUCER: The beginning is weak. But I haven't really looked at it closely. I'm not quite sure who could play the part of the kid. Any ideas?

WRITER: Well, I —

TELEVISION PRODUCER (interrupting): Doesn't matter now. There isn't even a script. Now, how much do you think this is going to cost? Remember, we have a budget. Listen, I'll put together a letter and get it out to you soon. Okay? Overall, it's not bad, but it will have to be fixed up. Listen, give me a call if you need help. Take it easy.

WRITER: Sure. Take it easy. [He puts his pen down, looks at his script, and wonders what to do with it.]

When giving criticism over the telephone, the following guidelines are recommended:

1. Plan to give criticism over the phone only if you absolutely can't do it in person.
2. When possible, have a pre-criticism telephone conversation in which you set up a specific date and time for the criticism session.
3. Prepare for the telephone conversation by taking notes about what you will say. Mentally practice your words.
4. Have your notes in front of you when you call.
5. Begin the criticism telephone call by pointing out that your purpose is to help resolve the criticism in question.
6. Every ten or fifteen seconds, try to elicit some type of response, no matter how small, from the target.
7. Set up a time for a follow-up telephone call and be sure to make the call.

Guideline number 1 is important for several reasons. First, it is always better when possible to criticize in person rather than over the telephone. A face-to-face encounter affords you the opportunity of making more personal contact and thus displaying the helping spirit. It also allows you to be visually privy to the nonverbal behavior that helps alert us to such factors as whether our criticism is being met nondefensively or, for that matter, whether the recipient is even listening. Face-to-face criticism allows the giver to choose the environment, and if a last-minute cue indicates that the timing is bad, the criticizer can delay the criticism until a more suitable time arises.

Second, when you criticize in person, it is much easier to build the criticism spontaneously into the flow of the conversation. This frequently has the effect of making the target more receptive because the criticism becomes part of a conversation that has already been in progress; the recipient is already in the mode of listening to the giver. In contrast, when criticism is given on the telephone, it is much more formal, since the sole purpose of the conversation is for the giver to give criticism; the recipient knows throughout that his or her work is going to be criticized. This formality (as in performance appraisals) frequently creates anxiety in both parties and sets the stage for a tense conversation. When criticism becomes the focus of the conversation rather than part of it, the recipient may begin to feel threatened and overwhelmed.

A third problem with criticizing by phone is that once the phone call is initiated, you must continue the criticism, even if you sense the timing and delivery are not working. True, you can say you will call back later, but if you have reached the point of needing to break off the phone call, you can imagine how the recipient will probably feel in the interim. For these reasons, it is recommended that you criticize in person when possible.

Yet there are countless situations when criticism in person is impossible. Whether they are between corporate and district office, a West Coast producer and an East Coast writer, a manufacturing plant and a distributor, many situations demand criticism over the telephone. The luxuries of small talk, getting physically comfortable, and relying on nonverbal behavioral clues are not available. Consequently, you must run the risk of giving criticism that may become a negative event.

You can begin to overcome these factors by adhering to the remaining guidelines. Prepare for the criticism telephone call by making a pre-criticism telephone call. This is useful because it allows the target to prepare, ensures that a time can be blocked off without interruptions, and, perhaps most important, makes the criticism a process instead of a one-shot event. In this telephone call, keep the tone positive so the recipient will not be overly anxious about the next call.

Mentally rehearsing your criticism will pay off when you execute it. Not only will it make your voice friendlier, but also it will make you less nervous when you actually make the phone call. Having notes in front of you will also be helpful because your notes will keep you organized, keep you on track. It's also a good idea to write little reminders to yourself like "Keep calm" and "Don't rush"; these help you manage your own tension and keep the tone of the conversation positive. The same is true for when you are taking criticism over the phone. Having notes in front of you will help you stick to the issues, remind you to ask for pertinent information, and minimize your own defensiveness. Tom Watson, Jr., for example, is said to have kept handy notes that reminded him to keep calm whenever Watson, Sr., criticized him over the telephone.

Begin the criticism phone call with a statement that indicates that you are in fact an ally. Point out that your purpose is to help resolve the criticism in question. This will set the tone for a positive experience. It will defuse the negative mental set toward the call that the target might have and get him or her to think of the call as a learning experience.

Since you can't see whether he or she is really tuning you in, it's a good idea to get the recipient to respond intermittently rather than just after you are finished. You can check for understanding or agreement after each key point. This strategy also allows you to make the phone call more of a dialogue, which makes the conversation less stressful. Getting the recipient involved personalizes the phone call, too.

Finally, it is good practice to follow up the criticism telephone call with an additional call. All of us can remember times when a criticism telephone call has demoralized us, leaving us feeling down for a few days. A follow-up phone call that emphasizes support and commitment creates the opportunity to make sure the recipient realizes that you are on his or her side. This makes it easier for the recipient to respond productively. The follow-up call shows that your desire is to help, not to reprimand.

Note the application of all the aforementioned points in the following conversations.

WEST COAST TELEVISION PRODUCER: Hi, George, it's Harry. How are you?

EAST COAST WRITER: Good, how are you?

WEST COAST TELEVISION PRODUCER: Fine. Listen, I have read the script and I am very excited about it. I want to go over it with you so we can get it moving. When is a good time for me to call back so we can go over it in detail?

EAST COAST WRITER: Now is fine, or tomorrow if you like.

WEST COAST TELEVISION PRODUCER: Tomorrow is better for me. George, it's going to be a great script. I'll speak to you tomorrow!

Next Day

WEST COAST TELEVISION PRODUCER: George, it's Harry. How are you?

EAST COAST WRITER: Good. Tell me what you think.

WEST COAST TELEVISION PRODUCER: Lots of good bits, George. My goal is to make this a great success. I'm preparing a letter for you that will be more detailed than our conversation. To get started, though, my concerns are with three things. Have a pen?

EAST COAST WRITER: Yeah, go ahead.

WEST COAST TELEVISION PRODUCER: Okay . . . [He explains.] That's it. What do you think?

EAST COAST WRITER: I think I agree with the first point. The last two I'm not sure about.

WEST COAST TELEVISION PRODUCER: Okay. Think about them and I will call you a few days after I send out the letter. George, I'm really excited about this. Don't worry about rewrites. I will help you as much as possible.

EAST COAST WRITER: Thanks, Harry. I'll look forward to your letter.

One Week Later

WEST COAST TELEVISION PRODUCER: George, it's Harry. I
wanted to see how you are doing.

EAST COAST WRITER: Good. Your letter made a lot of sense. Let
me tell you what I'm doing . . .

WEST COAST TELEVISION PRODUCER: Sounds much better.
Listen, let's speak in two weeks, and if you need any help or
have any questions, just call. Okay?

EAST COAST WRITER: Thanks, Harry. Speak to you soon!

Granted, this sounds idealized, but even a slight resemblance to
this is far better than the initial conversation, which is what most of
us usually experience.

Criticism Through Letters

A common practice in the working world is to criticize through
letters and memos. One situation in which it is appropriate to do
this is when distance separates the people involved, such as the West
Coast television producer and the East Coast writer. Another situation is when it's your job to criticize through letters, as it is for an
editor of a medical journal who, after reading each submittal, must
send his critiques back to each author. Other times, we're asked to
"drop a memo telling me what you think" on our co-worker's desk.

What makes giving criticism in writing especially troublesome is
that the sender has no way of knowing if the recipient interprets the
criticism as intended or if the recipient even agrees with the criticism.
A few days later, the sender may find out that the recipient interpreted
his criticisms differently than he intended. And even if his written
criticism ultimately is understood, the sender usually spends the next
few days or weeks wondering how the recipient will respond. For
most people, waiting for the target to respond can be very anxiety-
arousing, and the more significant the letter and the target, the greater
the anxiety. It is not uncommon for the stress of waiting for a response to interfere with work efficiency.

From the recipient's perspective, a similar problem is presented in
that there is not an immediate opportunity for him to ask questions
and respond to the criticism. The letter basically makes criticism a

monologue. With no outlet for an immediate response, the recipient is left to evaluate the criticism without assistance.

Although, as we have seen, recipients make a common practice of "leveling down" the importance of spoken criticism, criticism presented through letters is responded to differently. There is less chance for the recipient to level down because there is no dialogue to mediate the impact of the criticism; the recipient is not given the chance to say "Yes, I'll get on it as soon as I finish this other stuff." More often than not, after reading a letter of criticism the recipient feels either anxious, angry, or depressed, all of which make it difficult generally to work effectively.

One more point distinguishes giving criticism through letters, and it is the chief difference between criticism through writing and criticism that is orally communicated. Oral criticism occurs in a face-to-face encounter. Although the exact moment may be distressing, it passes, and the recipient is left to mull it over as part of the past. While thoughts about the criticism remain and may even be difficult to deal with, the recipient is not subjected again to the actual experience of being criticized. On the other hand, written criticism is recorded and, as such, is something tangible that shows the recipient she has been criticized. A letter, unlike a face-to-face encounter, is not transient. Quite the contrary, it is permanent, and this quality of written criticism is both its strength and its weakness. It is common practice for the recipient to reread the letter several times. On the down side, if the letter has a negative structure, the recipient becomes further demoralized with each rereading. On the other hand, if the letter is structured in a positive manner, the rereading of the letter serves as an educational process. Each rereading allows the recipient to see the benefits of the criticism better. Unfortunately, most of us have been subjected to negative criticism through letters, and it is the rare person who has not been discouraged or distressed by the written word.

An excellent illustration of the differences between productive and counterproductive criticism through letters is provided by the following two letters. The first was received by a prominent Los Angeles psychiatrist who had submitted an article to a prestigious medical journal. The second was sent by a New York book editor to her West Coast writer and discussed his first draft of a book. Note the difference in tone, opening, implied messages, specificity, and concluding statements.

> The article has received favorable comment and review and will be acceptable with revision. The major problem is with style. It reads like a talk. It needs a great deal of editing with removal of the first person. References must be more complete and keyed in to the text. No items in press. The figure is sloppy. It needs to be completely thought out and redone, and a legend must be provided. Please adopt our style. Watch your spelling. I look forward to a compulsively revised manuscript.

The recipient's reaction to the letter was "anger. . . . It was demoralizing. I had no sense of what to do. There were no comments on the manuscript. He made no changes, corrections, nothing. . . . All I got out of it was negatives. I don't understand why they want the article. He didn't tell me why they want it. . . . I think he didn't like it but maybe it met the journal's criteria for publication. . . . The word 'compulsively' turned me off immediately. . . . This is low on my priority list."

The second letter, excerpted because of its length, began like this (note the references to past successes à la Coach Riley):

> I am sure that this is going to be another one of your terrific and highly successful books. It is interesting, enlightening, and will be helpful. . . . Your advice is insightful, imaginative, and comprehensive. Thus, I consider this to be a strong first draft. I have gone through it accordingly, page by page, editing closely and making suggestions for additions and changes. I know that with not too much more work, you will have written an important book and one that will more than justify your already established reputation in this area.

The next few pages of the letter provided a very detailed description of changes to be made and how to make them. Here is how the letter concluded:

> I hope that you are not daunted by all of these requests for revisions, small and large. Please call me with any ques-

tions or concerns, but between this letter and the many tags on the manuscript, I think it will be very clear what you need to do to strengthen your manuscript. I think that the results will be well worth your efforts. This is going to be a wonderful book and one that will attract a large and enthusiastic readership.

The recipient described his reaction to the letter as "enthusiastic. . . . I knew she liked the book, that she was excited, that she wanted to publish it and thought it would be very successful. Now, the amount of revisions requested was much more than I had anticipated. However, she gave me specific examples and solutions so she made it easy for me. Also, I never felt I wrote something poorly. All of her specific criticisms were phrased in a very productive manner, like, 'How about saying it like this . . .' and then she would give a reason, sometimes grammatical, for the change. Actually, I learned a lot about writing from her criticisms. And she was right. Making the revisions was a major effort but well worth it."

The obvious differences in these letters — tone, emphasizing the positive, providing specific suggestions for how to improve — do not need elaboration. But what is interesting and probably representative of the reactions of most recipients of criticism letters is the attention paid to specific words, like "compulsively." This word had a negative effect on the recipient of the first letter; to him it implied a tremendous amount of work without offering any support for what he had already done or for the revisions he was being asked to make. The second recipient also paid close attention to the written words of his critic; he commented on how the exact wording of criticisms made him feel as though he had not written anything poorly. He consequently began to see each criticism as a way of improving the manuscript. Choice of words and overall phrasing, whether written or spoken, are crucial in giving criticism productively. The first critic discouraged his recipient to the point that he put the work on hold. The second author was inspired and responded as quickly and productively as his schedule permitted. Clearly, the second editor increased her chances of getting the Critical Edge.

Here are some guidelines to follow when you give criticism through

letters. Remember that your goal is to get the recipient to treasure
the letter.

1. State in the letter that its purpose is to help resolve the criticism presented.
2. Give several examples of the behavior you are criticizing but
   do not present them as prosecuting evidence. Use the examples to elaborate upon your criticism. Remember, you
   want to teach appropriate skills and knowledge.
3. Use the subjective tone.
4. Suggest that the recipient think over the content before responding.
5. When possible, include positives. Whenever you can, make
   sure that positives run through the letter rather than placing
   them separately at the beginning of the letter (the latter is
   equivalent to "Good but . . ."). Also, placing positives
   throughout the letter helps give it a positive tone.
6. Invite involvement by suggesting that the recipient call you
   if there are any questions.
7. Demonstrate commitment to help resolve the criticized behavior by stating that you will call in a week or two to follow up.

Receiving Secondhand Criticism

A nurse at Cedars Sinai Hospital in Los Angeles was told by another
nurse that she had heard the first nurse's work wasn't up to par.
When the first nurse asked who was the source of the criticism, her
co-worker stated, "I don't remember. I heard it a few days ago." An
accountant at a Big Eight firm had a similar experience. His co-
worker had "promised not to reveal the source." Both the criticized
nurse and the accountant reported that the experience made them
very "nervous that people were saying things behind my back . . . angry
because I wasn't told who said it. . . . I didn't think it was true and
didn't know who to speak to." Situations like these — hearing a
criticism about yourself through a third party rather than directly
from the source — are extremely troublesome and frequent occurrences.

When such a situation arises, the hurdle that the recipient encounters is that the criticism process is not a true interaction. Neither is criticism through letter, but here the recipient eventually has the opportunity to respond directly to the original source of the criticism and can carry on at least a written dialogue in which information can be modified, clarified, and validated. With secondhand criticism, the recipient is dealing with a surrogate who may or may not be giving the criticism accurately. Therefore, the information that is passed on must always be regarded as suspect. Furthermore, whereas criticism through letter identifies the source, in many cases of second-party criticism the surrogate refuses to identify the actual source of the criticism. As a result, the recipient does not have the opportunity to clarify or validate the criticism in question. For these reasons, the common response to secondhand criticism is anger and a feeling of helplessness, which cause the recipient to assume a defensive posture.

If you are subjected to secondhand criticism, here are some recommendations:

1. Assume an investigative stance rather than a defensive one. Assess the validity of the second party. Is he really reliable? Can you trust him? Do you have reason to doubt what he is saying? Thank him for the information and express appreciation for his not sharing it with others. (You have no control over whether he actually does share it, so your best strategy is to communicate your expectation that he will keep it between the two of you.)

2. If the second party will not identify the source of the criticism, encourage him to ask his source to speak to you directly.

3. Go to your supervisor and explain that you have heard criticism about yourself. Ask her for her advice about how you can find the source of the criticism. This step is a bit tricky, because you would not want to incriminate yourself with your boss by letting her know you may be doing something wrong. Therefore, you need to consider this step in the context of the relationship you have with your boss. If you know she will support you, take it. If not, be careful.

4. Most important, appraise the validity of the criticism. If it's valid, forget about the source and take the necessary productive actions.

Criticizing Somebody
for Culturally Motivated Behavior

An AT&T manager had a talented engineer whose ideas never got recognized. The problem was that the young man in question was rather reserved and rarely spoke up at meetings. The times that he did, he was so timid that the other engineers, a rather aggressive bunch, either did not pay attention to what he said or challenged him into silence. Wanting the young man to receive his due, the manager took him aside and explained that if he were ever going to make his knowledge known he had best speak up in a forceful manner. The engineer replied that in his culture, it was seen as inappropriate to express one's opinions so directly. The manager was stymied.

Stories such as these are becoming par for the course in corporate America. One manager from an aerospace company, for example, had four subordinates: an Indian, an Iranian, an Englishman, and a Korean. The manager was Japanese. The obvious problem is that different cultures have different rules of behavior, and accordingly, a criticism of how one acts may be valid in one culture but quite inappropriate in another. Consequently, many individuals resist certain criticisms because they ask them to go against their cultural norms. And if they do respond to such criticisms, they frequently feel as if they have betrayed their heritage. For cross-cultural criticism, the following strategies are recommended:

1. Never try to force a person to act in a way that contradicts his cultural norms. Most likely, he won't change his behavior anyway, and constant prodding is sure to create tension and hostile feelings.

2. Explain that the action required is job-specific — that it is appropriate in his current "work culture" and that doing it, or not doing it, at work does not mean that he has to do it all of the time.

3. Empathize with the fact that going against one's upbringing can be conflict-arousing. Listen to his concerns and show that you respect his position.

4. If the person seems to be unable to adapt to his working environment, point out to him how this difficulty is hurting his work performance. In other words, focus on how the issue is a work-

related rather than a cultural problem. This is justified because in the end, work results cannot be ignored.

5. Most important, when possible, make sure that everyone in the working group knows each other's cultural rules. Being aware of these differences helps each person learn the best way to respond to the other.

The aforementioned AT&T manager capitalized on this last point. Instead of trying to change his subordinate's belief that assertive expression was inappropriate, he explained to the other engineers that the man in question was hesitant to speak out for cultural reasons. He asked for their help, telling them to solicit their colleague's opinions actively. As they practiced this strategy, the engineer became more and more comfortable in spontaneously expressing his views. In fact, several months later at an important meeting, he went so far as to interrupt one of his colleagues.

Criticizing Friends at Work

Making friends at work can be a mixed blessing. On one hand, it's an attractive arrangement to be working with someone whom you like and are able to socialize with after hours. But for many people, the relationship sours as soon as criticism needs to be given at work.

> "Hey, John, when you go over that report, make sure you redo the graphs. They really need to be fixed up. What were you doing, watching TV or something when you were doing them?"
> "No! I think they're fine. Anyway, what the hell are you doing, giving me more work to do. I thought your last report stunk and I kept my mouth shut!"
> "That's not true. My report was good."
> "Fine, if you think so. I thought it could have been much better. The point is, I don't tell you what to do. I expect the same, friend!"

Most people say that criticizing a co-worker whom you've become friendly with is especially stressful because, now that you're friends, she expects you to look the other way or let her do as she pleases. Unfortunately, keeping your criticism to yourself may preserve your friendship, but at the same time, in some situations, it impedes your effectiveness at work.

It may be argued that criticizing a friend at work can be avoided simply by not making friends at work. However, considering that most people spend at least a third of their day in their working environment, this argument seems extreme. Not only is it natural to make friends at work, but also, many people go to work specifically hoping that they will make friends with their co-workers. Another possible way to avoid criticizing friends at work might be to choose your friends at work carefully, paying particular attention to where they are in the organizational hierarchy and what they can do for you. The more influential they are, the less you criticize. This recommendation fails on the grounds that it will cause you to keep your criticisms to yourself for fear of being offensive and losing your contacts. Furthermore, it goes against what we already know to be true — criticizing upward is essential to individual and organizational effectiveness. More important, these criteria are hardly the basis for a friendship. In fact, people who base their friendships on job status and connections are usually perceived as manipulative and untrustworthy, two qualities that create enemies rather than friends.

Therefore, the following pointers for criticizing friends at work are proposed:

1. Since thoughts affect behavior, clarify your attitude about making friends at work. If you believe that friends and work don't mix, your best bet is to make friends elsewhere, since you are sure to create problems for yourself. If you think you can handle the dilemmas that friends at work may bring, that the friendship is worth the problems it may cause, then feel free to make as many friends as you can, regardless of their job status.

2. When you have to criticize a friend, use the friendship to facilitate the criticism rather than letting it be an obstacle to the criticism. Do this by beginning with a statement along these lines: "One of the nice things about being friends is that you are able to communicate openly and honestly, even when it comes to criticism." You may even add that you wouldn't be a very good friend if you didn't help her do her work more effectively. While this sounds a bit sugar-coated, remember that it is the phrasing of the point that makes it effective,

and be sure to tailor your phrasing of these thoughts to each particular situation. A Merrill Lynch broker reported that he had criticized a close friend he worked with about the way he dressed by starting out with "Look, we're friends, right? You want me to give you the truth or a bunch of B.S.?" For insurance, throw in that as a friend, you certainly expect her to have the same attitude when it comes to criticizing you. This approach is extremely effective for two reasons. First, it is intellectually appealing. It is very hard for the recipient to make a case against you for telling her something that can help her, even if the information might be initially distressing. Second, it forces the recipient to acknowledge that you are criticizing her because you care about her. This helps minimize defensiveness and allows your friend to evaluate your criticism more accurately.

Making friends at work not only can make your job more enjoyable but also can enhance your success, especially when you and your friends criticize each other effectively.

Dustin Hoffman summarizes the point in talking about the friendship he developed with Warren Beatty when making the film *Ishtar*: "To me, a real friend is someone I know who really loves me but will be hard on me because he wants me to do my best. And that's Warren."

Criticizing in a Group Setting

At a nursing staff meeting, a head nurse has to criticize one of her subordinates for the way she is treating a patient. An advertising executive reviews a layout with a client, an artist, and two copywriters. He criticizes the artist. An engineer presents a software system to his colleagues. They find several glitches and criticize his oversights.

All of these situations represent one of the most difficult criticism encounters — giving criticism in a group. At the very least the recipient is embarrassed. And the giver runs the risk of injecting tension into the meeting, which all too often inhibits others from contributing their thoughts. Why take a chance if you might be criticized? Risk-taking behavior and innovativeness are stifled. Yet criticizing an individual in a group setting is a reality of work. What seems to make it a particularly stressful experience is that it goes against the popular opinion that criticism should be given privately. While this opinion is usually valid, the above situations and hundreds of others frequently demand that criticism be given in front of others. Two strategies can serve you well in these situations.

The first is to depersonalize the criticism by specifically directing comments to the work per se, not to the person who performed it. For example, the advertising executive would depersonalize his criticism by proclaiming, "Let's look at the layout. I think the graphics need to be more colorful" rather than specifically addressing the artist by saying, "The layout is good, except you need to make your graphics more colorful." The first phrasing focuses on the layout itself, while the second singles out the artist as the person who didn't do his part. With this strategy, behavioral logistics are very important. Imagine, for instance, that you are the advertising executive. You would put the layout on the table and have your staff sit around it. You would then "interact" with the graphics by pointing to them and making your criticisms at the same time. By acting in this manner, you focus attention on the work rather than on the individual who created it. The overall effect is to make the individual responsible more objective because you have detached him from the criticism interaction. You have made the target an observer (just like everyone else in the group) rather than a direct participant.

This strategy is effectively used by a major company in the communications technology business. In one of the company's research labs for developing software computer programs, the developers must have their work inspected by their colleagues. As you can imagine, the review process is loaded with criticisms. Their procedure adopts this strategy by having the inspecting computer experts sit around a table, each with a copy of the software program. A moderator reads the document, and each inspector offers criticism in turn. The moderator makes sure that the inspectors address their criticism to the document, not its designer. The actual developer is also present in the room but sits away from the table. His task is solely to listen and make notes. The behavioral logistics of his sitting away from the table helps everyone remember to focus on the software, not its designer, and at the same time helps the designer listen more objectively because although he is present, he is removed from the criticism process.

A second and more subtle way of offering criticism to an individual in a group setting is to turn the individual criticism into a group criticism by making the statement general. For example, let's suppose that at a staff meeting, a head nurse is reviewing the treatment of the patients on the ward. When the name of a particular patient comes up, she wants to criticize the nurse assigned to him for not spending enough time with him. In fact, the nurse in question spends too little time with all her patients. Instead of criticizing the nurse directly in front of her co-workers, which will probably elicit a defensive reaction such as "Well, he tells me not to bother him" or "I have too many patients," the head nurse can handle the situation by making this general statement: "It's really important that we all spend adequate time with our patients. It is something we value here and is one reason people come to this hospital." A statement such as this serves several purposes. One, it communicates to the nurse in question that it is indeed important to spend time with patients without letting her co-workers know that she is falling short of expected standards. Two, it emphasizes the desirability of the same behavior to the other nurses, and this is a bonus. If they are spending adequate time with patients, it reinforces their behavior. If they are not spending adequate time (though their supervisor may be unaware of it), then they, too, profit from the criticism. The pitfall, of course, is that the recipient may not perceive that she is performing the criticized behavior and thus would not apply the statement to her own behavior. Nevertheless, contrast this technique with the option of creating a roomful of red, embarrassed faces, and you'll see that the benefits can outweigh the risk.

A related criticism situation is one in which business demands that you criticize a group of workers. Examples are criticizing a small team for how they handled a project and criticizing an entire division for poor quality control. In such situations, use the same principles as those for giving general criticism. Be specific and encouraging, and express a vote of confidence in the group's ability to get the job done.

One particular strategy to use when criticizing a group is to apply a metaphor. Not only does the metaphor provide the means for communicating the criticism, but a group metaphor also builds cohesiveness, a quality that is apt to facilitate the functioning — and thus

improve the results — of the group. A Michigan high school basketball coach found success when he criticized his team for not getting
along, for too much bickering, for blaming each other for team losses.
He criticized them like this: "You know, a basketball team is just
like a hand. [He holds up his hand as he gives the criticism.]
Look . . . every hand has five fingers. Each finger can pretty well do
as it wants. But the hand only has use when the fingers work together.
When the fingers work together, they have strength. But if the big
finger yells at the pinky, and if the index finger ignores the thumb,
then the hand is nothing. Even if the fingers are strong, smaller hands
will have a stronger grip . . . because the fingers must work together
to become a hand."

The president of a hospital criticized his hospital's staff along these
lines: "We are like a body. Nursing services, X-ray technicians, doc-
tors, emergency room, discharge services, we all are parts of the same
body. We are all organs. We all need to be well, because if one part
of the body becomes diseased, it spreads to the others, and then we
have a real illness. Each organ needs to be in good condition. Then
the blood throughout will circulate much better. So each organ needs
to do a couple of things so our body becomes healthier."

However, criticizing a group through metaphor is not for everybody. It usually takes very good communication skills and a motivational style of delivery, since the members of the group have to
believe in the metaphor if they are to relate it to their particular
situation.

Another tactic to try when criticizing a group is to present the
criticism in a manner that forces the group members to come up
with the answer to the problem and resolve the criticism themselves.
Instead of "You guys are really screwing things up. The quality of
the department's product stinks. You better all shape up or you might
all be out of a job," try "Listen, the quality of the department's
product is way down. What do you all think can be done to improve
it?" This is similar to the technique of criticism through question
described in Chapter 5. It is effective with group members not only
because they usually come up with an answer that makes sense, but
also because the group problem solving makes them a more cohesive
unit. They begin to apply peer pressure on each other to implement
the solution and resolve the criticism. The art to develop when you

criticize a group is that of making the group more powerful than the sum of its parts.

Criticizing Clients and Customers — Without Losing Them

It might be true that the customer is always right, but there are plenty of times when to do your job right, you have to criticize the customer. The strategy to employ is to phrase the criticism in a manner that reflects your desire to provide better customer service. When this approach is taken, it immediately lets the customer know that changing her behavior is in her best interest because it will get her better service. A perfect example of this approach took place at Chicago's O'Hare airport. A ticket agent dealt with an overbearing customer by telling him, "Sir, if you just calm down and answer my questions, I will be able to take care of you right away. Otherwise, you might miss your plane!" The customer regained his composure, provided only the necessary information, got his ticket, and thanked the agent. This scenario is in marked contrast to one in which the ticket agent responds to the same customer with anger, defensiveness, and poor service, perhaps causing the customer to switch to another airline.

This strategy is also applicable to more long-term relationships, such as when the same client continually acts in a way that negatively affects your work. A junior partner in a Big Eight firm once had a client who was consistently late in reporting his tax information. This caused the accountant to have to file extensions, which his superiors did not want him to do. Although the client was influential, the accountant finally criticized him by saying "If you can get your tax information to me earlier in the year, I can devote more time to your returns and save you more money. Also, I won't have to keep filing extensions, so there will be less chance of an audit." The client responded by making sure that his information was given to the accountant on a timely, periodic basis, and the accountant's superior noted that the accountant was destined for partnership.

Sometimes it is absolutely necessary to criticize a customer, even if the criticism cannot be disguised as a route to better customer service and you run the risk of offending the customer or losing them. As an example, a passenger on a Delta Airlines flight was flirting with a flight attendant in a most obnoxious way, to a point where other passengers noticed and seemed to be feeling uncomfortable. The flight attendant finally spoke out, saying, "Sir, will you please mind your manners." He was a perfect gentleman for the rest of the trip. In this case, the flight attendant had strong grounds for criticizing, for she not only stopped a disruptive behavior but also let the other passengers know that she was in charge, a perception that makes passengers more comfortable.

There are other times when you criticize the customer because you find his behavior unacceptable and simply do not want his business if the behavior continues. A manager of a computer store in Santa Monica, California, recounts such an experience:

"A customer called up complaining about his computer printer. My service department tried to help him over the phone but he kept saying, yelling, actually, that he couldn't understand them — both service engineers are Korean. He became very abusive and the call was passed on to me. I tried to help him over the phone . . . instruct him what to do, but to no avail. He asked about a service call, and because he lived only a few minutes away from the store, I made the visit myself. I wanted to speak to him. When I got there, I fixed the printer — all it needed was a new ribbon. Apparently, when my service department told him to pick up the 'cover' of the printer, he thought they were saying 'coover' and had no idea of what they were talking about. Anyway, when he asked how much the service call was, I told him to forget it, that I wanted to talk to him. I said, 'Listen, my service department, as is the case with all my employees, does excellent work. The two gentlemen you spoke to are Korean, and they both do excellent work and provide excellent service. They are both learning English as best and as fast as they can. In fact, for most people, their English is not a problem. I want you to know that my staff is very important to me, and if you can't treat them with respect, then I would prefer that you go to another store.' Now, he became very apologetic and agreed that his behavior had been inappropriate. He even said he would call the service people and apologize. I told him that wasn't necessary, that I just wanted to let him know that my staff is very important to me and I expect customers to treat them with respect. Two days later, he walked into the store and apologized to the two Korean gentlemen. To top it off, he has remained our customer."

What is important here is that the manager, personal values aside, decided it was appropriate to criticize a customer and run the risk of losing him. He evaluated the situation and decided that if the customer was going to continue behaving abusively toward his staff, it would be better to lose the customer than to force his staff to tolerate such behavior. By criticizing the customer (and he told his staff that he was going to do that before he made his service call), he demonstrated to his staff that while the customer is important, he is not so important that the boss would let him abuse the staff. He used criticizing the customer as a means of building employee loyalty and protected his staff's self-esteem in the process. And let's not forget that he changed the customer's behavior, too.

Overall, though, the key to criticizing clients and customers is to do it, whenever possible, in a way that gives them what they want — better service.

Criticizing a Former Co-worker Who Is Now Your Subordinate or Boss

The strategy used here obviously depends on whether the change in the relationship makes you the boss or the subordinate. If you have become the subordinate, you should do nothing differently. You have already developed a style of relating to your former co-worker, and there is no reason to change it just because she is now your boss. If you perceive that her style of relating to you has changed, that she has become more "power"-oriented, then you should develop your skill in executive suite criticism. You should not confront your new boss and tell her how she has changed, because she is sure to attribute your comments, even if accurate, to envy.

The same basic strategy holds true if you become the boss. If your style of criticizing your co-worker has been effective, continue doing what works. However, if there has been conflict or disagreement, instead of having to settle for the standstill that is frequently the result of peer criticism, you now have the work power to ensure the results you want. The mistake that most newly appointed bosses make is to force their subordinates to change simply because they are now the boss. In other words, they abuse their power. A more effective means of handling disagreement is to explain to your former co-worker that you certainly respect his views but that you are now accountable for the results. Therefore, it is your responsibility to make the decision you think is best. In effect, what you have done is shift the emphasis from having power to taking responsibility.

A superb execution of this strategy was used by a staff writer for a network television series. After working as a staff writer for two and a half years, he was promoted to producer, which granted him more authority, including the first level of script approval. When one of his former co-workers finished a rough draft of the following week's script, the new producer made significant changes, which upset the staff writer. They had joined the show together, and the criticized writer was probably envious and angry that he hadn't received the promotion. The producer recounts the conversation that followed:

STAFF WRITER: Hey, I looked at the changes you made. I don't understand. What is it? You're the hot-shot producer now and want to take control?

PRODUCER: Are you saying you didn't like the changes? And by the way, you will notice that I didn't say these were final changes. I said for you to think about them and see what you can do with them.

STAFF WRITER: Yeah, I know. But still, what is it going to be? Now that you're the producer I have to run everything by you? First of all, there are a lot of lines that you put in that I think stink, to tell you the truth.

PRODUCER: Good! Make sure you underline them so I can do something about them. You know, you have to realize some things. First, just because I got a promotion doesn't mean I am going to tell you what to do. I have always given you criticism about your work, and you have always criticized my ideas, too. So that's not going to change. What will change is that because I have some authority, I can be more influential with the big boys. Maybe the quality of the show can be elevated to something that will really make a mark on the public. Also, I have worked with you for two and a half years. And I know that you are one of the best in the business. And if I have to use my power, if you want to call it that, to make you write your best scripts so that you can get the recognition and bucks that you deserve, then, dammit, I will. And if you want to be upset about that, then fine. My job is to be responsible for the quality of the scripts. And I expect you to be, as you have been in the past, open to my criticisms, and I expect you to continue to criticize my work, whether it's my script work or how I carry out my responsibilities as producer.

STAFF WRITER: All right, all right. If you think I'm so good, maybe you can help me get a promotion, too. Now, can we go over the script?

What made this encounter productive was that the producer did four things. First, he clarified the recipient's evaluation of the criticism by pointing out that the changes were not final. Doing this helped put the situation in perspective and keep it on track, directing attention to criticism of the script, not to the issue of giving criticism because roles had changed. However, the staff writer ignored this and began to escalate the argument: "There are a lot of lines that you put in that I think stink!" Second, the producer displayed the Critical Edge rather than getting caught up in a destructive dialogue — he turned the criticism into a positive opportunity and encouraged the staff writer to make detailed notes about the lines he questioned so that they could be looked at. This type of response kept the situation from escalating into a destructive interaction in which nobody would win. Third, without pausing (which was important, because he was coming off a positive sentence), he made another artful point by referring to some of the qualities that had made their relationship successful in the past — specifically, their productively criticizing each other — and noting that he expected that this would continue. Thus, he let the staff writer know that he would criticize all of his scripts and at the same time pointed out that he had been doing this for two and a half years anyway; it had nothing to do with being a new producer. Finally, the producer defined his job responsibility and strategically put it into the context of how it could benefit the staff writer by securing more money and more recognition for him.

While this particular encounter probably did not wash away the staff writer's deeper feelings of resentment and envy, it did clear the air and set the stage for a productive working relationship. In fact, several months later the new producer noted that the creative juices of the show were flowing better than ever and that the staff writer was doing his best work ever. Another month passed, and the writer had his contract renewed — ironically, for more money and a new title: coproducer of the show!

Two final recommendations: If you find yourself moving up the organization, become familiar with the pitfalls that your new position brings with it in terms of impeding criticism. And remember that many times, as in the preceding case, your former co-worker might once again become your co-worker, so do not abuse your new power and thereby offend him or her.

Criticizing Someone Who Responds with Anger

Anger is one of the most frequent responses to criticism. Regardless of whether it's your boss, peer, or subordinate who's angry, your basic strategy is always the same — manage your own anger. If you are unable to do this, the encounter will quickly escalate, and more often than not the recipient will quickly point out how angry you are becoming, which will probably make you even angrier. When you as the giver become angry, it provides the recipient with a means of sidestepping the original criticism situation, since he can make your anger and loss of control the issue rather than his criticized behavior, the behavior that precipitated the encounter. He can say, "Hey, I'm not going to listen to you shout at me. When you calm down, I will listen to you." In effect, he has made your anger the problem, not his own, and thus excuses himself from the criticism situation. Therefore, learn to manage your own anger. Some effective ways of doing this include practicing relaxation on a daily basis so that you can stay relaxed in the heat of the moment, using your self-statements as instructions to remind you to stay calm, and mentally rehearsing for the encounter by visualizing yourself handling it effectively. Once you can manage your own anger, you are more likely to be able to overcome the anger and defensiveness of others.

In managing the recipient's angry response to your criticism, the first thing to do is to ask yourself, "Why is he becoming angry?" Although you will probably never know for sure, the reason is probably that he is feeling threatened. In this context, his anger becomes his means of protecting his self-esteem. Therefore, your primary strategy becomes to reduce the perceived threat and thus overcome his defensiveness. Any of the following three maneuvers tends to be very effective:

1. Negate any irrational and defensive thoughts he may be having by saying something like "I hope you are not thinking that I am not going to give you another assignment, or that I am no longer interested in your services, because that is not true. I just want to make things better next time."

2. Help the recipient process what is going on temporarily by shifting the subject of the discussion from the criticism per se to what is then occurring: "It seems to me that you are getting angry [or "that it's hard for you to take this in"] and I'm wondering if you are feeling threatened by what I am saying, because that is not my intent."

3. Defuse the anger by saying "I can see that things are getting a little hot. Let's take a break and we will discuss it later."

All of these interventions help overcome defensiveness; they prevent the criticism situation from turning into a conflict that is bound to escalate. As a result, the criticism process can continue on course, thus increasing the chance that the recipient will eventually respond productively. At the very least, the interventions enhance the recipient's awareness of his anger and perhaps thus reduce it.

A word of caution: Do not tell the recipient "You are getting defensive" or "Stop being so angry." Such direct comments — which usually come out of our own anger — only fuel the fire.

Some nonverbal strategies you can employ are based on the fact that when one becomes angry, one's bodily responses — rates of heartbeat, breathing, perspiration, and respiration — speed up. As previously noted, when the body speeds up, a person becomes mentally rigid, which makes it more difficult for her to process information accurately and consider alternative viewpoints. This makes it harder for the angry recipient to keep an open mind and listen productively. Therefore, you can make it more likely that the angry target will hear your criticism if you slow her down. Ways to do this include getting her to speak more slowly, getting her to sit down while you are talking, and offering her a cold, noncaffeinated drink. These strategies are particularly useful because they decrease the recipient's anger without overtly pointing out that she is angry, which sometimes, no matter how skillfully done, makes the recipient more resistant.

Another effective way of minimizing the recipient's anger when you criticize her is to acknowledge at the start that you do not expect her to become angry or to compliment her in advance for not getting angry. For example, "I know you won't get angry when I tell you this" or "I appreciate your not getting angry when I tell you this. A lot of people would." The rationale behind this strategy is that the initial statement is a self-esteem builder. If the recipient responds with anger, she loses the compliment. Most people choose to keep the compliment by not getting angry.

What about when you are the recipient of your boss's angry criticisms? A secretary got tired of listening to her boss criticize her in an angry and abusive manner. He would incorporate insulting phrases into his criticisms of her work: "How could you be so stupid . . . You spell like a high school dropout . . . Sometimes I think you're deaf . . ." (These were the mild insults!) She finally responded by writing down all his pet insults on an index card. The next time he began his tirade, she whipped the card out and said, "Here, boss, I made it easy for you. Just go down the list." They both laughed, and the boss realized how inappropriate his behavior had been. He changed. While this is not a recommended tactic for every subordinate who is criticized by an angry boss, it does illustrate that there are many ways to handle a criticism situation.

To reiterate, there is no guaranteed way to keep a person from responding to criticism with anger, so in the end, your best bet to overcome an angry response is to manage your own. The answer is to stay cool, calm, and collected whenever you criticize anybody.

Being Criticized by Your Boss
for Something Your Subordinates or Peers Did

If it's your subordinate who you think is responsible, it is an error to tell your boss that it's not your fault, that it's the subordinate's fault. Making excuses won't help; they are repugnant to most bosses. More important, the work structure makes your subordinate's performance ultimately your responsibility and yours alone. Blaming subordinates will only suggest to your boss that you are not able to get them to perform efficiently.

It is much wiser for you to agree with your superior, accept the criticism, and keep to yourself the reason the job wasn't done. The necessary critical intervention is not between you and your boss but between you and your subordinate. Use productive criticism to motivate him so that the incident is not likely to occur again.

When your co-workers are involved, two different situations are possible. One is when your peers deserve to be criticized along with you. The other is when your peers deserve to be criticized instead of you. In the first case — when your co-workers deserve to be criticized, too — tell your boss that you agree with the criticism and that you will respond appropriately. Then recommend that the boss share the criticism with your peers, since the others would benefit, too. This is a good way to get your co-workers to hear the criticism without being an office snitch. On the side, you can approach these co-workers, share the criticism you got, and work out a plan so you can all avoid the criticism in the future. This usually works. A district manager of a large food chain passed on the criticism he received from his regional manager to his peers this way: "Listen, George is very disappointed that we as a district have not been getting our produce into our stores fast enough. He says we are all responsible. He recommended that we look into how we route the produce and how fast our suppliers get the stuff to us. To me that is a good idea. I am already getting my routes checked out. You might want to do the same." Note that the district manager who passed on the criticism simply communicated the information, using cooperative words — *we, our, us.* Most important, he did not attempt to tell the co-workers what to do (it was not his criticism) but simply told them how he personally was going to respond. If you find sharing the criticism doesn't work, improve your skill at peer criticism; at the same time, let your boss know that you personally are responding to the criticism.

The second situation — when your peers deserve to be criticized instead of you — is trickier. It may be best (you will have to size up the situation yourself) to accept criticism anyhow and promise to respond to it. Any other response may be seen as defensiveness or an attempt to put blame on your co-workers. Although you are taking the heat for something you didn't do, you are also showing your boss that you can accept responsibility. After all, your boss might be giving out the same criticism to other innocent co-workers, too, on the grounds that since you all work together, you all get criticized together. And besides, he or she may feel you are culpable because you are part of the team. However, if this response is not acceptable to you, then react by making the boss be very specific: "Well, what are you basing this on? . . . I am not quite sure why I am responsible for this . . ." or "Are you saying that this was my responsibility? . . ." Statements like these will help your boss clarify exactly what your role is in the situation and perhaps see that you are being undeservedly criticized. Whichever tack you take, ask your boss to pass the criticism on to the others. Then, follow the earlier suggestion of tactfully sharing the criticism with your co-workers so the situation can be prevented in the future.

Criticizing the Subordinate
Who Almost Always Makes Excuses

One of the most frustrating situations that a boss encounters is when a subordinate is constantly making excuses for the results he achieved. Whether it's as plain as "It's not my fault," a little more pointed — "Gee, Jack didn't get me the data on time . . . that's why the report is late" — or more elaborate — "Well, I spoke to the sales agent about three weeks ago, and he was supposed to call me back. When I didn't hear from him . . ." — the result is the same: The subordinate in effect denies the criticism because the reason that he gives is intended to justify his actions. Thus, "I know I was supposed to have the report finished on Thursday, but Mr. Smith gave me another assignment" really means "The report wasn't supposed to be finished on Thursday because Mr. Smith gave me something else to do."

In regard to the cause of the excuse making, UCLA psychiatrist Dr. Ronald Podell states, "Many times the excuse maker is coming from a position of being insecure. To him, if he admits he is responsible, he thinks he is a failure. By making excuses, he protects his self-esteem. However, there are probably countless other reasons why a person makes excuses." This is no doubt true. The strategy in any case is to minimize the chance that the subordinate will make excuses for his results so that he can instead realistically look at his work and begin to improve it. There are several ways you can do this.

The first approach to the situation stems from treating the excuse making concretely — as a defensive behavioral pattern of responding that has been used effectively over a period of time. The plan here becomes to break the defensive pattern. You can do this by voicing your criticisms and then, before the subordinate has a chance to respond, telling him to think about it for a few days. The logic here (as discussed in Chapter 5) is that if you slow his response down, he will be apt to appraise the criticism more accurately and recognize his responsibility in the situation at hand. Appropriate phrasing of this approach would be: "Listen, I am going to tell you something, but I don't want you to respond now. I want you to think it over for a few days and then we will discuss it at the end of the week." In this phrasing, the boss short-circuits the excuse making by telling the subordinate not to respond. Since the boss has work power, it is doubtful that the subordinate will respond at that moment. The boss also makes sure that the situation will eventually be discussed by stating that this will be done before the week is over. The drawback, of course, is that you would have to use this approach almost every time you criticized the subordinate. For obvious reasons this is not usually feasible.

The second approach, based on the theory that the excuse making comes out of insecurity, is simply to acknowledge to your subordinate that it is permissible to make mistakes and that while you expect him to function at his optimal level, you do not expect him to be perfect. This has the effect of making the subordinate feel that he does not have to prove that he is not at fault every time he is criticized. It is also good policy to point out that mistakes provide a good opportunity to learn how to do something better. When you try this approach, you are giving permission to fail, which, if you recall, is one of the ways a superior can help a subordinate build a COTE of armor.

The third and most direct way of dealing with the excuse maker is to criticize him directly for constantly making excuses for his results. This can be combined with the delay tactic mentioned above: "Listen, I want to tell you something and I don't want you to respond now . . . I want you to think it over. A lot of the times I criticize you, you have reasons for why something didn't happen as planned. And a lot of times those reasons make sense. But rarely — I can't think of one time, maybe you can — do I recall you saying that it was your responsibility, that you made a mistake. I find this makes it hard for me to help you develop, because part of developing is acknowledging that you make mistakes. I also think that it prevents you from fairly evaluating your own strengths. Don't respond now. Think about it and we will discuss it later on in the week."

There are several points to note about this approach. First, the boss pointed out that some of the subordinate's excuses were valid; failure to do this would probably cause the recipient to cite examples of legitimate excuses and thus discredit the overall criticism. At the same time, she stated that although there have been legitimate excuses, she couldn't think of any times that the subordinate took responsibility, and she invited the subordinate to cite one. She knew the subordinate wouldn't be able to come up with one either, thereby confronting the subordinate with the fact that he makes excuses almost always. This is a neat way to imply "always" without actually stating "always"; overtly stating it usually triggers defensiveness. The third point to note is that the superior did not lean too hard on the subordinate; rather, she implied that she sees the subordinate as someone who has the ability to develop, but only if he takes responsibility for his results. This puts the subordinate in a bind: If he doesn't accept responsibility for his results, then in his boss's eyes he can't improve. The only way he can improve is to acknowledge that he is responsible for his results.

Finally, anytime an excuse maker owns up to his results, you should do two things. First, don't reprimand him for making a mistake. This is equivalent to smacking a five-year-old child for telling you the truth — you can bet he will choose to lie next time. In fact, do the opposite by telling him how much you appreciate his taking responsibility for the results and telling him that you admire it. When you respond like this, you increase the likelihood that he will take responsibility for his results in future. Second, immediately move on to discussing how to improve the situation. This lets the subordinate see that in most cases, once you accept responsibility for your results, you can simply move on to making things better.

Deciding Whether to Criticize Unethical Behavior When It's Not Your Place to Do So

One of the most trying experiences that people have at work is observing something that goes against their personal ethics. Some examples: a bank teller seeing a loan officer stretching the rules so the customer, who is the loan officer's friend, can get a loan; a sales rep witnessing a co-worker padding their business expenses from their recent trip; an electrician knowing that his boss is recommending a particular type of wire to a customer because it is more expensive than another type that is equally good for the project; an employee hearing the president of the company touting the company's stock even though business is bad; a nurse seeing a doctor suggesting a particular operation for financial reasons instead of medical reasons.

These situations are tough because the other person's actions clash with your own sense of right and wrong. The situations are even more complicated to deal with because these behaviors reflect ethical judgments, which traditionally are a personal matter and not appropriate for others to criticize. Furthermore, if you do criticize, the usual response is either "Look, mind your own business" or "You do what you think is right and I will do the same." The exception, of course, is if you are the boss criticizing a subordinate. In that case, you can use your work power, if need be, to prevent the criticized (unethical) behavior from recurring. If you are not the boss, what then? And what do you do if it's your immediate boss or someone higher up who, in your eyes, is acting unethically? There are three choices to ponder.

The first is to do nothing. Get angry, talk to your friends, maybe even a few co-workers, but in the end say nothing. You simply accept the situation and perhaps rationalize, "Well, that's business. Everybody does it." Many people take this position on the grounds that while they don't like what they see, they had better not say anything if they want to keep their job.

The second choice is to quit your job. If you find the situation unbearable, you can always leave. Being able to implement this choice obviously depends on whether you need the job; whether you can find a new job; and whether any other problems would result.

The third choice is to voice your criticism to the person involved. The drawback here is not that you will be told that you are out of line (maybe you won't if you practice the art of criticism) but that in some extreme cases you will actually be fired for blowing the whistle. For example, take the case of Roger Boisjoly, an engineer at Chicago-based Morton Thiokol Inc., the company that used faulty O-rings in its solid-fueled rocket booster for the space shuttle *Challenger*. Boisjoly believed that something was wrong with the O-rings before the fatal launch and went to his superiors with the information. Unfortunately, his bosses didn't listen. After the *Challenger* disaster, Boisjoly was demoted and then went on extended sick leave from Thiokol. Despite the strained circumstances, he says he would risk his career again for his conscience. "I couldn't live with any self-respect if I didn't," he says. This illustrates an important point about criticizing unethical behavior: Do what you must, but be prepared to accept the consequences of your decision.

Criticizing Someone for Personal Hygiene

Criticizing a worker for personal hygiene is a dirty business, and most people break out into a sweat at the thought of doing it. Nevertheless, as you know if you have ever worked with someone with body odor, it's a necessity. Here are a couple of methods that people have found to be effective.

Katy Smith, corporate training manager for A & S Restaurant Corporation, a subsidiary of Pillsbury Company, recalls that one of her managers handled the situation by explaining to the offender that his odor was "getting in the way of his doing his job," because colleagues stayed clear. The approach defused any defensiveness, she says, because the manager didn't attack the individual or say things like "You stink" or "You are doing a lousy job because you stink."

Although this approach was effective, it may be a little too direct for you. Therefore, you might want to try the "perfume" approach. A group of secretaries couldn't stand the smell of one of their co-workers. All of them were reluctant to say anything for fear it would hurt their peer's feelings. One of them came up with a plan. They all chipped in for some expensive toiletries. They then drew straws to see who would have the task of delivering the criticism, which was presented along these lines: "I am going to say something to you that embarrasses me and might embarrass you, but I am going to say it anyway. You might not be aware of it, but you have body odor. Please don't take it the wrong way. I wanted to tell you because it's becoming a problem. The other girls notice it, too. Now, we like you and we wanted to show you that we are sincere, so we all got you a gift. Use it in good health." A month later, the secretaries reported that their co-worker was no longer fouling up their work. The key point to extract from this delivery is that when giving a particular criticism is apt to be embarrassing for either or both the giver and the recipient, acknowledge it — it breaks the tension.

If neither of these approaches works, try Johnny Carson's suggestion: Put an eight-foot-tall can of Right Guard next to the person's desk!

Criticizing the Co-worker or Boss
Who Almost Always Criticizes Negatively

If there is one thing at work that nobody needs, it's a co-worker who is always passing out unproductive critical comments about one's work. Moving your desk, ignoring her remarks, or showing your displeasure are usually not sufficient answers to this unpleasant problem.

A more effective strategy is not to try to get your co-worker to stop criticizing you, but to make her do so productively. Just as the jujitsu expert uses an opponent's power and applies reverse leverage to overcome him, so you must plan to take advantage of what your co-worker is already doing. A window designer for a national retail company implemented this principle perfectly. Her co-worker was always telling her negative things about how she displayed the store's merchandise in the window. Sometimes the colors were wrong, other times the "scene is too crowded," but most of the time it was "It looks lousy." The criticized window designer thought about her goal — what she wanted to happen — and formulated a way to best criticize her critical co-worker. The next time she was faced with her co-worker's critical comments, she asked her, "How can I do it better?"

This response aptly demonstrates how communicating criticism can be effectively reduced to one sentence. Look what happens. If the negative criticizer tells you what you've asked, you are the winner. On the other hand, if the response is along the lines of "I don't know," your best bet is to explain, "I'm doing the best I can. I would appreciate it if you would keep your criticisms to yourself until you can tell me how to do it better, because, after all, I do welcome your productive criticism." In effect, you are not telling your co-worker not to criticize you; rather, you are asking her to change how she criticizes you.

If her critical comments continue, it is probably necessary to be more direct. You can point out that while productive criticism is appropriate, her being constantly and unproductively critical is not helping you to do your job, nor is it making you feel good, and that if it continues, the boss will have to be informed. Of course, it is wise to suggest that an alternative is the two of you sitting down together and making a cooperative effort to better the situation. The second choice is usually picked. The fact that you even offer this as an option also serves to show your co-worker that you want to have a good working relationship with her. However, while going to your boss may make you uncomfortable, it may be what it takes in some cases to make your life easier.

A derivation of this strategy is particularly helpful with the boss who is almost always (and exclusively) pointing out what you do wrong. Since a governing rule of the boss-subordinate relationship is that you don't tell the boss what to do, your reaction to unproductive criticism should be to structure the criticism process. Ask your boss to set aside a time in which he can criticize you productively. Instruct him in which of the areas of your work you wish to be criticized. Emphasize that knowing what he likes is just as important to you as knowing what he thinks needs to be improved. Assuming that all goes well, or at least better, in this productive session, at the end of the meeting express your sense of the benefits of the session, express your desire to have such sessions on a continuing basis, regardless of how infrequently, and remember to implement his criticisms. In essence, you are teaching your boss how to criticize you, and in the process, everybody wins.

Changing negative behavior by making use of the negative behavior itself reflects the art of criticism at its highest level.

If, having criticized the above solutions, you think you are getting good at managing the impossible, you're ready to develop the Critical Edge. Practice by generating your own strategies and techniques for the following criticism dilemmas. Come up with several tactics for each one and then criticize each move you have planned. Remember, there is no one way. Your success will be enhanced if you keep in mind that your goal is to take each criticism to TASK.

- A co-worker almost always brings up irrelevant subjects in meetings, and nobody else is saying anything, not even the meeting leader.
- A subordinate continually plays up to you and tells you everything he thinks you want to hear.
- Your boss frequently gives you tasks that have nothing to do with your job, and you find some of them demeaning.
- Your boss starts to share information about her personal life, and you don't want to hear it.
- A client always drinks too much at lunch and gets out of hand.
- A subordinate comes to you and says that his co-workers do not respect him.
- Your office mate makes personal telephone calls all day, which prevents you from concentrating and getting your work done.
- Your boss continually gives you work at the last minute and expects you to meet the deadline.
- You worked hard on a project, but your boss takes the credit.

In sum, the art of criticism is putting it all together — being able to give and take criticism productively in any situation. Yes, the quality of your work will be better if you can master this art. Yes, your working relationships will be better. Yes, you will increase your chances for moving up the organization. Yes, you will get successful results. Yes, you will have the Critical Edge.

Conclusions:
Aristotle Revisited

THIS BOOK has brought together a wide body of knowledge for the purpose of teaching you how to use criticism productively on the job so that the quality of your work, working relationships, job satisfaction, and overall results improve. Some important points have emerged about criticism. A review of them is best accomplished with the help of some great critics.

When Aristotle coined the word "criticism," he was probably well aware that he was on to something, and indeed, criticism has prevailed throughout the ages. Cultures, the evolutionary process, and, most especially, particularly visionary people have all interacted to affect criticism — how we think about it, how we practice it. These ghosts of the past are powerful shades for today; they help us see more clearly those aspects of criticism that give us the Critical Edge.

First we must remember the function, or intent, of criticism. As I. A. Richards wrote in his 1929 work, *Practical Criticism*: "Finally, apart from what he says, his attitude to what he is talking about, and his attitude to his listener, there is the critic's intention, his aim, conscious or unconscious, the effect he is endeavoring to promote." Most of today's critics seem to think the function of criticism is to point out what is wrong. As we have seen, the common synonyms for criticizing are *flaw finding, fault finding, blaming, reprimanding,* and other words and phrases that by association imply that when you criticize, you look for the worst. The prophecy becomes self-fulfilling. Those who want the Critical Edge need to remember that the intent of criticism must always be to improve. They will need to develop and practice a new criticism vocabulary so that criticism becomes associated with improvement, helping, care, trust, productivity, and support.

R. P. Blackmur's essay "A Critic's Job at Work" recalls a second point: that criticism is a subjective evaluation. He wrote, "Criticism, I take it, is the formal discourse of an amateur." By this statement, Blackmur did not mean that the critic should be a dilettante but that he should be the opposite of a professional insofar as he is not "professing" a doctrine. Modern critics often forget this and present their criticism as if they are professionals who know right from wrong and know exactly how the job should be done. When criticism is presented so dogmatically, the recipient loses the chance of being the initiator of new modes of behavior; criticism becomes the death of, not the instigator of, insight. Getting the Critical Edge means using all the knowledge you have but, at the same time, remembering to discount the doctrine that goes with it and make room for other people's frames of reference.

A third issue repeatedly associated with criticism is that of criteria. A practice originally introduced by Plato, criticizing on the basis of criteria is essential. As Aristotle pointed out, employing criteria is a multifaceted concept; we have seen its importance in formulating criticism, appraising criticism, and assessing when it's appropriate to criticize. Stephen Pepper, in his book *The Basis of Criticism in the Arts,* makes the point cogently: "A thoroughly competent critic is one who has both intimate experience with the [work] . . . he is judging and a possession of reliable criteria of criticism." Criticisms that we give today are often based on our whims of the moment, and this reduces criticism to sophistry. True, even the objective criteria that we can choose to base our criticism on entail an initial subjective choice; good critics nevertheless have criteria, know how to evaluate their criteria, and are continually reevaluating their criteria.

A fourth point is that criticism is a complex task. To offer opinions, to have them accepted, to effect results, to avoid hurting the recipient, are not simple endeavors. Nineteenth-century poet and critic Matthew Arnold underlined just how complex criticism is:

> Criticism must maintain its independence of the practical spirit and its aims. Even with well-meant efforts of the practical spirit it must express dissatisfaction. . . . It must not hurry

on the goal because of its practical importance. It must be patient, and know how to wait; and flexible, and know how to attach itself to things and how to withdraw from them. It must be apt to study and praise elements. It must be apt to discern the shortcoming. . . . And this without any notion of favoring or injuring. . . .

Today, critics ignore the complexity of criticism by giving it at inappropriate times, in inappropriate settings, and without carefully thinking about what they want their criticism to accomplish, how to get criticism to fulfill its TASK. To attain the Critical Edge, you must look at criticism as much more than just the act of judging.

Respect is the fifth keynote. Plato and Aristotle were said to spend days formulating their criticisms; it is safe to assume that they treated criticism as something not to be taken lightly. But throughout the ages, respect as an ingredient of productive criticism has broadened to mean more than recognizing the activity as important. Respect has an interpersonal connotation that can best be described as being sensitive, recognizing that the recipient of your criticism has feelings, and recognizing that those feelings are not impervious to a critic's words. Most modern critics forget this point and pepper their criticism with name calling and other put-downs that communicate a lack of respect to the person they say they are trying to help. This is in marked contrast to how a great critic operates, even when there is strong disagreement between him or her and the recipient. Note how American poet and critic John Ransom demonstrated respect for the recipient of his criticism:

> Mr. T.S. Eliot is an extraordinarily sensitive critic. But when he discusses the so-called metaphysical poetry, he surprises us by refusing to study the so-called conceit which is its reputed basis. . . . Now there is scarcely another critic equal to Eliot at distinguishing the practices of two poets who are closely related. He is supreme as a comparative critic when the relation in question is delicate and subtle.

Compare this with how a Steven Brill or a George Steinbrenner would describe the recipient of their criticisms. To get the Critical

Edge, you must always respect the recipient of your criticism as well as the importance of the criticism process.

Sixth, criticism must be allowed. Plato, Aristotle, Darwin, Galileo, and Freud revolutionized the world because their criticisms were, albeit sometimes with resistance, allowed to surface. As history and practical experience have shown, when critical thinking is blocked, stagnation occurs, and eventually a violent reaction to the suppression results. In today's world, criticism is often blocked because people perceive it as a threat, unlike the great critics, who saw it as a means of positive stimulation. Individuals, organizations, and societies that want the Critical Edge must allow criticism to flow readily rather than block it for fear of offending or being wounded or, perhaps, for fear of its truth. The last stanza from Alexander Pope's "Essay on Criticism" puts it succinctly:

> The learned reflect on what before they knew:
> Careless of censure, nor too fond of fame;
> Still pleased to praise, yet not afraid to blame;
> Averse alike to flatter, or offend;
> Not free from faults, nor yet too vain to mend.

Finally, it must be remembered that criticism is an art, since there always remains in criticism an element of personal vision. Above all, it is the ability to transfer that vision to others that gives individuals, organizations, and societies the Critical Edge.

Bibliography

BOOKS

Adams, Hazard, ed. *Critical Theory Since Plato*. New York: Harcourt Brace Jovanovich, 1971.

Arnold, Matthew. "The Function of Criticism at the Present Time." In *Critical Theory Since Plato,* edited by Hazard Adams. New York: Harcourt Brace Jovanovich, 1971.

Bennis, Warren, and Bert Nanus. *Leaders: The Strategies for Taking Charge*. New York: Harper & Row, 1986.

DeVries, David, et al. *Performance Appraisal on the Line*. Greensboro, N.C.: A Center for Creative Leadership Publication, 1986.

Garfield, C. *Peak Performers*. New York: William Morrow, 1986.

Geneen, Harold, and Alvin Moscow. *Managing*. New York: Doubleday, 1984.

Grove, Andrew. *One-on-One with Andy Grove: How to Manage Your Boss, Yourself and Your Coworkers*. New York: Putnam, 1987.

Iacocca, Lee, and William Novak. *Iacocca: An Autobiography*. New York: Bantam, 1985.

Kaplan, Robert. *Criticism and Power*. Greensboro, N.C.: A Center for Creative Leadership Publication, 1985.

Kohn, Alfie. *No Contest: The Case Against Competition*. Boston: Houghton Mifflin, 1986.

Lefton, Robert, et al. *Effective Motivation Through Performance Appraisal: Dimensional Appraisal Strategies*. New York: John Wiley & Sons, 1977.

Levinson, Harry, et al. *CEO: Corporate Leadership in Action*. New York: Basic Books, 1984.

Olivier, Laurence. *On Acting*. New York: Simon and Schuster, 1986.

Pascale, Richard, and Anthony Athos. *The Art of Japanese Management*. New York: Simon and Schuster, 1981.

Pepper, Stephen. *The Basis of Criticism in the Arts*. Cambridge: Harvard University Press, 1956.

Pope, Alexander. "An Essay on Criticism." In *Critical Theory Since Plato,* edited by Hazard Adams. New York: Harcourt Brace Jovanovich, 1971.

Richards, I. A. *Practical Criticism*. New York: Harcourt Brace Jovanovich, 1929.

Riesman, David, ed. *The Lonely Crowd: A Study of the Changing American Character*. New Haven, Conn.: Yale University Press, 1973.

Righter, William. *Logic and Criticism*. Washington, D.C.: Chilmark House, 1963.

Townsend, Robert. *Up the Organization*. New York: Alfred A. Knopf, 1970.

Weisinger, Hendrie. *Dr. Weisinger's Anger Work-Out Book*. New York: William Morrow, 1985.

Weisinger, Hendrie, and Norman Lobsenz. *Nobody's Perfect*. Los Angeles: Stratford Press, 1982.

Zilbergeld, Bernie, and Arnold Lazarus. *Mind Power: Getting What You Want Through Mental Training*. Boston: Little, Brown, 1987.

NEWSPAPER AND MAGAZINE ARTICLES

Ajemian, Robert. "Inside the Diaries and the Mind." *Time,* June 2, 1986, 36. Quote from Mario Cuomo, Chapter 4.

Darrach, Brad. "On the Road to *Ishtar*." *People,* May 25, 1987, 106. Quote from Dustin Hoffman, Chapter 9.

Erickson, Milton. "Two-Level Communication." *Journal of Clinical Hypnosis* 30 (1973): 83. Quote from Dr. Erickson, Chapter 5.

Farber, S. *Vis à Vis,* April 1987. Information about Woody Allen, Chapter 4.

Goodwin, Doris Kearns. "Batting Champ Wade Boggs Hits with a Cool Eye, a Hot Hand, and a Resolve to Help His Sister Overcome Illness." *People,* June 16, 1986, 104. Quote from Wade Boggs, Chapter 4.

Harris, Kathryn. "Diller's Hands-on Efforts Pull Firm off the Critical List." *Los Angeles Times,* April 19, 1987. Quote from Jonathan Dolgen, Chapter 7.

"How Companies Pick New CEOs" (excerpt from *Passing the Baton,* by Richard Vancil), *Fortune,* January 4, 1988, 74. Quote from Richard Vancil, Chapter 8.

"How to Succeed Without Even Trying." *Psychology Today,* September 1986, 22. Quote from Spiro Agnew, Chapter 7.

"Jack Welch: How Good a Manager." *Business Week,* December 14, 1987. Quote from Roger Schipke, Chapter 7.

"Jackie Collins Husbands Her Energies to Turn Out Steamy Hollywood Saga." *People,* January 12, 1987, 80. Quote from Jackie Collins, Chapter 4.

Krier, Beth Ann. "Norman Vincent Peale: Positively 90." *Los Angeles Times,* June 5, 1988. Quote from Norman Vincent Peale, Chapter 1.

Lazarus, Richard. "Thoughts on the Relation between Emotion and Cognition," *American Psychologist* 37 (1982): 1019.

Litsky, Frank. "Lewis Comes Back to Silence Critics," *New York Times,* June 20, 1987. Quote from Carl Lewis, Chapter 4.

Los Angeles Times, November 30, 1986. Quote from Cary Grant, Chapter 4.

Los Angeles Times, May 24, 1987. Quote from David Puttnam, Chapter 2.

Los Angeles Times, June 1, 1987. Quote from Pat Riley, Chapter 5.

"Michael Gould Finds There's Life After Robinsons." *Los Angeles Times,* August 28, 1986. Reference to Michael Gould, Chapter 1.

PSA Airline Magazine, October 1986. Quote from Henry Rogers, Chapter 3.

Reibstein, L. "What to Do When an Employee Is Talented — and a Pain in the Neck." *Wall Street Journal,* August 8, 1986. Quote from Katy Smith, Chapter 9.

"Rogers's Tough Report Card." *U.S. News & World Report,* June 16, 1986. Information about William Rogers, Chapter 2.

Roman, Mark. "Beyond the Carrot and the Stick." *Success,* October 1986, 42. Quote about Mark Shulman, Chapter 5.

Shales, Tom. "Woody: The First Fifty Years." *Esquire,* April 1987, 88. Quotes from Woody Allen, Chapter 4.

Sky Airline Magazine, October 1986. Quote from Stanley Marcus, Chapter 2.

Small, Michael. "With *Top Gun* and *Legal Eagles,* Two Long-Distance Screenwriters Make Hollywood's Big League Draft." *People,* August 4, 1986, 86. Quote from Jack Epps, Jr., Chapter 7.

USA Today, February 13, 1986. Reference to Jan Kemp, Chapter 1.